TALKIN' 'BOUT A REVOLUTION
Music and Social Change in America

TALKIN' 'BOUT A REVOLUTION

Music and Social Change in America

Dick Weissman

Backbeat Books

An Imprint of Hal Leonard Corporation
New York

Published in 2010 by Backbeat Books
An Imprint of Hal Leonard Corporation
7777 West Bluemound Road
Milwaukee, WI 53213

Trade Book Division Editorial Offices
19 West 21st Street, New York, NY 10010

Credits can be found on pages 371–372, which constitute an extension of this copyright page.

Printed in the United States of America

Book design by Mark Lerner

Library of Congress Cataloging-in-Publication Data is available upon request.

ISBN 978-1-4234-4283-7

www.backbeatbooks.com

Contents

Introduction   xi

**1 Songs of the Immigrants and Songs in American
   History and Politics**   1
  Arrival   1
  Songs of the Immigrants   2
  Songs About the Immigrants   5
  The Revolutionary War   7
  The Postcolonial Era   9
  The War of 1812   10
  The Mexican War   11
  The Period Before the Civil War   14
  The Civil War   15
  The Spanish-American War   16
  World War I   17
  Other Early Political Songs   19

2 Native American Music and Social Issues   21
  The Inadvertent Host   21
  Conquest and Removal   23
  Nineteenth-Century Indian History   28

Indians in the Twentieth Century   33

Traditional Music   39

Twentieth-Century Music   40

Musical Fusions by Various Indian Artists   51

White Commentary on Indians   53

Indian Classical Music   60

The Business of Indian Music and a Look at the Future   61

3 **African Americans**   63

The Slave Trade   64

Early Music   64

The Development and Evolution of Slavery   68

Religion   68

The Civil War and Its Aftermath   72

The Period of Maximum Oppression: 1880–1914   73

Secular Folk Music   73

Minstrels, Ragtime, and Broadway   75

Birth and Evolution of the Blues   78

White Blues and White Audiences   89

World War II to the Sixties   94

Gospel Music   95

Pop and R&B   97

Motown and Stax Records   98

Soul   101

Jazz   104

Rap   109

Songs by White People About African Americans   123

Race: An Ongoing Issue   128

4 **Women's Lives and Songs**   131

The Role of Women   131

World War I and Women's Suffrage   135

Between the World Wars   137

The Fifties and Sixties   141

The British Invasion, the 1650 Broadway Songwriters, and
  Motown 143
Feminism and the Women's Movement 145
Enduring Women's Issues, from the Seventies On 153
Eighties and Nineties Ladies 157
The Nineties and Beyond 161
Women in Jazz 167
Women's Roles in Music 168
Songbook Analysis 169
The Music Industry and Women's Music 170

5 **Protest Songs: Music as a Tool for Social Change** 171
Joe Hill 174
Songs of the Miners and Textile Workers 175
Conservative Songs 177
Music and the Communist Party 178
The Radical Schools of the Thirties and Black Protest
  Music 180
The Spanish Civil War and Protest Music 181
Changes in American Life and the Union Movement 182
The Almanac Singers 184
Professional Protest 185
The Hitler-Stalin Peace Pact 186
Alan Lomax and Woody Guthrie 189
Leadbelly 193
Protest Music and Audiences 196
World War II and the Almanacs 197
Pete Seeger and People's Songs 198
Josh White 199
The Red Scares, the Election of 1948, and the End of People's
  Songs 200
The Weavers 202
The Effects of the Blacklist on Political Music 204
Folk-Pop Crossover 204

The Kingston Trio   205
Music and the Civil Rights Movement   207
Protest Singers of the Sixties   209
Protest Music Today   216
The Future of Protest Music   225
Why Folk Music? Then and Now   226

6 **Spanish-Speaking Groups**   231
The Southwest   231
Immigration   234
Political Militance   236
Mexican American Music   236
Evolution of Musical Style in Mexican American Music   243
Mexicans in Anglo Music   246
Puerto Rican Life and Music   247
Cuba and the Exodus   249
What's Going On: Chicano Consciousness and Music   253
Ry Cooder   262

7 **Rock and Roll**   265
Why Rock and Roll?   265
Rock and Roll History   266
"Rock Around the Clock"   269
Elvis and Sun Records   269
Rock and White Supremacy   271
Cover Records   273
"The Sound of Young America"   275
Politics of the Sixties   275
Peace, Love, Flowers, Drugs, and Music   276
Peace, Love, and Disillusionment   279
Disco   279
Punk   280
Hard Core   282
Straight Edge vs. Punk's Underbelly   283

Heavy Metal and Eighties Rock   284
Grunge   286
Jokers in the Deck   288
Mainstream Artists   289
Rage Against the Machine   290
Rock and Roll and Race   291
Women and Rock   293
Rock and Roll Today   294

8 **The Music of Hate**   295
Anti-African American Music   295
Neo-Nazi Music   297

9 **The Two Gulf Wars, 9/11/2001, and Afghanistan**   301
The Gulf War of 1991   301
9/11   304
The Second Gulf War   306
Iraq and Vietnam   313

10 **Music and Social Change**   315
Omissions   315
Music, Celebrity, and the Political Process   316
Situations Where Music Had Influence   318
Can Music Cause Social Change?   321

Bibliography and Discography   323
Index   349

Introduction

In the early 1990s I was teaching in the music department at the University of Colorado at Denver. The School of the Arts was just beginning to separate from the broader College of Arts and Sciences, and was eager to expand its offerings to attract more students. Laura Cuetara, the Acting Dean of the college, asked me if I could put together a class that would meet the university's multicultural diversity requirement.

Since I have degrees in music, black studies, and the sociology of music, and a long-term interest in American music and how it relates to politics and ethnicity, I came up with a class called Social and Political Implications of American Music—but could not find an adequate textbook to cover the subject matter. While there are many books that deal with the relationship between music and social change, most lack a broad approach to American music history, focusing instead on a style (such as blues, hip-hop, punk, or folk music) that the author is comfortable writing about. Some of these books are truly remarkable, but they are extremely subject-specific. Other books weigh in heavily on social theory, but are so abstruse and philosophical that they are difficult for most students to follow.

In 1996, a fellowship from the University of Colorado at Denver allowed me to write a workbook to meet the goals of the class I had created. I always wanted to turn the textbook into a book that would be useful for the general reader, but during the intervening years, I was interrupted by various writing projects and my own career as a performing musician. This work fulfills my ambition and expands my original vision of including music by and about Native Americans, African Americans, Spanish-speaking groups, and women, as well as music specifically designed to encourage or initiate social change. Subsequently, I have added material on the music of immigrant groups, songs celebrating patriotic events, and the political aspects of jazz and rock and roll.

Although this is a book about music, most of the emphasis will be on the lyrics of songs. Musical styles will only be discussed when they bear some relationship to the book's subject matter, such as some of the angry instrumental music of post-bebop jazz.

For the most part, I have omitted Canadian, British, and other foreign artists, even though they are clearly part of the American music panorama. To include them would have required delving into other musical cultures, such as the French-Canadian music world, that I felt were beyond the province of this book.

Thanks to John Cerullo of Hal Leonard for encouraging this project, to editors Bernadette Malavarca and Sarah Gallogly, and to the many people with whom I have discussed various aspects of the book, especially Frank Jermance, Larry Sandberg, and Harry Tuft. Special thanks to Susan Planalp for her proofreading and editing skills.

Dick Weissman
December 2009

I

SONGS OF THE IMMIGRANTS AND SONGS IN AMERICAN HISTORY AND POLITICS

Arrival

The first people of what is now the United States were the American Indians, whose music is the subject of the next chapter. This chapter will address the music of immigrants dating from the earliest European colonists, beginning with Spanish and followed by British and other Western European settlers. They in turn brought Africans to this country through the slave trade, sometimes directly from that continent, sometimes from the West Indies. I will cover the music of African Americans in considerable detail later in the book.

Drawn by the prospect of a huge, relatively unpopulated country with enormous natural resources, immigrants facing economic difficulty or religious persecution at home sought opportunity in America particularly during the nineteenth century. According to Victor Green's fascinating survey *A Singing Ambivalence: American Immigrants Between Old World and New, 1830–1930*, three and a half million Germans, and almost as many Irish immigrants came to the United States from 1830 to 1930. Other large groups of settlers arrived from the various Scandinavian countries, Italy, Poland, Hungary, China, and Mexico, as well as Jewish immigrants from Russia and other Eastern European countries.

Immigrants at Ellis Island, 1908

Songs of the Immigrants

Each group brought their own music and musical style along with them on their travels. In many instances they also brought musical instruments on the ships, singing and playing to pass the time and to take their minds off the voyage and their anxieties about what awaited them in a far-off foreign land. The prevalent themes of their songs were

Desire to return home
Sorrow at parting with family, friends, lovers, or spouses

Aspirations to make a fortune in America before returning home
(rather than seek further economic opportunities by staying)
Difficulty adjusting to the English language and American
customs
American suspicion of immigrants' lifestyle and behaviors
Discomfort at the materialism of American culture

There is not space in this book to print songs that delineate each
of these attitudes. The reader is referred to Green's book, and to Jerry
Silverman's *Immigrant Songbook*, which, unlike Green's, includes
music along with the words to a variety of immigrant songs. In the
appendix of this book is a list of songbooks that deal with the songs
of specific groups.

While many of the immigrants' songs reveal nostalgic feelings for
the homeland, they also protest the conditions that drove them to
seek a better life abroad, and express hopes of peace and plenty at the
end of their journey. McKee's "Farewell to Ireland" describes Erin's
"daisy hills," but at the same time laments the starvation, high rents
and taxes that plagued the Irish people. In a later example, Jerry Silverman prints the song "Poor Cambodia," credited to Sam Ang Sam.
This song depicts the blackhearted Khmer Rouge Cambodians, who
were responsible for the genocide of millions of their countrymen
from 1975 to 1979.

The "Farewell Song for German Emigrants Going to America,"
like many similar compositions, looks forward to prosperity in the
New World with scenes of "clover growing three feet tall" and "butter and meat enough for all." Meanwhile, the Norwegian American
song "Oleana" makes fun of both America and the attempts of Norwegian violinist Ole Bull to found a utopian colony in 1852. It depicts cows who milk themselves and salmon who leap into the kettle
to serve a group of happy, well-stuffed citizens who do not need to
work to enjoy the good life.

A much bleaker satire comes through in the mid-nineteenth-
century Irish immigrant song "Drill, Ye Tarriers, Drill," which

Steelworker in Homestead, Pennsylvania

describes unfair bosses and poor working conditions in America: the protagonist, Big Jim Goff, is blown through the air by an explosion, and his wages are docked "for the time you were up in the sky." A more serious Irish lament, "No Irish Need Apply," complains about a job advertisement containing those very words.

Anti-Irish sentiment was common in this period, especially in the northeastern cities where there was a substantial Irish population. Chinese immigrants, many of whom settled in the San Francisco area, also encountered discrimination, both in the city and in the California gold fields. Greene prints a song about a Chinese laundry man that protests the way Christian patrons looked down on the laundry business. It includes the line "I can wash handkerchiefs with sad tears." And the composer Morris Rosenfeld, who arrived in New York from the Russian-Polish border in 1886, deplored the New York sweatshops that cost so many immigrant girls their youth and health. Some of Rosenfeld's songs (unlike the other immigrant songs just described) were published in sheet music, and recorded by a variety of artists.

Rochelle and Robert L. Wright's book *Danish Emigrant Ballads and Songs* presents another aspect of the songs of the immigrant. Virtually all of the songs in the book were published in Denmark, many by the prolific songwriter Julius Strandberg, who published about ten thousand songs by himself and others. Featuring many of the themes of the immigrant songs discussed above, these songs suggest that similar ones must have been published in many of the immigrants' home countries.

Songs About the Immigrants

The immigrants were not always accepted by the people who were already settled in this country. There is a certain irony to this, given that the only true natives in America were the American Indians, and even they had come long ago from Asia. To put it another way, Beau Allen, in a song about people moving to Colorado, used the line "Everyone wants to be the last one in."

Specific stereotypes developed around the behavior, dress, and alleged characteristics of various ethnic and religious groups. This negative stereotyping reached its height in descriptions of African Americans, as we will see in the discussion of African American music. More recently, Mexican Americans have received similar treatment. However, other groups were not exempt from these attitudes. The sort of stereotypes that prevailed include the following:

Irish: Drunken thugs
Italians: Dirty, gangsters
Jews: Greedy, untrustworthy money-grubbers
Germans: Dumb, fat, speak with accents
Chinese: Suited only to be laundry workers, untrustworthy
Poles: Dumb
Scots: Cheap

Jon W. Finson, in his excellent *The Voices That Are Gone: Themes in Nineteenth-Century American Popular Song*, prints the lyrics to a number of songs that portray immigrant groups in a negative light. This genre of song varied from mildly poking fun at ethnic groups to offensive uses of dialect and downright insulting descriptions of a given group's behavior. Two New York songwriters named Edward "Ned" Harrigan and David Braham, writing mostly in the late nineteenth century, specialized in these songs; according to Finson, they wrote almost two hundred songs that dealt with ethnic and racial interaction in New York City. One of the most extreme was "The Skidmore Guard," castigating Irish, "Dutch" (Germans), and Italians and asking for "stricter quarantine or stronger fumigation." Lingenfelter, Dwyer, and Cohen print a nasty anti-Chinese song called "Get Out, Yellow Skins, Get Out" in their book *Songs of the American West*. The song boasts of stealing gold mined by Chinese miners, and threatens to repeat that act unless the Chinese leave.

Some of the same suspicion that greeted immigrant groups attached itself to the new and growing Mormon population in America. (Joseph Smith founded the Mormon church in New York state in 1830; later his followers moved to Missouri and Illinois to escape persecution. After Smith's death Brigham Young moved the church's headquarters to Salt Lake City.) Lingenfelter, Dwyer, and Cohen include thirty-five such songs, ranging from idyllic portraits of the

Mormon colony in Utah ("Wish I Was a Mormon," 1863) to denunciations of Mormons and their leaders ("In the Midst of These Awful Mormons," 1872). The influx of new cultures in the young nation of America was bound to spur tensions, some of which lead to major political happenings that shapes culture and people—wars.

The Revolutionary War

The imposition of taxes on colonial America by the British was one of the primary causes of the Revolutionary War. Various songs celebrated tax resistance on the part of the colonists, including a song about the repeal of the Stamp Act in 1766. One of the most celebrated events in early American history was the Boston Tea Party of 1773. The British had passed the Tea Act, which gave the British East India Company a monopoly on tea in the colonies. In Boston a group of rebellious colonists dressed up like Indians, boarded British ships, and threw their cargo of tea overboard. Vera Brodsky Lawrence, in her book *Music for Patriots, Politicians, and Presidents: Harmonies and Discords of the First Hundred Years*, reprints a song that describes how the colonials boarded the ship and disposed of the tea.

The American Revolution soon followed, and other songs celebrated the battles of Lexington and Bunker Hill in 1775. One of the unusual aspects of the songs of the Revolutionary War is that a number of the political leaders of the rebellion, including Samuel Adams, Benjamin Franklin, and Thomas Paine, wrote songs to assist the cause. It is difficult to imagine contemporary political figures writing songs to galvanize their supporters; still, a handful of American politicians since the time of the Revolution, including Senator Orrin Hatch, Louisiana governor Jimmie Davis, and West Virginia fiddler and senator Robert Byrd, have used music to bolster their political campaigns. Quite a few of these early songs did not use original melodies, but were parodies of existing (often British) popular songs.

One of the most famous songs of the period was composer William Billings' renowned song "Chester," which declares the new country's trust in God, deplores British generals Burgoyne and Clinton and Admiral Howe, and describes "generals yielding to beardless boys."

Other songs celebrate leaders like General "Mad Anthony" Wayne and Vermont Green Mountain Volunteer leader Johnny Stark. The latter song, "The Bennington Riflemen," has been reprinted in many songbooks, with its stirring chorus "Oh the rifle, oh the rifle in our hands will prove no trifle."

As a substantial number of colonists sided with the British during the war, not all of the songs of the period were anti-British. Lawrence prints the song "Bunker's Hill, a New Song," which celebrates the British fight against the rebels and praises the "great Howe, our brave commander." Yet another wrinkle was the rebels' fascination with Major John André. André was a British spy who recruited the traitor Benedict Arnold to convert to the British cause. The Britisher was caught after a meeting with Arnold and was executed as a spy. The song "Death of Major André" praises André's courage and his demeanor to the very moment of his death. It even expresses the wish that André could have been freed and Arnold killed in his stead. According to Lawrence, songs and poems about André's fate continued to be written for years after the event.

As was later the case with the songs of the Civil War, some songs were used by both camps, with different sets of lyrics. The song "Yankee Doodle" is a prime example. According to Lawrence, the original version of the song dated to the French and Indian War, fought in the 1750s, when the American people were still loyal British subjects. The original lyric was a condescending description of the American colonists. It was written from the viewpoint of British soldiers, and questioned the courage of the Yankee soldiers. The later, pro-rebel version, which is the one we sing in American schools today, celebrated the heroism of George Washington and his American soldiers.

"Johnny Has Gone for a Soldier," one of the earliest antiwar songs, dates from the Revolutionary War. Peter, Paul, and Mary recorded it almost two hundred years later, and it also appears in various song collections, including Jerry Silverman's *Folk Song Encyclopedia, Volume II*. The song expresses the viewpoint of the soldier's wife or girlfriend, who is "crying her fill" and laments that she is heartbroken.

The Postcolonial Era

The Revolutionary War ended in 1783, and the United States became an independent nation. George Washington, the general who had led the United States Army to victory, became the country's first president.

Although not everyone was enthralled with his agenda, Washington's status as a national hero enabled him to govern relatively smoothly. After his second term of office, two political parties battled for control of the government. The Federalists represented a comparatively conservative, aristocratic group who believed in a strong central government, while the Democratic-Republicans, under the leadership of Thomas Jefferson, espoused more liberal views.

When John Adams became president in 1796, Congress passed the Alien and Sedition Acts. The Naturalization Act, which fell into this set of laws, established that to be a citizen one had to have been a resident of the United States for a minimum of fourteen years. Only citizens were allowed to vote. The Sedition Act made it a crime to oppose any government measure in speech or print. The penalties were fines and jail terms. Some Republicans were in fact jailed under this measure.

Both parties advocated their views in songs. The Federalists' favorite was "Hail Columbia," adapted from an earlier work by lyricist Joseph Hopkinson. It throws in the name of everyone's hero, George Washington, and describes threats to the country's existence. Another song that has retained some presence in American history is the pro-Jefferson song "Jefferson and Liberty," which has the catchy and very singable chorus

> Rejoice, Columbia's sons, rejoice!
> To tyrants never bend the knee,

> But join with heart and soul and voice,
> For Jefferson and liberty.

According to Lawrence, the first printing of the song occurred in January 1801, at about the time of Jefferson's inauguration as president.

The War of 1812

Toward the end of the eighteenth century, America experienced difficulties with both France and England. Both countries attempted to intercept American ships and, in England's case, to remove American sailors. This "impressment" was undertaken by using the argument that Americans were really British citizens.

In the late 1790s the United States came close to war with France, but when Napoleon came to power in 1799 he brought these hostilities to a close. In the case of England, conflict was less easily avoided; Britain yearned to restore America to its kingdom, while on the American side imperialists agitated for war, believing that if we defeated the British again we could also wrest Canada from their control.

An odd artifact of the war is the song "James Bird," printed in Ethel and Chauncey O. Moore's *Ballads and Folk Songs of the Southwest.* Bird's story resembles that of Benedict Arnold. Bird fought bravely during the War of 1812, but then deserted and was captured, tried, and executed. This long ballad begins by describing Bird as noble, graceful, and manly, acknowledging in a letter to his parents that he has deserted the ship and must suffer for it. The song concludes with the execution and the burial of Bird's "mangled corpse" on Lake Erie's "distant shore."

Possibly the most significant musical event of the war was the birth of what became America's national anthem, "The Star-Spangled Banner." As Vera Brodsky Lawrence tells the tale, on September 5, 1814, Washington, D.C. attorney Francis Scott Key boarded a British ship to negotiate the release of his friend Dr. William Beanes, who had been taken prisoner. While this transaction was taking place, the British were bombarding Fort McHenry, an event that Key witnessed firsthand. That night Key wrote his lyric, which was set to an old British tune called "Anacreon in Heaven." The original lyric had several verses that are rarely, if ever, sung today, but the verse and refrain are known by every schoolchild in America.

The war ended in a complete stalemate, with neither side able to claim victory. In fact, the Battle of New Orleans, which gave the Americans their greatest triumph of the war, took place on January 8, 1815, eleven days *after* the end of the war. In 1959, almost 150 years after the war of 1812, Johnny Horton recorded a long ballad written by a high school principal from Timbo, Arkansas named Jimmy Driftwood, called "The Battle of New Orleans." The lyric refers to Andrew Jackson, "Old Hickory," who had commanded the victorious army, and the bravery of the American soldiers. It sounds like an authentic folk song, and in fact the verse uses the melody of an old fiddle tune called "The Eighth of January." The song became a runaway hit record, and was awarded a Grammy in 1960 as 1959's Song of the Year. Aside from the national anthem, it is certainly the best-known song about the War of 1812.

The Mexican War

In 1803 Thomas Jefferson negotiated the terms of the Louisiana Purchase with France. For slightly more then twenty-three million dollars the United States acquired some fifteen states, including a large part of the Midwest and portions of what became the Rocky Mountain states.

The purchase marked the beginning of an aggressive expansionism that came to be known as "Manifest Destiny"—a phrase coined in support of America's proposed annexation of Texas in 1845. Mexico, which owned most of the American Southwest, now stood in the way of plans to extend the young nation from the Atlantic Ocean all the way to the Pacific.

Texas had fought a war of independence with Mexico in 1836 and was operating as an independent republic, but Mexico still claimed ownership. In 1846 the United States, which had granted

Texas statehood, invaded Mexico, defeating the Mexicans in little more than a year. In 1848 a peace treaty was signed, and Mexico, in exchange for fifteen million dollars and a debt relief package, relinquished Texas, New Mexico, Arizona, California, and portions of what later became Colorado to the United States.

Later in the book I will discuss the music of Mexican Americans in detail. The songs on the American side of the conflict include a tribute to General, and later President, Zachary Taylor, entitled "Hurrah for Rough and Ready," and "Strike for Your Rights, Avenge Your Wrong," a call to arms that marshals American troops against the jails of Santa Fe, where their countrymen are in "captivity." The song "Maid of Monterey" pays tribute to a Mexican woman who nursed the American wounded during the war, even though she favored the Mexican cause. Many Americans, too, sympathized with Mexico, and several thousand American soldiers actually defected to the Mexican side.

Davy Crockett and Other "Heroes"

Davy Crockett, known as an "Indian fighter" (one who fights American Indians), is one of the most identifiable pioneer heroes in American history. He fought against the Creek Indians in 1813–14, served in the U.S. Congress, and died at the Alamo in the fight for Texas independence that ultimately led to the Mexican War.

The Lomaxes print a song called "The Ballad of Davy Crockett" in their book *American Ballads and Folk Songs* that pays tribute to Davy's strength. The sheet music for a song called the "Crockett Victory March" appeared in 1835, and in 1846 a minstrel song titled "Pompeyu Smash" depicted a knock-down, drag-out fight between Crockett and a slave named Pompey. The result was a stalemate. Davy surfaced again with a 1954 Disney TV show, with Fess Parker playing the title character. The theme song became a hit record in three different versions. The most popular version was by Bill Hayes; Tennessee Ernie Ford had a country hit with his version, and Parker's version also made the charts. The long ballad describes Crockett's political career and his heroic death at the Alamo, and even touches on his legend with the final phrase describing him as "king of the wild frontier!"

Another Indian fighter, William Henry Harrison commanded a thousand American troops at the battle of Tippecanoe in 1811, defeating the poorly armed Indian forces. His 1840 presidential campaign slogan, "Tippecanoe and Tyler Too" (referring to the battle and to Harrison's running mate, John Tyler) also became the title of a popular song.

The Hutchinson Family Singers

The Hutchinson Family Singers were a family of New Hampshire musicians who sang contemporary lyrics often set to well-known tunes. Directed by Jesse Hutchinson, the group consisted of five family members who traveled in New England and New York, later crossing the Atlantic to perform in London.

Like many Americans, the Hutchinson singers opposed the war with Mexico, rejecting it as an attempt to extend the geographical reach of slavery. Their song "Eight Dollars a Day," written by J. J. Hutchinson, denounces the United States Congress—"fiddling to the tune of eight dollars a day"—and their "mad cry of war." The Hutchinsons were active in the antislavery struggle, and also sang for the temperance movement, which is covered in the chapter on women and music.

Incidental References

All of the songs discussed in this section have been composed songs, but a handful of folk songs that have survived also make incidental references to the Mexican War. Jean Ritchie sings a song that mentions "a little trouble down in Mexico, nobody hurt by Jeremy Taylor-o." The rest of the song consists of square dance calls, and has no bearing on the war. The sea shanty "Santy Anno," in which ships travel around Cape Horn to the California gold mines, contains one verse that refers specifically to General Santa Ana:

Santy Anno was a good old man, heave away, Santy Anno,
Until he went to war with his Uncle Sam, all on the plains of
   Mexico.

Some other versions attribute heroic qualities to the Mexican general and his men, and some even picture him as being victorious.

The Period Before the Civil War

At the time of the Civil War, which was fought in from 1861 to 1865, two basic issues divided the North and the South. One was the issue of slavery, which continued to be important in most of the Southern states but was now widely condemned in the North. The other was

The Hutchinson Family Singers

the notion of states' rights in opposition to the power of the federal government.

While some Northerners took up slavery as a cause, believing that it violated American principles of freedom and democracy, many others, basically indifferent to the plight of African Americans, simply recognized that the institutions of slavery did not suit the needs of the industrial North.

As new states opened up for settlement in the Midwest, Northern and Southern settlers clashed over whether the state should permit slavery. In 1820 the Missouri Compromise dealt with the issue of slavery in the area acquired through the Louisiana Purchase. Anything north of latitude 36° 30' was declared closed to slavery. The Kansas-Nebraska Act of 1854 specified that in the states of Kansas and Nebraska (which would have been free states under the Compromise) the voters could choose whether they wished to permit slavery. Antislavery forces, seeing the law as a concession to Southern slaveholders, formed the Republican Party in opposition to the act and ran a candidate, explorer James Fremont, in the 1856 presidential election.

The election was a three-way contest between Fremont, Democrat James Buchanan, and former president Milllard Fillmore, running as the candidate of the Know-Nothing Party. The latter group was opposed to Catholic immigration, and worked to curb immigration and naturalization generally. The party eventually split over the issue of slavery, and the dominant, antislavery bloc joined the Republican Party.

Lawrence prints a number of songs supporting the various factions (and often insulting the opposition). An odd sidelight of the campaign was that the famous songwriter Stephen Foster's talents were enlisted in the Buchanan cause, because Foster's sister was married to Buchanan's brother.

The Civil War

The Civil War was a unique event in American history. Although it was not really fought over the issue of slavery, but rather the question of states' rights, it resulted in the freeing of the slaves. As countless movies, novels, and songs attest, it pitted brother against brother and friends against one another, and resulted in four years of continuous warfare that threatened the very existence of the United States as a single nation.

There are so many Civil War songs that several published books consist entirely of songs of the Union and Confederate forces. Willard A. and Porter W. Heaps printed hundreds of these songs in their authoritative work *The Singing Sixties: The Spirit of Civil War Days Drawn from the Music of the Times.*

As the reader has seen in other songs of America's wars, the songs express admiration for military heroes, longings for home and family, the sadness of the constant specter of death and wounds, and even a feverish desire for an end to the conflict. The latter notion is seen in "The Cruel War," with the line "The cruel war is raging, and Johnny has to fight." The Union forces sing, "We'll hang Jeff Davis from a sour apple tree," while the Confederates respond, "Our soil's been tramped by hostile foes."

Many of these songs contain hidden ironies in their history, if not in their lyrics. For example, the song "Dixie" was written by Northerner Dan Emmett, but became the ultimate anthem of the South. A similar fate befell "All Quiet Along the Potomac"; written by a Confederate soldier to commemorate a comrade killed on picket duty, the song was also adapted by the Union side. Clearly, this descriptive narrative of a seeming lull on the battlefield that ends in the death of a soldier resonated with on the armies of both sides.

The Spanish-American War

The Spanish-American War was a short-lived conflict (109 days) that sprang from America's involvement in Cuba's fight for independence from Spain. When the U.S.S. *Maine*, sent to Havana to protect American interests there, blew up in the harbor, Spain was blamed and Congress passed a resolution authorizing military force in Cuba.

Spain declared war in April and sued for peace in August, turning over Puerto Rico, the Philippine Islands, and Guam to the United States.

The songs of the war celebrate the American victories, and in particular Theodore Roosevelt's exploits on San Juan Hill. They also respond, not favorably, to some Filipinos' wish to obtain independence rather then to assume an identity as an American colony. "In Mindanao," printed in Jerry Silverman's *American History Songbook*, depicts the hardships of insect bites and the physical labor of clearing the land of stumps. Another song of the period, printed in Carl Sandburg's *American Songbag*, denounces the "damn Filipinos." "Damn the Filipinos" is a postwar song that is even more explicitly anti-Filipino, accusing its subjects of stealing and lying.

Other songs of the period include the 1900 tribute to Theodore Roosevelt "When Teddy Comes Marching Home," and various versions of the song "The Battleship of Maine" that describe the war and the sinking of the ship. The folk revival group the New Lost City Ramblers famously performed the latter, which includes the chorus "At war with that great nation Spain . . . it was all about that battleship of Maine." Other versions of the song have been collected in Arkansas and North Carolina.

World War I

World War I was a conflict between England, France, and Russia, allied against Germany and the Austro-Hungarian Empire of the Hapsburgs. When the Russian Revolution occurred in October 1917, the Russians withdrew from the war. President Woodrow Wilson had actually run his re-election campaign on the slogan that he had kept the United States out of the war, but nevertheless he soon convinced the U.S. Congress to enter it.

World War I was a controversial war in the United States, and some left-wing American political factions opposed our participation in what they referred to as an "imperialist war." Isolationist groups, who believed in staying out of world conflicts, also decried U.S.

involvement. In 1915, Alfred Bryan and Al Piantadosi wrote the song "I Didn't Raise My Boy to Be a Soldier." It contained the lyrics

> Ten million soldiers to the war have gone,
> Who may never return again.
> Ten million hearts must break
> For the ones who died in vain.
> Head bowed down in sorrow
> In her lonely years,
> I heard a mother murmur through her tears:
>   *(Chorus)*
> I didn't raise my boy to be a soldier,
> I brought him up to be my pride and joy,
> Who dares to place a musket on his shoulder
> To shoot some other mother's darling boy?
> It's time to lay the sword and gun away,
> There'd be no war today,
> If mothers all would say,
> "I didn't raise my boy to be a soldier."

The song concludes with the line: "Remember that my boy belongs to me!"

Still, a raft of patriotic songs supported the war, and some are still well-known today, almost a hundred years later. Many of them were written by professional songwriters, such as George M. Cohan's 1918 song "Over There," with its impassioned cry that "the Yanks are coming." Another example is Robert Levenson and E. E . Bagley's "That's What the Red, White and Blue Mean," whose chorus attributes distinct virtues to the colors of the flag. The "Marine Corps Hymn" wasn't copyrighted until 1919, but the lyrics refer to the Mexican War and to the undeclared wars with the Barbary pirates of North Africa in the early nineteenth century. The tune comes from Offenbach's "Two Gendarmes," published in 1859, but the lyrics appear to be the result of various additions over the years. The end of the song describes Army and Navy troops observing the Marines on guard in Heaven.

Other Early Political Songs

Every election has enlisted music in the cause of its participants; Irwin Silber prints many of these long-forgotten songs in his book *Songs America Voted By*. The contents include positive songs favoring a particular candidate, and negative ones attacking the opposition.

The positive songs tend to refer to the candidate's patriotism, especially battlefield experience. Examples include:

Heroism—leading the troops or enduring wounds

Love of country

Down-to-earth characteristics, even a nickname, such as "Old Hickory" for Andrew Jackson

The negative songs charge opponents with:

Cowardice—fleeing a battle or losing one

Snobbery—aristocratic dress or mannerisms

Associations with "bad" people, such as a song about William McKinley, associating him with the corrupt party boss Mark Hanna

Racist stereotypes, especially anti-African American references after the Civil War

In addition to bravery in battle, prominent leaders' deaths in peacetime have been commemorated in song, as in a folk song recounting the assassination of President Garfield, with its pitiful description of Garfield's widow at the dying man's bedside.

The songs of later wars, which often relate to more contemporary issues than the ones discussed here, will feature in the corresponding sections of this book.

2

NATIVE AMERICAN MUSIC AND SOCIAL ISSUES

The Inadvertent Host

Most Americans see the history of American Indians from the view-point of the Western Europeans who settled in the United States in the sixteenth and seventeenth centuries. Europeans came to America seeking economic opportunities, searching for religious or political freedom, or simply because they felt that any change might represent a possible improvement in the quality of their lives.

When these early immigrants arrived in the New World, they found the land was already occupied. This did not represent a military challenge to the invaders, because the Indians were spread out in many separate tribal groups. Some tribes were sedentary, some nomadic. There were tribes who were tied together in a sort of loose political confederation, notably the Iroquois, and others who fought each other. Many tribes were so geographically removed from one another that they had no interactions with any other group.

The Indians had no understanding of who these "visitors" were or exactly what had brought them to America. If the Indians had been a unified group, and had immediately sensed that their lives and land were in danger, perhaps they would have mounted some sort of unified offensive against the invaders and been able to defeat them. Even granting this scenario, the defeat would only have been a temporary one because of the white man's superior firepower and unified military force.

This course of action simply did not occur to the Native Americans, for the most part. During the 1760s the Ottawa chief Pontiac united tribes in the Great Lakes area in hopes of driving the British back across the Allegheny Mountains, and later the Shawnee chief Tecumseh attempted to convince a number of tribes to unite against the white invaders. He traveled all around what is now the Midwestern United States from 1808 to 1811, in an attempt to get Indians to form a united front against the white man. His efforts were unsuccessful, and ultimately he was betrayed by his own brother. Chief Black Hawk forged an alliance of several tribes in Illinois, but he was betrayed by one of his alleged allies, and captured in 1832.

Some sixty years later a Paiute Indian named Wovoka created the Ghost Dance religion, which was intended to unite the Indian tribes to defeat the white man. This led to the disastrous massacre of the Sioux at the battle of Wounded Knee. That event signaled the end of any unified Indian overthrow of the white man. Details of all of these events and the many battles between Indians and whites are thoroughly discussed in Dee Brown's classic book *Bury My Heart at Wounded Knee: An Indian History of the American West.*

Before we take a brief look at the events that followed white settlement, it is important to comprehend that the ethnic groups that immigrated to the United States all proved to be useful to the country's overall economic development. But the Indians did not appear to be of similar use to the white settlers. There were some attempts to enslave Indians, and in a few cases the Indians themselves marketed their captives as slaves, often selling them to the white man. One historian, J. Leitch Wright Jr., reports that there was a relatively extensive trade in Indian slaves, especially during the seventeenth century. Wright claims that many of these slaves were exported to the West Indies, but that thousands remained in the South from the sixteenth to the eighteenth centuries.

Folklorist Roger Paradis has collected a ballad about a young Indian slave named Lisa. Although the song is in French, Paradis's recorded versions of the song appeared on the American side of the Canadian border. Paradis collected eight different versions of the ballad. The story begins with a young Indian maiden sold at auction. Despite her desperate pleas to be allowed to return home she is sold to a captain. She continues her pleas for freedom to no avail. Paradis makes a detailed analysis of the American and Canadian versions, but, as he points out, the significance of the song is that it is the only Indian song about slavery. Possibly there were others, but no collector has discovered them.

Problems arising from the spread of diseases from the white population and the Indians' ability to disappear from plantations contributed to the difficulties of using Indians as slaves. Ultimately the African slaves proved to be a more efficient labor force, and because they came from different groups with different languages and cultures, for the most part they were unable to resist captivity in any inter-tribal way that united different groups. The Africans were also in a foreign land, and, unlike the Indians, had no knowledge of where they could go if they ran away.

George Washington and Thomas Jefferson wanted the Indians to become farmers. When the Cherokees began to successfully cultivate their lands in the nineteenth century, some of them assumed the role of successful slaveholding planters. When the Cherokees were forced off their land and removed to Oklahoma, their careers as aristocratic planters came to end.

Conquest and Removal

The Spanish were the first white settlers in the United States, founding St. Augustine, Florida, in 1565. The English settled Virginia in 1607, the Puritans came from England in 1620, and the Dutch founded New York in 1623. There are numerous tales of the Indians providing native crops, such as corn, that enabled the settlers to survive. The relationship of the European settlers to American Indians from the sixteenth though the nineteenth century can be summarized as follows:

> Coexistence followed by conquest and open warfare
> Spread of disease (sometimes intentional)
> "Purchase" of land
> Treaty negotiations, usually followed by ceding of lands for minimal financial compensation
> Indian relocation to outlying, seemingly undesirable territory

The Indians did not passively accept their annihilation or removal. They fought back in Virginia and Massachusetts, only to be decimated. In the Revolutionary War and the War of 1812, sometimes Indians chose to side with the English and had to suffer the consequences. Those who supported the Americans were not especially

Wichita Indians in war song

rewarded for their loyalty. The bloody American Civil War of 1861–1865 might have provided the Indian with a timely opportunity to fight against the white man, but by this time there were too many white settlers.

Disease and Land Purchases

Contact with the white man introduced new strains of disease that had never previously afflicted the Indian. Charles Wilkinson, in *Blood Struggle: The Rise of Modern Indian Nations*, mentions ninety separate epidemics of smallpox, diphtheria, typhus, cholera, tuberculosis and cholera from the early sixteenth century until the beginning of the twentieth century. In addition to the natural occurrence of these diseases, there were incidents of settlers or troops deliberately selling Indians infected blankets that carried smallpox.

The extent of these deaths is difficult to estimate, because the estimates of the original Indian population vary wildly. What we do know is that by 1880, when the U.S. Government declared that the Indian wars were over, there were only 248,253 Indians remaining in the United States. Even accepting the lowest population estimate of one million, this means that three-fourths of the Indians were decimated by diseases.

Rationale for Conquest and Removal

The following rationalizations were used to justify the removal of Indians from their land:

1) Indians were regarded as children who lived in a primitive culture. They were not thought capable of operating in a modern world, with "enlightened" European settlers.

We can only speculate on why the pop songs of the nineteenth century would paint the Indian in romantic and attractive terms, while folk songs tend to focus on his alleged savagery. Of course, the pop song authors were sitting in cities like New York, and the only Indians they had ever

U. S. ZOUAVES.
WITH BUFFALO BILL'S WILD WEST.

Buffalo Bill's Wild West Show

seen were probably in Buffalo Bill's touring Wild West show. The folk songs were presumably born among the peoples of the frontier, or at least people whose parents, siblings, or neighbors had the experiences described in the songs.

There were parallel romanticized descriptions of Indian life in the novels of James Fenimore Cooper and the poetry of Henry Wadsworth Longfellow. Wild West shows, beginning in 1837, also portrayed the Indian as a quaint artifact of a passing way of life. At one time there were fifty touring shows, with Buffalo Bill's show being the best known of the lot. Indians were duded up in sequins, plumes, and spangles. George Catlin's paintings in the 1840s, and Edward Curtis's photographs in the early twentieth century, established the visual image of the Indian as a sort of noble primitive.

The song "Indian Outlaw," written by Tommy Barnes and Gene Simmons, was a career-making record for Tim McGraw in 1994. The song depicts the hero as living in a teepee, and capable of shooting a buffalo or a deer with a bow and arrow at a range of one hundred yards. The oddest thing about the song is its wholesale co-opting of the bridge of a song by John D. Loudermilk called "Indian Reservation." That song is entirely favorable towards the Cherokees, painting a picture of dignity and pride, rather then buying a collection of white folks' clichés about Indians.

The pop song "The American Indian Girl," written in 1835 by J. M. Smith and Charles Edward Horn, refers to its heroine as "the simple native forest child."

A number of the songs printed in folksong collections describe the demise of Indians with a combination of sympathy and a sense of inevitability. In other words, it was perceived as necessary for the poor, naïve Indian who lived the idyllic life to yield to the encroachment of modern civilization.

2) The Indians were viewed as bloodthirsty savages and libertines, unable to control their sexual urges and their desire to destroy white settlements and kill the settlers. Several songs portray Indian women as submissive and sexually available, but not to be classed with white women, who possessed manners and social graces.

The song "Little Mohee" is about a white settler meeting an Indian maiden who immediately falls in love with him and asks him to marry her. Although her father is a chieftain, and riches are implied in the offer, the settler goes back "over the sea" to his fiancée. It turns out that she has been unfaithful to him, so he decides to return to his "little Mohee." The song, which praises and patronizes the Indian maiden, discloses white settlers' ambivalence about Indians.

3) The Indians possessed land and minerals, and the settlers wanted and needed these resources.

4) Jefferson felt that all Indians should give up their nomadic ways and turn to farming. If they were unwilling to make these adjustments, whites felt justified in acquiring Indian land by force.

5) General Andrew Jackson was one of many who held that the white settlers could and should do whatever they wanted, and if the Indians didn't like it, they were welcome to fight!

After Andrew Jackson enacted the Indian Removal Act of 1830, the Cherokees, Choctaws, and Creek Indians were all forcibly removed to Oklahoma. The Cherokee removal in 1838 went down in history as particularly cruel; four thousand Indians died during this famous "Trail of Tears" march.

Nashville singer-songwriter Randy Handley recorded his song "Trail of Tears" in 1998. The chorus disparages Andrew Jackson and uses "a trail of tears . . . a trail of pain" as a metaphor for the injustices chronicled in the verses. At the end of the song, Handley changes the chorus to say that the trail of tears remains.

In the same year that "Trail of Tears" was recorded, Cherokee Indian composer Lee Johnson released a long piece called *Trail of Tears.* This vocal and instrumental work includes a Cherokee choir and a large, mostly string orchestra, along with spoken-word selections.

Nineteenth-Century Indian History

The period from 1850 to 1900 was the period of subjugation, removal, and annihilation. The Indian Appropriation Act of 1854 gave Congress the right to establish reservations. The completion of the transcontinental railroad in 1869 sounded the death knell of the buffalo, the animal that had provided virtually total sustenance for Plains tribes like the Pawnee. In her 1970 song "Now That the Buffalo's Gone," Buffy Sainte-Marie, one of the earliest Indian protest singers in the American folk music revival, compares the treatment of Indians to the German Holocaust, and challenges self-declared Indian sympathizers to take a stand.

In 1876 General George Custer was defeated by the Sioux at the Battle of the Little Big Horn. A year later the United States violated its treaty with the Sioux and seized the Black Hills. In the same year Chief Joseph of the Nez Perce surrendered after an epic but fruitless march. Joseph's small band of Indians evaded the United States Army for months, and fell just short of escaping to Canada. In 1881 Sitting Bull surrendered, and the bloody massacre of Wounded Knee in 1890 concluded what Custer had initiated. The Apaches had their last stand with the surrender of Geronimo in 1886. The Indian wars were now officially over.

General Custer has remained a symbol in the history of the western United States. From one point of view, he was a heroic figure who gave his life fighting against a large Indian force. From another vantage point, he represents the bullheaded militarism that appears a hundred years later in Pete Seeger's song "Waist Deep in the Big Muddy." There are a number of songs that celebrate or describe Custer's last stand. H. M. Belden printed two in his 1940 collection *Ballads and Songs Collected by the Missouri Folk-Lore Society*.

"The Last Fierce Charge" relates a conversation between two of Custer's soldiers, with one sensing that he is about to die. He asks the other soldier to write to the woman who has promised to marry him, and to his mother. His mother has already lost her husband and another son in the service of his country. The song ends with both men being fatally shot by the "jeering" enemy.

The second song, "The Soldier Boys," has a similar story line; after the first soldier's request, the second soldier asks that his comrade do the same for him if he is the one who dies. This song devotes a few more verses to the actual battle, which is described as "the fight they could not gain." Other versions of the song have been discovered in Georgia, Kentucky, Texas, Minnesota, Massachusetts, Oklahoma, and Nova Scotia, though some concern battles of the Civil War instead of Custer's demise.

Eddy Arnold, the popular country music crooner, recorded the song "Battle of Little Big Horn," which depicts Custer's men as noble heroes, fighting against the Indian hordes. The late Porter Wagoner recorded another version of the same song.

In 1964 Johnny Cash recorded a different kind of album of songs about Indians, called *Bitter Tears*. On this recording, which has been reissued on CD, Cash recorded a number of songs by Indian protest singer Peter La Farge. One of the songs is "Custer," a sarcastic song about the general. It depicts him as a savage who killed "women, dogs, and children," and uses the refrain "the general he don't ride well anymore."

Jack Gladstone is a contemporary Blackfoot singer-songwriter who performs multimedia shows, combining music with projected visual images. His 1993 song "Valley of the Little Bighorn" is a song about Custer's defeat written from the point of view of a white soldier, concluding, "We found a trail of thorns in the valley of the Little Bighorn." In contrast, the 1969 song "Custer Died for Your Sins," by the late actor-singer Floyd "Red Crow" Westerman, takes its title from a well-known book by Indian activist Vine Deloria Jr. The song delineates various grievances that Indians have accumulated over the years, and has the refrain "Custer died for your sins, a new day will begin."

The Reservation System and Allotments

The nineteenth century marked the beginning of the reservation system as we know it today. The Indians became dependent upon the federal government for food and medical care. The buffalo were gone, the transcontinental railroad was built, and in 1871 the government declared an end to treaties with Indian tribes. Congress could now pass statutes regulating Indian affairs that did not require approval by Indian tribes.

The Dawes Act of 1887 was designed to break up the reservations. It gave the head of a family 160 acres of land and prohibited the sale of this land for twenty-five years. The goal was to destroy Indian tribal structure, and to make the Indians into landowners, just like the white settlers. According to Robert Utley, in his book *The Indian Frontier of the American West*, four years after the passage of the act Indian land was reduced by 17,400,000 acres, or about one-seventh of Indian lands. By 1933 the Indians had lost about 60 percent of the 130 million acres they had owned prior to the Dawes Act. Trading posts run by white entrepreneurs were established on the reservations. They sold goods to the Indians, and later became outlets for selling Indian arts, crafts, and artifacts to white tourists.

"Navajo, Navajo," a 1903 song written by Harry N. Williams and Egbert Van Alstyne, is a strange vaudeville "coon" song, making fun of blacks. In this song a Navajo woman is courted by a black suitor. The Navajo had a "face of a copper shade," and the "coon" who visits her says he will help her string her beads. The racist chorus says,

> Nava, Nava, my Navajo
> I have a love for you that will grow,
> If you'll have a coon for a beau,
> I'll have a Navajo.

The Ghost Dance and the Peyote Cult

In 1890 a Paiute Indian named Wovoka created a new pan-Indian religion, combining aspects of Indian spiritual beliefs with some Christian dogma. He promised a new faith that would unite all Indians. This religion spread among various Indian tribes, including the Sioux. Indians wore "Ghost Shirts," which were supposed to be resistant to bullets. The unfortunate massacre at Wounded Knee marked the end of the Ghost Dance's credibility.

Lingenfelter, Dwyer, and Cohen's 1968 book, *Songs of the American West,* includes the song "The Indian Ghost Dance and War," credited to W. H. Prather. The song was published in the 1892–1893 report of the Bureau of American Ethnology, and reprinted in two later publications by folklorist Levette J. Davidson. The song describes the Indians leaving their reservation to fight, in the belief that their ghost shirts were invulnerable to bullets. Other verses depict the battle and attribute great courage to the American soldiers. The song concludes with the lines "The settlers in that region now can breathe with better grace; / They only ask and pray to God to make John hold his base."

Later we will see a number of songs by Indian artists and white sympathizers that refer to the battle of Wounded Knee in the context of the confrontation between the FBI and the American Indian Movement almost a hundred years later.

At about the same time as the Ghost Dance religion was spreading, the ingestion of peyote became more widespread among Indian tribes. Although peyote had been used among the Plains Tribes as early as the 1840s, an Indian named John Wilson of mixed Delaware and French stock was responsible for this particular revival. After Wilson died, the use of peyote became associated with the Native American Church. The eating of peyote with its accompanying visions was believed to cause a mingling of the Great Spirit with Jesus Christ.

By the 1960s the use of peyote had become a fad among literary and "hip" types who sought hallucinogenic experiences. Indians have maintained that their use of the drug is a sacred rite, and part of a religious ceremonial. Indians have received permission to use peyote for religious purposes, but some controversies still exist, such as the Indians' desire to have the use of peyote legalized for prison inmates. Peyote songs will figure later in the section on American Indian musical styles.

Schooling

On the reservation Indian culture and language was eroded through a combination of enforced attendance at the white man's schools, and the rise of schools run by religious missionaries. Some Indians were sent to boarding schools such as the Carlisle Indian Industrial School, where students from all tribes were compelled to take new English names and were beaten for speaking their native languages. Children were sent away at the age of six or seven, and often did not return until they were seventeen or eighteen years old. Some parents refused to allow their children to attend these schools, and by 1902 enrollment had shrunk to just over sixteen thousand students.

John W. Troutman's book *Indian Blues: American Indians and the Politics of Music, 1879–1935,* describes the attempts by both the Office of Indian Affairs and the Christian Indian boarding schools to keep the Indians from singing and dancing. These institutions discouraged any form of tribal identity or heritage. The goal was to get the Indian to assimilate into Anglo culture. In direct contradiction of these aims, the Office of Indian Affairs allowed Buffalo Bill Cody to hire hundreds of Indians to sing and dance in his Wild West shows. In a sense these Indians were playing at being Indians for white folks, just as the African American minstrels were doing.

In the early part of the twentieth century various pieces of legislation further restricted Indians' rights to land ownership, and prohibited alcohol consumption on reservations. However, in response to ethnomusicologists collecting Indian music, the restrictions against students performing Indian music at such institutions as the Carlisle Indian School began to be lifted.

By the 1950s and 1960s the Bureau of Indian Affairs (BIA), which had pressured Indian families to send their children away, had begun to establish day schools on the reservation, and boarding schools became a rarity. Besides the BIA schools, an alliance of Congregational, Presbyterian, and Dutch Reform Churches set up schools starting in 1820. They were usually vocational schools, designed to teach Indians a trade. By 1868 there were 109 of these schools.

Indians in the Twentieth Century

In the twentieth century, several wars and social movements shifted paradigms and restructured society in a relatively short time and had a major cultural impact on Indians.

The New Deal and the Indians

When Franklin Delano Roosevelt took office in 1932, he appointed a pro-Indian activist as head of the BIA. Collier promoted tribal governments, and he shepherded the 1934 Indian Reorganization Act. This legislation abolished the allotment program and authorized funding for tribal land acquisition.

Collier was a pro-Indian official, but he had difficulty understanding that not all Indians wanted to be organized into their own equivalents of white governmental structures. In 1935, 172 tribes voted to follow Collier's model, but 73 tribes voted to be excluded from the program.

World War II

World War II created profound changes in the social structure of the United States. Early in 1940, at a time when the war was raging in Europe the United States still ostensibly maintained a neutral position in the conflict. The Civilian Conservation Corps (CCC) arranged classes in welding, auto mechanics, sheet metal work and carpentry on the reservations. According to Donald L. Parman, writing in the book *The Twentieth Century West*, during World War II forty thousand Indians got jobs off the reservation, and per capita income soared from $400 in 1940 to $1200 in 1945.

The end of the war brought the return of thousands of war veterans who had glimpsed a world that they had never experienced before. Of course this was equally true for African American and Mexican American solders. Soldiers served side by side with members of different ethnic, religious and economic groups. The Army also cut across social classes. Members of a single company might include a university professor serving alongside a person with a fourth-grade education. Risking one's life for one's country also left a soldier with little desire to continue living a life defined by unemployment, disease and a low life expectancy.

The returning Indian soldier was outraged that he could not legally buy alcohol on the reservation, a situation that prevailed until 1954.

Johnny Cash had a hit record in 1964 with the song "The Ballad of Ira Hayes." Hayes, a Papago Indian, was one of the men who raised the flag at Iwo Jima in the famous photo by Joe Rosenthal. He returned home after the war, and he became a hopeless drunk, arrested fifty times. Peter La Farge, who was the first artist to sing and write songs supporting Indian rights, recorded the song in 1962, but Johnny Cash's version got to #3 on the Billboard charts. Antonino D'Ambrosio's fascinating book *A Heartbeat and a Guitar: Johnny Cash and the Making of Bitter Tears,* points out that initially Columbia Records, for whom Cash recorded, offered no support for the song, and it got no airplay. Cash himself hired promotion people and took a full-page ad in *Billboard,* the music trade paper, castigating radio people for their cowardice in not playing the song. It has been covered by numerous other artists, including Bob Dylan, Pete Seeger, Kinky Friedman, and Townes Van Zandt.

The song tells the story of Ira Hayes, beginning with the white man's theft of the Pima Indian's water rights. Ira enlisted in the Marine Corps and returned from the Pacific a hero. He was briefly honored and then returned to his home, where he proceeded to drink hard. As La Farge puts it, "At home nobody cared what Ira's done / And when do the Indians dance?" The song ends with Ira's death in a few inches of water in an irrigation ditch. It is probably the best-known Indian protest song ever written.

Postwar Developments

In 1953 Congress passed the Termination Act, which simply dissolved certain Indian nations, such as the Menomee and Klamath Tribes. By the late 1950s, 109 Indian nations had been terminated through the application of this law. The Relocation Act of 1956 set up job training centers off the reservation and offered individual financing for relocation. At the same time, funds for similar programs on the reservation were denied. Those who enrolled in the relocation programs had to sign agreements stipulating that they could not return to the reservation to live.

The Sixties, the Civil Rights Movement, and Indian Activism

The late 1950s and the 1960s saw the beginnings and growth of agitation for equal rights in the African American community. Indians became aware of sit-ins, voter registration campaigns, and confrontations with state and local governments in the southern states.

Taking similar action was more difficult for Indians, because they were a large part of the population in only a few towns that bordered reservations, such as Gallup, New Mexico; Rapid City, South Dakota; and Flagstaff, Arizona. Furthermore, the issues that concerned Indians, such as the forced sterilization of women in BIA hospitals and the removal of Indian children from their homes by state social workers who placed them in white foster homes, did not seem to interest the media. Neither did widespread alcoholism on the reservation, fetal alcohol syndrome in Indian children, the high degree of diabetes among Indians, or their low life expectancy. The affected population was simply too small and localized to attract media attention.

Vine Deloria Jr. dates the start of organized Indian activism to the 1969 blockade by Mohawk Indians of the bridge from the United States to Canada. The Mohawks were protesting demands by the Canadian government that they pay customs duty on goods brought back from the United States, as well as bridge tolls.

Clyde Bellecourt had attempted to organize Indians in Minneapolis as early as 1964. Initially he had little success, but he and several other activists, including Dennis Banks, organized the Concerned Indian Americans in 1968. When they realized that the acronym representing their organization would be CIA, they changed their name to the American Indian Movement. The four young leaders of the organization were all ex-convicts who were particularly concerned with police violence, unjust arrests, and alcoholism.

A series of protests exploded around the country. On November 9, 1969, Indians occupied what was formerly Alcatraz Prison, reclaiming it as Indian land and agitating for the creation of an Indian cultural center there. Rock group Creedence Clearwater Revival donated a boat to the cause.

Other protests involved fishing, land rights, treaty rights, and the struggle to obtain equitable royalties for the extraction of minerals. Activists fought against the clear-cutting of forests on the reservation, demanded the right to use peyote in religious rituals, and worked to stop the desecration of burial sites and the removal of sacred objects.

In October 1972, AIM activists occupied BIA headquarters in Washington. The government agreed to consider the Thirty Points that the protesters had raised as their agenda and allowed the occupiers to leave the building, giving them $66,000 designated for "return transportation."

Perhaps the most dramatic protest with the most far-reaching consequences occurred on the Pine Ridge Sioux Reservation in South Dakota. Dick Wilson, the dictatorial Sioux tribal leader, maintained a private army to suppress any resistance to the exploitation of mineral rights. Traditional leaders asked AIM for assistance, and the decision was made to occupy Wounded Knee. This decision was rife with symbolism for the Sioux, because it was the site of one of the worst massacres in the bloody history of white and Indian relations. Armed confrontations developed between AIM leaders and supporters, and Wilson's goons. Eighteen homicides were recorded on the Pine Ridge reservation in 1975 by the Commission on Civil Rights. Many people sought arms, and the FBI became involved in assisting Wilson. On June 25, 1975, the FBI entered an AIM compound and in the resulting firefight, two FBI agents and one Indian were killed.

In total, 562 of the AIM faction were arrested, of whom only 185 were actually indicted and 15 were convicted. Most of the convictions were on charges of interfering with a federal officer, or on contempt of court. Leonard Peltier, who fled to Canada and was extradited to the United States, was convicted in the shootings and currently serving a life sentence in a federal prison.

There is an entire CD of songs recorded in honor of Leonard Peltier. The artists range from Indian singers, including Buffy Sainte-Marie, Mitch Walking Elk, and Joanne Shenandoah, to white supporters of Indian rights, including Jim Page, Larry Long and Canadian singer Bruce Cockburn. Most of the songs are specifically about Peltier, but several others are about Anna Mae Aquash, an Indian activist who was murdered on the reservation. Shenandoah's song, "Please Sign Here," is a plea to gain signatures on a petition to free Peltier. Buffy Sainte-Marie's song, "Bury My Heart at Wounded Knee," draws a parallel between the massacre of the Sioux in the nineteenth century, and the confrontation with the FBI. The CD concludes with a message from Peltier himself.[*]

---

[*] For those who wish to know more about the Peltier case, Peter Matthiesen has written a superb and lengthy book titled *In the Spirit of Crazy Horse*. Peltier's appeals have been denied, and currently his only chance for freedom is through executive clemency. This can be granted only by the president of the United States.

Anna Mae Aquash   AIM still exists, but it appears to be hopelessly factionalized, with much of the controversy devoted to the murder of Indian activist Anna Mae Aquash. Anna Mae was murdered at Pine Ridge in 1976, and the investigation into her death has dragged on for over thirty years. John Graham, an Indian member of AIM, was tried for her murder, but he was acquitted in 2009. AIM was thoroughly infiltrated by the FBI, and some believe the FBI murdered her, or that AIM itself disposed of her because she knew too much about the organization's purchases of guns, use of drugs, and possibly even murders committed by AIM members. Other people allegedly involved in the murder are still awaiting trial. Because AIM has split into various factions on this issue, it is extremely difficult to separate facts from conjecture in the case.

Current Developments: Casinos and a Flowering of Culture

The newest wrinkle in Indian country is the development of casinos. The Indian Gaming and Regulation Act of 1988 allowed tribes to regulate gambling, subject to regulation by states where reservations are located. The Seminoles started bingo games in 1979, and by 1985 ninety recognized tribes were operating some sort of games of chance. By 1991 the number had grown to 150, and a September 29, 2008 article in the *New York Times* by Jo Becker and Don Van Natta Jr. puts the current figure at 423 Indian-owned casinos. In 1994 gambling had become a $3 billion business, but the current value, according to the article cited above is $26 billion. According to Charles Wilkinson, whose book was cited earlier, Indians net about 30 percent of this money, or almost eight billion dollars a year.

There is a great deal of lobbying in Washington for and against Indian casinos. Various state governments, existing white-owned casinos, and entrepreneurs argue that Indians have an unfair business advantage because they do not pay taxes.

There is a certain irony in Indians hustling money from white gamblers, since throughout history the money and natural resources have all gone in the opposite direction. Many tribes have used their income from the casinos to build reservation businesses, and some have distributed royalties to tribal members.

This is a book about music and politics, but I would be remiss not to mention that the last twenty or so years have seen the flowering of numerous Indian novelists and poets, visual artists, playwrights, and filmmakers. Sherman Alexie, in particular, has distinguished himself in film, music, poetry, and fiction. He has coauthored the music for a number of songs in his films, and he also has written *Reservation Blues*, a novel that depicts delta bluesman Robert Johnson returning from his supposed death to live on an Indian reservation.

Traditional Music

Music pervaded the life of the American Indian. A few songs by Canadian Indians appear in French publications as early as 1609. Several others were printed in the eighteenth century, but for the most part the white settlers had little interest in Indian music. Theodore Baker studied the music of the Seneca tribe in 1880. Alice Fletcher studied the music of the Omahas in 1884, and later Fletcher's student Frances Densmore studied the music of numerous tribes. The first audio recording of Indian songs was made in 1889.

Music was an integral part of Indian life. Frederic Burton's 1909 book *American Primitive Music* pointed out that "every conceivable thing in which [the Indian] has an interest becomes the subject of a song"—friends, enemies, sacred events, forests, lakes, fires, teepees, babies, whiskey, clothes, etc.

Traditional Indian music is generally classified according to regional styles. Ethnomusicologist Bruno Nettl, for example, describes an Eastern style that contains short phrases and call-and-response patterns, as well as a Navajo-Apache style with a large vocal range, nasal tone production, and even rhythm patterns. Songs can be further classified by performer and function—some songs were limited to performances by either men or women, and some had roles in specific ceremonies.

A special caveat about collections of Indian music is that they reflect not only researchers' individual taste and bias but also their rapport with informants, who may have declined to share songs tied to rituals or ceremonials not open to those outside the tribe. It should also be remembered that folklorists and ethnomusicologists often focused on collecting older songs before they disappeared forever, and missed or ignored contemporary compositions. Yet the collectors mentioned above were working at a time of new influences in Indian music. In the church schools, Indian children were learning vocal harmonies that had been rare in traditional Indian music. And as the tribes were pushed out of their original geographic areas, they began to meet other groups and to exchange musical ideas. The Ghost Dance discussed earlier in this chapter provided another forum for this sort of cultural interchange.

Twentieth-Century Music

The following tables list the forms and musical subjects that flourished in the Indian musical community over the course of the twentieth century.

Traditional songs: Often unaccompanied, or accompanied by percussion only.

Peyote songs: Also sung in Indian languages, these songs often contain vocables—syllables without a specific meaning. Peyote songs may describe the hallucinogenic visions produced through the use of the drug. More recent peyote songs are sometimes sung in harmony.

Powwow (49er) songs: Powwows are inter-tribal gatherings, and sometimes have a white audience. The songs often mix Indian languages and English, and may contain vocables. Many powwows are large annual events with prize money awarded in singing and dancing contests. There are hundreds of these events in Indian country.

Country and western: There are some Indian country and western bands that are quite popular on specific reservations, such as the popular longtime Navajo band the Sundowners.

Blues, reggae, and rock: A number of Indian bands, including XIT, Red Thunder, Burning Sky, and Walela, work in these styles found in American pop music.

Folk, country, and rock: A number of Indian artists cross over into all of these categories. Keith Secola, whose powwow song "Indian Cars" was a big hit on Indian radio (there are twenty-six Indian radio stations on or near the reservations), is among these, as are Bill Miller and Jack Gladstone, who perform widely for white audiences. Joanne Shenandoah has been referred to as the "Indian Joan Baez."

New Age: New Age culture in white society has brought about a sort of faddist interest in Indian flute music. Such players as Ed Wapp and Kevin Locke are fairly tradition-oriented, and some, like R. Carlos Nakai, are more experimental. Nakai has recorded many albums as a soloist, with his jazzy group Jackalope, and with non-Indian New Age pianist Peter Kater. He has also recorded a number of works by Arizona State University professor James de Mars. Some of the Indian flute players are Anglos, and fall into the category that poet-scholar Wendy Rose refers to as "white shamans."

Chicken scratch: This is a hybrid of German-Mexican, rock, and Indian music featuring accordion and saxophone. It is popular among the Tohono O'odham Indians of southern Arizona.

Protest music: Protest music is not a musical style, but an ideological idiom that deals with social issues. A number of artists and groups, such as Julian B., John Trudell, and Red Thunder, perform spoken word to rhythm backgrounds in the style of rap or rock and roll. The earliest protest singers of the 1960s and '70s, especially Peter La Farge and Buffy Sainte-Marie, performed in a country-folk style.

Hybrids: Categorizing music by style or subject is convenient for critics and scholars, but it is less useful for many musicians who enjoy leapfrogging musical styles and genres. Artists like Keith Secola or R. Carlos Nakai are not easy to pigeonhole, because their curiosity and creativity may lead them in many different musical directions.

I have separated the songs to be discussed below by theme, as follows:

Historical, nationalistic, and pan-Indian: "Nationalistic" songs express solidarity within a tribe, while "pan-Indian" songs proclaim solidarity with Indian tribes in general.

Lifestyle commentary: Songs about various aspects of life, such as cars, dance, or pow-wows.

Mystical: Songs that refer to the sacred, dream-like visions, and oneness with the earth.

Protest, selling out, and solidarity with other groups: Protest songs invariably indict the white man, to whom an Indian might be in danger of "selling out" his own people or culture. Songs of solidarity make common cause with other oppressed groups, usually black or Hispanic people.

Historical, Nationalistic, and Pan-Indian Songs

Many of the historical songs, such as songs about Custer, spill over into protest subject matter. Cherokee Rose and Silena's "Visions of History" is a song of retribution, the price to be paid for taking an Indian's life. The lyric states that "visions of history haunt me in my dreams."

Buddy Red Bow's "Wounded Knee" describes the acts of brutality perpetrated by white soldiers in that battle and ends with the burial of the 267 men, women, and children who died there. Another of Red Bow's songs is about Ben Black Elk, an Indian who greeted tourists at the foot of Mount Rushmore, where the heads of several

American presidents are carved into the face of the mountain. Red Bow asks why there are no Indian faces up there with them.

Two sets of songs relate to the notion of Indian unity. One set refers to specific tribes, usually the tribe that the singer belongs to. While many tribes have passed down traditional songs that were intended to bring the tribe together, particularly for purposes of fighting against other tribes, Joanne Shenandoah's song "We Are the Iroquois" is a contemporary song that encourages loyalty to elders and tribal unity. Part of the lyric states,

> We are the Iroquois
> We are proud and we are strong
> We've held on to our culture now
> Oh for so long.

There are a number of songs, like Tom Bee's "Let My People Dance," that refer to "our people" in a more general context. Such songs can be interpreted either as pertaining to a specific tribe, or as representing all Indians.

Beginning with World War II, many Indians served in the U.S. Armed Forces. A number of songs pay tribute to the contributions of Indian "warriors" to these struggles. Vincent Craig's "Navajo Code Talker" describes the use of the Navajo language in World War II as a means of communicating secret information. The Japanese never succeeded in breaking this code.

Bobby Eagle, a Sioux veteran, wrote "Vietnam," a song that pays tribute to Vietnam War veterans. The chorus includes the lyric "Vietnam, a place to die young, / Vietnam, color didn't matter at all." And the group Apache Spirit recorded "In the Persian Gulf," a song about the Persian Gulf War.

Lifestyle Songs

Lifestyle songs describe social conditions rather than political ones. Keith Secola's "Indian Cars" is the classic song of this genre, with lyrics like "My car is dented, the radiators steam / One headlight don't work, the radio can scream" and "I got a sticker that says Indian power / I stuck it on the bumper, that's what holds my car together."

Buddy Red Bow and others have written songs for and about pow-wows, which are well-attended social events with dancing ("49ers") and drinking. Tom Bee wrote and recorded a song called "Nothing Could Be Finer Than a 49er" that tells of dancing around the fire with a bottle of wine and taking his girlfriend home after the dance in his "one-eyed Ford." In her popular autobiography, *Lakota Woman*, Mary Crow Dog prints a fragment of a 49er song that includes the lines

> One drunk Indian yells 'cause he's being mugged,
> Some young Indian complains his phone is bugged—
> What's your beef?
> Ugh, ugh, big chief, how, how,
> Hio, yana-yanah-hioh.

These lines are typical of 49er songs in their combination of slightly silly poetry, vocable syllables, and the acknowledgment of the white man's tendency to call all Indians "chief."

Alcohol   Alcohol is a serious problem on the reservation and in neighboring towns. One of the most powerful and upsetting songs on the subject is A. Paul Ortega's "Chicago." Ortega sets the lyric to the old cowboy song "The Streets of Laredo." Instead of a cowboy all wrapped in white linen, Ortega gives us an Indian. Instead of Laredo, the song is set in Chicago. After the opening chorus, Ortega delivers a long recitation about a drunken Indian staggering down the sidewalks of Chicago. He has come to the big city "because they told me life was going to be easier." Instead he is shunned because of his race. The song includes the Pledge of Allegiance, reworded to say, "There is one nation which is enslaved, because it has not had its liberty and freedom." At the end of the song Ortega returns to the Laredo melody, concluding with "I know I must die."

Ortega also recorded some duets with Joanne Shenandoah. In the song "Lovin' Ways" they address not only alcohol, but also domestic abuse. In general, however, the subject of alcohol is one that contemporary Indian novelists and poets have examined in much greater depth than singers have chosen to do.

Mystic Songs: Dreams, Visions, and the Earth

Traditional Indian music incorporates a sacred identification with "Mother Earth" wherein man's death is a return to whence he came. This identification is probably the aspect of Indian music that resonates most with the followers of New Age philosophy. Like the African American spirituals of the eighteenth and nineteenth centuries, contemporary Indian songs with spiritual overtones offer hope in a world beyond the everyday difficulties of contemporary human experience. Songs like Buddy Red Bow's "Winds of Life" tell of a peace and contentment not available on the earth, in a time without hunger and a place where children gather, singing songs of love.

In their song "Three Generations," the Song Catchers express reverence for their elders and for the sacred mountain that guards their grandfather's grave. They conclude the song with the lyric

> And my father became my grandfather
> And I became as he.
> In the shadow of the sacred mountain
> My son becomes me.

Another song by the same group, "Walk Your Road," not only identifies with the earth and the spirit world, but also warns against the white man's destructive practices: "They have poisoned precious waters / They have filled the sky with holes."

The imagery of eagles and feathers appears in many Indian songs. In Tom Bee's "Anthem of the American Indian," recorded on XIT's

Silent Warrior album, the eagle is presented as a wild and untamed bird. Knifewing Segura's "The Indian and the Eagle" proclaims that "the Indian and the eagle are one." Since the eagle is at once an endangered species and a patriotic symbol of American life, this identification with a proud but disappearing bird represents a complex set of images and ideas.

Bill Miller's song "Reservation Road," cowritten with John Flanagan and Brent Holmes, combines a whole panoply of symbols in a song that tells a tragic story from Miller's childhood. The album notes inform us that Miller's grandfather was killed by a drunk driver on the reservation. The song tells of a promised land where the grandfather's spirit soars, "beyond a place where eagles fly." The singer's identification with the earth is enforced by his grandfather's admonition: "He said don't make promises that you won't keep / Don't betray the earth beneath your feet."

Protest Songs and Solidarity

Indian protest songs inveigh against the theft and destruction of Indian lands, conditions of economic disadvantage, loss of native culture and languages, educational deprivation, problems associated with relocation to the cities, and genocidal practices—and lodge complaints against the U.S. government and the capitalist system.

Earlier in this chapter I discussed Peter La Farge, Buffy Sainte-Marie, and Johnny Cash's *Bitter Tears* album. In the pop-rock genre, XIT, in the mid-1970s, was the first Indian group that performed rock music with socially relevant lyrics. There are also examples of such songs written by sympathetic white performers, such as Bruce Cockburn or Marty Stuart.

Theft and Destruction of the Land   Protests against environmental violation provide a rich counterpoint to the many songs that speak of honoring the earth. In "So This Is America," Don Martin says the eagle's heart is broken because there is no harmony with the earth. Robby Bee's "Let's Save Our Mother Earth" complains about corporate control of the Environmental Protection Agency, citing nuclear plants "leaking radiation," the depletion of the ozone layer, and a variety of other environmental issues.

Economic Disadvantage   Peter La Farge's song "Alaska 49th State" asserts that

> The Indian isn't hired,
> They import white skins;
> The Indian can't hunt,
> Being there first was
> Original sin.

Some other protest songs present economic issues as being only one facet of an overall pattern of racism and genocide.

Racism and Genocide   Indian protest artists probably picked up the word "genocide" from black rap artists, and the Indian songs I have encountered that use that word are rap songs. Without Reservations' song "Mascot" protests the stereotyping of Indians in sports names or nicknames. It describes this behavior as "Indian bashing at the highest level / A racist attack disguised as the devil." Another song by this group, "Was He a Fool (Columbus)," describes both economic discrimination and genocide: "Left my people in poverty they starve / To me a genocidal catastrophe." Julian B. is a young SOAR artist whose album cover shows him swinging a tomahawk. The album's title is "Once upon a Genocide." In the song "Genocide in Progress" he derides, "Another little triple K town / Built on the graves of a lot of native slaves." In "Indian Fan," Julian B. raps about the police: "Do the cops care what tribe you're from? When they hide behind their badge, don't be dumb."

Language and Culture, Education and Relocation   The late actor-singer-songwriter Floyd Westerman commented on virtually every aspect of American life that affects Indians. His "Missionaries" advised, "Spoil the mind and spare the rod."

In "BIA Blues," he took on the government: "You know this land is our land, they stole it all away. / You must think we're some kind of fools, to let you carry on this way." Tom Bee's song "Relocation" describes the loneliness and frustration of the relocated Indian: "Iron ponies called the automobile / On a tombstone highway where the earth has died." And Robby Romero's song "Heartbeat" on the *Red Thunder* album expresses similar sentiments: "As the people sunset, are we really here alive? / On the Main Street of the wind, relocated from our homes."

General Complaints and Humor   Richard Cyr, in "Land of the Free," suggests: "If you've got some garbage, won't you send it to America, / That's what they're serving in the land of the free." Joe Manuel, in "Revolution Daze," predicts the coming of a new day:

> Your people are runnin' around
> Wonderin' what's comin' down
> It's just a big revolution you see.

Frank Montano writes in the wry "Commodity Blues":

> We eat commodity eggs for breakfast, commodity beans for
>   lunch,
> Commodity stew for supper, and we snack on peanut butter and
> Crunch.

Buffy Sainte-Marie summarized it all in her moving 1966 song "My Country 'Tis of Thy People You're Dying." In a laundry list of grievances she outlines the loss of native languages, the shipping of students to boarding schools, the "gift" of blankets carrying small-pox, and the destruction of the environment. Sadly, the song is still timely today.

The Flagstaff group Primitive Tribes plays punk rock with great strength and considerable volume. Their song "The Trail of Tears" is an impassioned condemnation of contemporary American capitalism, and a litany of complaints against racism and bigotry. This is an unusual recording for Indian music, because it is musically closer to punk rock then to rap music, country-rock, or more typical rock and roll. This is a self-produced cassette project, and I suspect that there are other Indian "garage bands" that are operating in a similar musical style.

Although this book mostly avoids dealing with Canadian Indian music, part of the pan-Indian movement is the pooling of Canadian and American Indians in various musical groups or recordings. The record *I Am an Eagle: The Music from the Legends Project* is a Canadian album recorded in Nashville, using musicians from various tribes. It is also an unusual album because it contains four instrumentals and ten songs. Some of the songs are sung in English, while the others are in various Indian languages. Some of the songs are protest songs, some historical, and some mystical. The song "Thunder Warrior" describes Custer riding into the Sioux camp "with unbraided hair crying out for wisdom." "Indian Giver" is another historical protest song, outlining how the Indian helped the white man, and was rewarded for his efforts by the theft of his land and his mineral rights.

Selling Out   A few songs commemorate the selling out of Indian values. Buddy Red Bow's "My Indian Girl" describes a troubled streetwalker as "My once Indian girl, living in a white man's world." The band Without Reservation recorded a song titled "To the Sell Outs." The song talks about selling out for money, and Indians who are ashamed of being Indians. The song ends with the dedication "For the one who sold his soul to the other side, / Here's your grave, punk, your only place to hide."

John Trudell   John Trudell was an AIM leader who was involved in the 1972 Indian occupation of the U.S. Treasury building in

Washington. Prior to that event, he had received threats about the safety of his wife and four children, who later died in a fire under mysterious circumstances.

I have chosen to discuss Trudell's work separately because he covers virtually all of the subject areas that we have already mentioned, yet seems to work in another dimension that goes beyond categorization or analysis. In addition to social protest songs, Trudell writes about personal confusions and romantic situations in music that lies halfway between spoken word with jazz accompaniment and rap. He records and tours with a six piece band that includes Quiltman, who sings Indian chants while the rest of the band plays impassioned rock and roll. Trudell narrates the lyrics, and on some songs the band sings parts of the song, or sings background vocals while Trudell is reciting the lyrics.

On his album *A.K.A. Graffiti Man*, the song "Somebody's Kind" describes a failed marriage between a white cowboy and an Indian woman:

> Once they shared the same dream
> Ends up they both had canvas of their own
> And they saw they only brought one canvas
> Her part of the dream alone was bigger then that.

As politically oriented as Trudell's work is, there is also positive energy. In "Rockin' the Res," released on video by the label Ryko, there is energy reborn out of long defeat: "Rockin' our hearts, rockin' the res, / No chance we'll ever give up."

On *Johnny Damas and Me*, Trudell takes on the subject of women's oppression in the song "Shadow over Sisterhood," explaining that

> The laws of justice
> Are business decisions
> Gender and class
> Cut with surgical precision.

In "Blue Indians," the title song of his 1999 album, he speaks about "blue" Indians "Being pulled into melting pots."

His song "Carry the Star," from the album *Bone Days*, declares,

> The more evil the empire,
> The more paranoid the society.
> Hanging from the cross,
> Indians are Jesus,
> Hanging from the cross.

All in all, John Trudell is a unique figure in contemporary American Indian music. He has managed to combine traditional Indian music with rock and roll, to express anger and bitterness and to advocate for positive change, to sing of romance and to "rock the res." Yet, because of his uncompromising political stance, and his involvement in AIM, Trudell gets little or no radio play.

Common Cause   As some Indian artists adopted the rap style, it was inevitable that they would include black musicians. Michael D., the "Ebony Warrior," is a member of Robby Bee and the Boyz from the Res. Their song "Ebony Warrior" proclaims, "Heart of a warrior and good to go. / Red and black warriors are good to go." Robby's song "Land of the Wanna Be Free" makes common cause with blacks: "The abuse you have put on our people / Is like the beating of Rodney King."

Mitch Walking Elk recorded an anti-apartheid song, and Russell Means in his "Class of '73" describes how Jews, Christians, and other friends of the Indian came to support AIM at Wounded Knee. The band Primitive Tribes' song "Humanism" expresses common cause with "black or white, gay or straight."

Musical Fusions by Various Indian Artists

Though there is only space below to address some of the major artists and musical trends, interested readers can turn to Brian

Wright-McLeod's *The Encyclopedia of Native Music*, which contains
439 pages of listings of recordings by American Indian and Canadian
"First Nations" artists.

Robert Mirabal is from the Taos Pueblo. He sings, writes songs,
and plays the Indian flute and percussion instruments. He also is a
published poet and photographer and makes and designs flutes. He
played in a world music multicultural band with African and Hai-
tian musicians before returning home to record a string of albums,
mostly for Silver Wave Records. His 2007 CD *In the Blood*, on his
own Star Records label, includes several songs sung in Mirabal's Tiwa
language, and others sung in English. Many of the songs are cowritten with white songwriters, but are about Indian life. Most are
somewhat reflective and philosophical, rather then bitter or angry.
On the other hand, the selection "Uncle Theo" describes Mirabal's
Uncle Theo, who served in Vietnam and lost his leg. His wounds
were inflicted not by the enemy, but by a sergeant "who they say was
in the Ku Klux Klan."

Robbie Robertson, born to a Mohawk mother, was a member of
the folk-rock group the Band. While the Band's songs mostly concern events in the history of white America, all the members of the
band except one were Canadians. Starting in the nineties, Robertson
began to make music that reflected his Indian heritage. In 1994 he
did an album that contained soundtrack music for a three-part Ted
Turner TV production called *The Native Americans*. The song "Ghost
Dance" tells how that dance was outlawed, but concludes that "We
shall live again." Robertson integrated his folk-rock music with a
number of Indian artists, including vocal groups Ulali, Walela, and
the Silvercloud Singers.

In 1998 Robertson continued in this direction on his album *From
the Underworld of Redboy*. Once again he used several Indian artists
on the recording—"Peyote Healing" features the vocal harmonies of
Indian peyote artists Primeaux and Miraj, and "Sacrifice" ("Take away
your language, cut off all your hair") sets an extended narration by
Leonard Peltier against a rock track. Scottish electronic music composer and trip-hop producer Howie B. also contributed to the album.

The women's vocal trio Ulali have released two albums of their own music, and were also featured on the Smithsonian Folkways anthology *Heartbeat: Voices of First Nation's Women*. On the later album, Ulali sings the song "Going Home" with the lyric "Return the land and heal our pain."

Ulali's leader, Pura Fé, is an actress and a dancer as well as a singer. She has a Tuscarora Indian mother and a Puerto Rican father, and has recorded three solo albums. On her 2007 album, *Hold the Rain*, she performs a number of songs in a sort of soul-rock vocal style. The stirring first track of the album *My People, My Land* (also included, in a different version, as the final track) features a sort of pan-Indian vocal group, recorded in North Carolina with members of five different tribes.

Walela is a vocal group that consists of the Coolidge sisters, Rita and Priscilla, and Priscilla's daughter Laura Satterfield. The Coolidge sisters have sung on many other people's recording projects. They are part Cherokee, and their recordings incorporate gospel and spiritual influences with New Age overtones. Most of their songs do not delve into political or social issues, but their 1997 Mercury album features the song "Bury My Heart at Wounded Knee," which refers to the massacre in which "A baby's blood was a soldier's pay."

White Commentary on Indians

Plenty of songs that portray Indians have been written by white artists.

Humor and Novelty Songs

Like the folk songs and older pop music songs mentioned earlier in this chapter, more recent songs continue to portray the Indian as a romantic and/or childish figure.

Johnny Preston's 1960 hit song "Running Bear," composed by J. P. Richardson (the Big Bopper) is about two Indian lovers who belong to tribes that are hostile to one another. In order to meet they dive into the "raging river" and die together. The song ends with the reassurance that they will always be together "in that happy hunting ground."

In the same year Larry Verne recorded a song written by Charlie Drake called "Please Mr. Custer." This song is about a soldier who begs General Custer to excuse him from going into battle. The song makes fun of the 7th Cavalry, and it includes the immortal lyric "There's a redskin waitin' out there, / Fixin' to take my hair."

Sucking noises simulating the sound of arrows are interspersed throughout the song, and one of the arrows kills a buddy of the singer.

Racist Sentiments and Stereotypes

In 1962 Rex Allen Jr. recorded a song called "Don't Go Near the Indians," composed by Lorene Mann. This long and convoluted story is about a white boy who meets an Indian maiden on the reservation. He falls in love with her, but when he asks the chief for her hand, the boy discovers that his own father was an Indian. The lyric goes on to tell how he was stolen by his white stepfather in retaliation for the scalping of his son. His stepfather then discloses that "I love you just as much as my own little feller that is dead." If this is not enough drama for the reader, the poor boy finds out that the girl that he wishes to marry is in fact his own sister!

Indian-White Romances

The song "Half Breed," written by Mary Dean and Al Capps and recorded by Cher in 1972, details the story of a woman who is not accepted by either whites or Indians: "both sides were against me since the day I was born." In another part of the lyric, children at her school taunt her, saying, "Give her a feather, she's a Cherokee."

Merle Haggard's 1976 "Cherokee Maiden" has an almost vaudeville flavor, and concludes that the singer will spirit the Cherokee maiden to Paradise.

John Mellencamp's 1987 song "Hotdogs and Hamburgers" tells the tale of an Indian girl hitching a ride. The white driver tries to trade goods or money for sex, but she complains that he is trying to "Get something for nothing, like the pilgrims in the olden days." When the driver finally lets her out, she meets an old Indian man who intuitively knows what has occurred. The driver realizes that

> To him I was the white man
> The one who sold him something that
> He already owned.

The driver continues on to Los Angeles, where he gets down on his knees and asks for forgiveness.

Reverence for Earth

The cowboy song "Home on the Range," a setting of a poem that dates from 1873, contains a nostalgic verse about the demise of American Indians, conjuring up images of their "flickering campfires" amid the "wild prairies" and "glittering stars."

Elton John's "Indian Sunset," written by John and Bernie Taupin in 1971, conjures up romantic images of yellow moons. It ends with the hero dying from a bullet as the Indians are being dispossessed from their land.

The rock group Kansas in Kerry Livgren's 1975 "Song for America" tells the lengthy story of a virgin land plundered by the white man. The same writer's 1976 "Cheyenne Autumn" contains similar idyllic visions of the land. The singer senses the "howling winds of war" on the horizon, and with them his impending doom. A female singer concludes the song with the lyric "Oh, we cannot endure like the earth and the mountains, / But there's more lives to keep, / For a new song is rising."

Chris Williamson is a feminist singer-songwriter whose Indian grandmother's flight with Chief Joseph is depicted in the 1984 song "Grandmother's Land." In the same year Williamson wrote and recorded the song "Prairie Fire," expressing reverence for the earth and describing her own "cowboy and Indian" heritage.

Social Problems, Social Protest, and Lifestyles

In addition to the song "Trail of Tears," discussed earlier in this section, Randy Handley also wrote and recorded the tune "Wind River Song." The song concerns a pregnant woman on the Wind River Reservation, whose young husband is not destined to return home. The last verse gets to the heart of the matter:

> How long can you give a people no hope at all
> If you weren't born white, then your ways are all wrong,
> The girl feels something kicking, and she knows
> That Davy is not coming home.

For the most part I have elected not to include the work of artists who were not born or do not live in the United States, but Bob Marley's 1983 "Buffalo Soldier" deserves some mention. Buffalo soldiers were African Americans recruited to fight Indians. The Indians referred to them as "buffalo soldiers" because of their nappy hair. The song never specifically mentions Indians, but makes common cause between Rasta men and the buffalo soldiers.

The Indian group Burning Sky paid tribute to Canadian singer-songwriter Bruce Cockburn by recording his song "Indian Wars" on their 1995 album. They also printed the lyrics on the CD booklet, prefacing them with the comment "the treaties were broken but we remain strong." The song refers to broken treaties, and the "pit of disgrace" that the white man has dug for himself. The chorus uses the repeated refrain "You thought it was over but it's just like before / Will there never be an end to the Indian wars?"

Tom Russell is a singer-songwriter whose songs are often set in the Southwest. His 1989 song "Blue Wing" depicts a longtime outlaw who ends up drinking himself to death in Los Angeles. The singer dreams that halfway through the funeral Blue Wing speaks of flying away "beyond these walls above the clouds where the rain don't fall, on a poor man's dream."

Bob Marley

Russell's 2004 album *Indians, Cowboys, Horses, Dogs* includes Peter La Farge's song "The Ballad of Ira Hayes," as part of a medley that also uses the songs "Bacon Rind" and "Chief Seattle."

Symbols

Neil Young's song "Broken Arrow" was written in 1967 and recorded by the Buffalo Springfield. The song creates a bridge between the life of the pop performer and the contemporary Indian, described as "empty-quivered" and holding a "broken arrow." The song touches on growing up in white Canada or America, and tells of a mythical wedding where the king and queen "married for peace and were gone." To the earth-oriented hippie movement that many folk rockers identified with, the Indian was a stirring and romantic figure, a sort of vestige of the last remnants of the noble tradition of a pristine America with old-growth forests and clean water.

Michael (Martin) Murphy recorded his hit song "Geronimo's Cadillac" in 1972. The song, cowritten with Austin poet John Charles Quarto, depicts Geronimo as a jailhouse inmate who has been given a Cadillac in exchange for the Indians' land. The white man, Murphy says, stole the Indians' land and won't give it back, but they "sent Geronimo a Cadillac." On the album's cover Murphy comments, "Let me ride with you, Geronimo. In prison, on a horse, or in a Cadillac, you fought them."

Murphy's 1976 song "Cherokee Fiddle" is a more specific complaint about the loss of traditional values. The hero is a Cherokee fiddle player who used to play for passengers at the railroad station. Murphy tells us that the fiddler played music for whiskey, and "good whiskey never let him lose his place." Later in the song Murphy comments sardonically that the Indians are "dressing up like cowboys, and the cowboys are putting beads and turquoise on." The song concludes with an analogy between the disappearance of the busking fiddler and the end of the railroad itself.

In 1992 John Anderson wrote and performed the haunting country-folk song "Seminole Wind." It mourns the death of the once-pure

Everglades, and the swamp drained by the Army Corps of Engineers. Anderson says that the last time he went to the swamp he "heard the ghost of Osceola cry." Osceola was a Seminole chief; many of the Seminoles were never conquered by the white man, but lived and hid in the Everglades.

Marty Stuart

Marty Stuart is a well-known country artist who has spent quite a bit of time on the Lakota Sioux reservation. In 2005 he recorded an entire album devoted to Indian issues—the first by a non-Indian since Johnny Cash's *Bitter Tears* album of 1964—called *Badlands: Ballads of the Lakota*. The songs range from Indian chants to spiritual tributes such as "Walking Through the Prayers." The song "Badlands" cites the contradiction between Indians and whites keeping and breaking treaties: "We never broke a treaty, / They never kept one." The song "Crazy Horse" pays tribute to that chief: "He was the last warrior standing, / Defending the old way of life."

Stuart's song "Casino" is the only song I have encountered on that subject. Considering the importance of the casino industry on reservations today, this seems a bit strange. In the song Stuart outlines the moral demise of a reservation gambler who has lost all his money and his good reputation. He pawns his silver, a "beautiful ring from the Black Hills gold mine," spends time in jail, and loses his wife. The song concludes with the singer questioning the existence of God. While casinos have brought money to the Indian people, inevitably some Indians will ruin their lives through gambling, succumbing to the same temptations as the tourists.

Hybrids

Cargo Records' 1991 compilation *Till the Bars Break* sets the poems of Jeanette Armstrong to various musical backgrounds, including the work of avant-garde guitarist Henry Kaiser. The white artists on this album tend to work in the folk ballad tradition. There are two songs about the death of Anna Mae Aquash, discussed earlier in this section. Black rap artist Chuck D says that "at least American Indians know how they've been fucked over." Other songs range from the semi-humorous "Hi Tech Teepee Trauma Mama," by performance artist Rebecca Bellmore ("Souvenir seeker, you are not a bad person / Free me from this plastic") to "Buffalo Jump," by Seventh Fire (What does it take to be a chief, anyway? / No one's going to come and terminate me").

In 1996 Amy Ray produced a compilation double album of songs benefiting the Honor the Earth Campaign for her Daemon label. The album honored indigenous people whose lands were endangered by the encroachment of "progress." A number of the songs deal with the loss of Indian land. The artists include a broad range of both rock and folk performers, including Bruce Cockburn, the Indigo Girls, the Latin Playboys, and Bonnie Raitt, as well as native artists Jim Boyd, poet-musician Joy Harjo with her band Poetic Justice, Indigenous, Keith Secola, John Trudell, and Ulali. There are two different songs about Wounded Knee, as well as a number of other songs that are about more general environmental issues. The Indigo Girls' song "Blood Quantum," which uses the word "genocide" as a chant, refers to boarding schools, colonization, and white attempts to Christianize Indians. All of the songs are from previously recorded albums, and were donated by the artists.

Indian Classical Music

There isn't space in this book to cover the numerous Indian classical music composers and musicians. Louis W. Ballard has taught workshops on Indian music all over the United States and composed music partially based on Indian themes. Other contemporary Indian composers include Ramon Chacon, Brent Michael Davids, and Jerod Tate. British composer Tony Hymas has written several ambitious works that feature various Indian artists, including John Trudell and Tom Bee. In the late nineteenth and early twentieth centuries, a number of American composers, including Edward Macdowell, tried to incorporate Indian music in a quest for an American classical music identity.

The Business of Indian Music and a Look at the Future

Larger record stores (like Amoeba Music in California; Twist and Shout in Denver; Music Millennium in Portland, Oregon; and Waterloo in Austin) generally carry a dozen or so recordings by Indian artists, or some of the non-Indian Indian flute players. The two primary producers of recordings of Indian music are Canyon Records in Phoenix, and SOAR in Albuquerque. Canyon has a large catalog that goes back over fifty years and includes most every genre of Indian music. It is a white-owned company, started by Ray and Mary Boley in 1951 when Ed Lee Natay, a Navajo singer, asked to make a record at their studio in Phoenix. They were so entranced with the music that they started Canyon in order to make Natay's record commercially available.

SOAR was started by an Indian singer-songwriter named Tom Bee who had recorded for Motown Records some years earlier with his band XIT. SOAR also covers every genre of Indian music, and has branched out into the production of some videos.

Folkways Records has issued a number of albums of traditional Indian music, as part of their huge collection of world music recordings. More recently they have produced two albums of American Indian women artists, whose musical range extends from traditional to contemporary music. Indian House is a label based in Taos, New Mexico, that has devoted itself to producing albums of traditional Indian music.

Silver Wave Records in Boulder, Colorado has produced several Indian music recordings, including some albums by Joanne Shenandoah. The label also produced albums that include Indian flute music, and New-Age style recordings of Native musicians collaborating with pianist Peter Kater.

Other labels devoted to Indian music include Makoche in Bismarck, North Dakota, and the Canadian company Arbor, in Winnipeg. Four Winds Trading Company is a Colorado-based distribution outlet that sells records and books of American Indian recordings.

Many Indian artists produce their own recordings on their own labels. These recordings are primarily sold by the artists themselves, or they may be available in towns located near the reservations.

In an October 1996 interview with Tom Bee, the CEO of Soar Records, Mr. Bee told me that 60 percent of his company's recordings were sold to non-Indians. If we assume that relatively little of the non-English-language traditional music is being bought by whites, except for purchases by scholars or libraries, the figure probably approaches or even exceeds 60 percent for Indian music sung in English. This is similar to the percentage of rap records journalists have concluded are bought by white suburban kids.

As world music in general has become increasingly accessible, and musicians and fans have developed an interest in it, it would not be surprising to see more non-Indian musicians incorporating Indian music or Indian musicians into their compositions and performances. As long as Indians continue to live in First World America under what could be described as Third World conditions, we can expect to see Indian protest music continue to be written and recorded.

3

AFRICAN AMERICANS

Of all the groups that we will discuss in this book, the African Americans came to this country under the most adverse conditions. They were sold into slavery against their will, herded like cattle by white slave traders and enemy tribesmen, and packed tightly together in suffocating proximity on oceangoing ships. On board the ships, the slaves were kept in chains with virtually no air to breathe. Many perished during the voyage. Because the slaves came from different tribes and spoke different languages, the possibilities of real communication among them, let alone the chances of revolting, were minimal.

Somehow, out of these impossible conditions a body of incredible music was born. This music has had a profound influence not only on the shape of American music, but on the music found in virtually every corner of the world. Spirituals, work songs, hollers, blues, ragtime, jazz, rhythm and blues, gospel music, soul and rap have spread to every corner of the planet, and provided the foundations of rock and roll. Discussing each of these musical styles in the context of the social conditions that framed them is a formidable task. There are many excellent books about specific styles of African American music, but our focus will be a more general one, including a number of musical genres.

The Slave Trade

Portuguese, Dutch, French, and English vessels carried slaves from the fifteenth through a good part of the nineteenth century. From 1481 to 1888 an estimated fifteen to fifty million Africans were removed from their homelands. The precise number is a matter of some controversy and conjecture, in the same way that authorities differ on the number of American Indians who lived in North America before the Europeans arrived. Historian Arthur Jones went so far as to claim that four slaves died in transit for every one who arrived in North or Central America. Some of these shipboard deaths were suicides, captives who threw themselves overboard rather than accept life as a slave. To use a rap simile, it was "all about the benjamins." In the late eighteenth century a ship carrying 250 slaves could net a harvest of seven thousand British pounds.

Initially the Central and North American colonists attempted to use Indians as slaves, but because white men's diseases decimated the tribes, and because the Indians had no concept that paralleled the white man's notion of work, Indians were regarded as a poor source of slave labor.

Early Music

Slaves were not allowed to bring instruments from Africa on the slave ships, so initially the music on the ships was entirely vocal music. An English surgeon who went on four slave-trading voyages reported that the slaves sang songs that appeared to be laments about exile. What dancing there was took place during the time when slaves were allowed on deck to get a breath of fresh air. Even when they were allowed (or, in some cases, forced, in an effort to make them more tractable) to dance, the slaves were kept in chains!

We know that slaves played the banjo and the fiddle not long after they were conscripted to the United States, but there was relatively little interest in the music of the slaves up until the Civil War, with the exception of the music adapted by the white minstrel shows. Music historian Dena Epstein reports references to slaves playing the banjo dating from 1754 and 1774. Quills or panpipes were also used, and by the eighteenth century black fiddlers were a normal part of the plantation's music scene. Slaves entertained at various plantation functions, but they also played for other slaves. When slaves escaped, newspaper advertisements soliciting their return included their musical skills as part of the description of particular slaves.

The history of the banjo is particularly intriguing, and it illustrates the interactions between white and black musical traditions. Banjos came in different string configurations, generally using four or five strings. Although the original players were certainly black, today the banjo is played almost entirely by white musicians.

The four string banjo is used in Dixieland jazz, while the five-string instrument is used in the music of the Southern mountains, and in bluegrass. The five-string has an unusual configuration of strings, with the fifth string only going up about three-quarters of the length of the instrument. It acts as a high drone string, or constant tone, against the picking of the other strings. This is an unusual configuration for a string instrument, because against all logic it places the highest and lowest string adjacent to one another. The usual pattern in string instruments is that each successive string is tuned higher than the one next to it.

Research in African music has revealed that the Wolof tribe of Senegal has a five-string lute with exactly such an arrangement of strings. It is called the halam, and it is usually played with the fingernails of the index and middle fingers of the right hand, as well as the thumb. This instrument appears to be the "grandfather" of the five-string banjo.

Stuart Jamieson and Margot Mayo collected music for the Library of Congress from black five-string banjo players during the 1930s. This music was not widely available until it was released by Rounder Records some fifty years later. It was assumed at the time of Jamieson and Mayo's work that the banjo had become anathema to African Americans because it was associated with the image of the "happy Negro" promoted in minstrel shows. In fact, although the guitar became much more popular among black musicians, beginning in the 1920s, there was a tradition of black string bands that continued to play mountain music. Today a young black string band called the Carolina Chocolate Drops continues this tradition, and blues musician-songwriter Otis Taylor recorded an album called *Recapturing the Banjo*, with a number of musicians including himself playing traditional and new banjo tunes.

The Uses and Dangers of Allowing Music

There were arguments for and against allowing slaves to play and sing, or to dance. On the positive side from the slaveholder's point of view, music could serve as a form of harmless entertainment that could take the slaves' minds off their lot. In addition, it could provide a source of amusement for the master and the mistress. A happy slave was thought to be less apt to consider insurrection, and he might work harder as well. On the negative side, the master never knew exactly what the songs were about. If the songs were sung in any sort of African dialect, dangerous information could be spread through the medium of the lyrics. Even without the use of African languages words could develop coded meanings, or specific slang words could have double meanings. And the slaves' adaptations of the English language may often have been difficult for whites to understand.

Two songs that represent the use of coded messages are "Follow the Drinking Gourd" and "Run to Jesus." The drinking gourd was the Big Dipper, and by "following the drinking gourd," slaves could run away to the North. "Run to Jesus" was a favorite of abolitionist hero Frederick Douglass, and its refrain, "I don't expect to stay much longer here," could certainly serve as a coded message from one slave to another.

Dance might represent an even more dangerous medium. Dance is intrinsically sensuous and potentially erotic, and the planter class was always ambivalent about black eroticism, at once tempted by it and viewing it as a form of primitive and potentially immoral behavior that might interfere with a stable work environment.

Underlying the life of the slave system was the owners' fear that the slaves would revolt. From time to time this did indeed happen. In 1810 a rebellion of four hundred slaves took place in Lexington, Kentucky. In 1822 Denmark Vesey led a South Carolina slave revolt, and Virginia saw Boxley's rebellion in 1825 as well as Nat Turner's in 1831. All of these revolts were suppressed and most of the perpetrators were killed Chris Seymour, in an article in the magazine *Nonviolent Activist* posted at www.peoplesmusic.org, claims that Denmark Vesey and his followers sang a parody of "Hail Columbia" that suggested that God was on their side, and that every Negro would "drive each tyrant from the land!" Folklorist Russell Ames believes that the song "Steal Away" may have been composed by Nat Turner himself. The last two lines of the song, as collected by Lawrence Gellert are: "But you can't keep the world from movin' around, / And not turn her back from the gaining ground." Gellert maintained that the words "turn her" referred to Nat Turner himself.

The Minstrel Show

Jon W. Finson dates the beginning of minstrel songs to 1830. The first minstrel songs were written by white entertainers who adapted some of the tunes, subject matter, and vernacular used by slaves. Some of the songs made fun of white high society, and others reflected poorly on the appearance and living habits of the slaves. The minstrels dressed up in exaggerated costumes and wore blackface. They also imitated the way that the slaves danced, and they often used banjos, fiddles, and tambourines to perform the music.

Some of the songs that the minstrels adapted were in turn rearranged by traditional black musicians, and passed back into oral tradition as traditional songs. Later on black composers began to write songs for minstrel shows, and even formed their own touring companies, often owned by white theatrical producers.

The minstrel image of African Americans was ultimately a negative one. Even the songs that portrayed the hard lot of the slaves presented them in a paternalistic, patronizing way. It is difficult to imagine that blacks enjoyed seeing or hearing parodies of themselves. It is difficult, however, to fault the black entertainers who participated in this genre, when one considers how few economic opportunities were available for black musicians or performers.

The Development and Evolution of Slavery

Slavery was initially found all over colonial America, but it quickly became centered in the southern states. This occurred for both economic and social reasons. The development of large farms in the south was ideally suited to the use of large numbers of slaves. The New England states lacked these conditions, and harbored a certain amount of anti-slavery sentiment, put forth by such groups as the Quakers.

Some of the more progressive southern planters, like Thomas Jefferson, were aware of the contradictions between a free American nation, won at great cost in the Revolutionary War, and the lot of the slaves. Jefferson maintained that he would free his slaves once his debts were cleared up, but neither event occurred.

Even in the South there were freedmen-slaves who were freed by their masters, or who purchased their freedom because they were skilled tradespeople who managed to work part-time for money for other employers in addition to their normal work obligations as slaves.

Religion

Religion represented a source of conflict for the slave owner. The planters wanted the slaves to worship their God and to forget or renounce the deities or religious practices of their countries of origin.

Organized religion, however, presented the problem of slaves gathering in large groups outside the work environment. Such gatherings might be conducive to revolts or refusals to obey orders, and produce the sort of solidarity that slave populations had been mixed to prevent. On the other hand, an emphasis on religion might prove useful in taking the slaves' minds off their immediate problems, and emphasizing the rewards of the afterlife.

Initially southern preachers were white, but some black preachers emerged, especially among the Baptists. The other religious groups preferred to use white preachers so that they could control the content of the sermons.

The Great Awakening of the mid-eighteenth century was a religious revival that took place throughout the American colonies. The sterile pessimism of the Puritan tradition was transformed into a joyous event. Black and white adherents attended the same religious gatherings, although they were segregated.

Origins of the Spiritual in Black and White

Throughout the twentieth century, controversy raged as to whether white hymns or white spirituals came from Negro spirituals, or vice versa.

This argument inevitably involved racial overtones. The proponents of the white origin of spirituals were, by implication, arguing that the African American did not possess sufficient powers to create music without the aid of whites' superior inventiveness. The black scholars who insisted on a black origin for the music had the opposite idea. From their point of view, the African American was a relentlessly inventive human being who despite his humble economic situation emerged as a more creative force than his white compatriots. Although scholars on neither side presented their viewpoints in quite the way that I am summarizing it here, the implications seem fairly obvious

The foremost advocated of the white origin of spirituals was George Pullen Jackson. In his book *White and Negro Spirituals, Their Life Span and Kinship*, he relates the tunes of several hundred African American spirituals to tunes found in the British Isles. He even claimed to find parallels in the use of the flatted third and seventh notes of the scale. These attributes are the basis of the blues, and most scholars attribute them to African Americans. The problem with Jackson's theories is that he ignores song texts, focusing only on melodies, and that many of the transcriptions of African American songs were notated by white scholars who made the tunes conform to Western European songs. Jackson also did not seem to understand that the tunes changed in performance, some through deliberate improvisations, and others because the singer forgot a tune or simply embellished it.

Black musicologist Miles Mark Fisher stands Jackson's theory on its head, claiming that white singers in the Appalachian mountains adapted spirituals as a protest against slaveholders.

Black scholar John Lovell Jr. claimed that the spirituals started in the seventeenth century, and that white spirituals didn't exist until the first quarter of the nineteenth century. Lovell regarded the black spiritual as a folk song, but the white spiritual was not.

Dena Epstein believes that there probably was an exchange of songs in the nineteenth century at camp meetings attended by both whites and blacks.

We will probably never know how many of the spirituals originated. We can only wonder whether there was some sort of transitional music leading to the creation of the spirituals, and whether that music was partly African or African-influenced. Since black spirituals were rarely, if ever, heard by white people, and because white people would most likely have had little or no interest in them, we cannot make these sorts of judgments with any confidence. What we do know is that the African American seems to have contributed call-and-response to the idiom. In call-and-response singing, the song leader "lines out" the words, and the congregation or choir repeats them. The song leader added the elements of improvisation, and possibly the more extreme emotive aspects of performance commonly found in the performance of white music, but not generally present in white religious singing.

After the Civil War, fund-raising tours were organized by the Fisk Jubilee Singers, and later by a similar group from the Hampton Institute. These choruses were sent out to raise money for their colleges. They performed rather formal arrangements of traditional spirituals, with much of the raw emotion and spontaneity removed from the songs. This established a tradition that frequently required black art singers like Paul Robeson, Marian Anderson, and Jessye Norman to perform and record albums of spirituals, usually with piano accompanists.

What the Spirituals Said

In most instances, the life of the slave was not a pleasant one. Slaves were expected to work six days a week, and a master could break up families by selling off one or more members. Dena Epstein mentions a song printed in a book in 1859, entitled "Sold Off to Georgy." It contains the lyric "Farewell, fellow servants . . . my poor heart is breaking."

Consequently, many of the spirituals focus on ultimate joy in the afterlife, rather than dealing with the events of everyday life. There are many references to biblical heroes, especially those who were underdogs, such as Daniel in the lion's den, or David's battle with Goliath.

Many songs can be interpreted in more than one way. For example, in the 1867 collection *Slave Songs of the United States*, the song "I Want to Go Home" contains such lines as "no sun to burn you, no hard trials." The white editors of this collection say that after Emancipation such verses as "no more whips a-crackin', and no more slavery in de Kingdom," were added to the song. These lines gave more specific meaning to what previously had only been implied.

Other songs were so explicit that they had to be sung in secret. Many of these songs are lost or forgotten, but the above collection printed the song "Many Thousand Gone." It contains the lines "no more driver's lash" and "no more mistress call for me." The same authors report that blacks in Charleston were jailed during the Civil War for singing, "We'll soon be free, we'll fight for liberty."

The Civil War and Its Aftermath

Just prior to the Civil War, in the year 1860, there were 488,000 free blacks in the United States. Forty-six percent lived in the Atlantic south, forty-four percent in the industrial north, and the rest lived in the western or central states. A variety of slave codes limited the activities of these "free" blacks. Their schooling was restricted, as was their movement and their ability to socialize with their enslaved brothers or sisters. During the period from 1810 to 1835 their right to vote was also eliminated.

When Lincoln emancipated the slaves in 1863 his intent was to create chaos on the plantations, and to encourage slaves to run away and to fight with the Union Army. By the end of the Civil War, 180,000 blacks had served in the Union Army. Some of the Union generals also confiscated southern land and gave it to freedmen. After Lincoln was assassinated, the more conservative president Andrew Johnson restored half of this land to its original owners.

The radical Republicans attempted to impeach Johnson. Though they failed by a single vote, Congress did pass the Thirteenth, Fourteenth, and Fifteenth amendments to the constitution, which provided for equal protection for blacks and gave them the right to vote A number of black government officials were initially elected, including sixteen black congressmen, yet this was a short-lived adventure.

The southerners responded with the founding of the Ku Klux Klan in 1866. Starting out as a Tennessee social club, the Klan soon took shape as a terrorist organization designed to intimate the newly freed black population. It assassinated its enemies in Arkansas and South Carolina, and it was involved in lynchings, floggings, and assorted acts of violence.

During the 1930s, the WPA (Works Progress Administration) conducted an extensive series of interviews with ex-slaves. These interviews revealed that they had viewed the end of slavery as a time of hope and possibility. Their hopes had turned to bitterness as they realized that they were not going to receive any land, that their very lives were endangered, and that their voting rights were being eroded by onerous literacy tests or property ownership requirements. Although schools were established for the freedmen, they were segregated from white schools, and generally underfunded. The emergence of the black church and families that were allowed to stay intact provided the base for the modern civil rights movement.

The Period of Maximum Oppression: 1880–1914

By the 1880s the U.S. government had turned more conservative, and had little interest in the "Negro problem." The early reformers in the South were portrayed by some people as Northern carpetbaggers come out of economic opportunism, ready to take advantage of poorly educated blacks and poor whites when the slaves were freed and the aristocrats who had dominated the economy were forcibly removed from power. New laws and state constitutions in the South effectively barred blacks from voting by instituting poll taxes and literacy tests but exempting voters descended from those who had held the franchise before the war—in other words, whites.

Large landowners instituted the sharecropping system, renting farms to tenants and advancing them seed and equipment in exchange for a share of whatever they produced. At the end of the growing season the two settled up. The tenant generally received little or no money for a year of backbreaking work, often incurring a deficit that would be charged against the next year's income. In many instances the tenant was in effect enslaved, because he could never escape his burden of debt. If he wanted to leave the farm he would have to sneak away in the dead of night, and move to another county or state.

Secular Folk Music

The primary musical styles that typify African American music emerged in the nineteenth century, during this period of maximum oppression. Most every genre of music that later developed and influenced the music of the entire world appeared in African American culture during the last half of the nineteenth century. Work songs, hollers, blues, ragtime, and even the building blocks that would lead to jazz all appeared during this time. As the dreams and hopes of the recently freed slaves turned into nightmares of repression, persecution, and prosecution, music became an increasingly important avenue for the transmission of ideas, emotions and dreams.

Our knowledge of how this music developed is limited because of nineteenth-century musicologists' lack of interest in investigating it. What information we have comes from the printed page, when in fact it is the dynamics of performance, improvisation, and reinvention that made this music so dynamic.

Most of what we *think* we know about work songs, field calls, and hollers comes through the work of early folk song collectors. Their field work started in the early part of the twentieth century. John Lomax, Dorothy Scarborough, Newman White, Howard Odum and Guy Johnson were all active collectors. All printed numerous texts, and Odum even wrote three novels based on his work with Left Wing Gordon, a blues singer who was one of his informants. Lomax, who later was joined by his son Alan, recorded many African American singers for the Library of Congress, and the two produced a number of songbooks. The other authors printed many texts, but included little or no music with them.

It is interesting, if unfortunate, that every one of the collectors listed was white. Although they certainly developed some rapport with their informants, there were certain limitations on the material that they collected. First of all, there was a certain amount of censorship imposed by the collectors. They tended not to be interested in anything that they regarded as popular music, because they felt that such music tainted the folk process. Second of all, they were frequently unwilling to collect material that they considered to be bawdy or obscene, and even less willing to print it. A more critical problem is the question of whether black singers or musicians would willingly share songs that protested against working conditions or white bosses, since doing so might endanger the lives or welfare of the singers, and perhaps of the collectors as well. Many of the Lomax recordings were done in prisons, with guards or prison wardens in attendance.

A bit later we will discuss the activities of Lawrence Gellert, a white man who collected over five hundred songs in the south during an extended residence there. Over two hundred of the songs were protest songs, far exceeding what any of the other collectors found.

Many of the work songs used the call-and-response pattern that is one of the primary characteristics of African music. Bruce Jackson points out that work songs are not simply *about* work; they are songs that help a person *do* work. This is because the songs have a rhythm that sets a tempo used in the work itself. In the southern prisons a song leader was an important component of the crew, because he stimulated the men to do the work, and because the singing itself helped to keep the workers' minds off their work. Some of the song leaders had a set repertoire of songs with very specific rhythmic patterns. Others used a more improvisational approach, varying the length of the line and the content of their words. Some seemed to construct their songs using the "assembly" concept found by Alfred Parry Lord in Serbia. The topic of the song is predetermined, but the specific content of verses and even the number of verses varies according to the mood of the singer.

Minstrels, Ragtime, and Broadway

The early minstrel shows were based upon white actors' observations of African Americans. The most famous of these early characterizations was Thomas D. Rice's "jumping Jim Crow." Rice had seen an old black slave whose shoulder and left leg were deformed, and his song-and-dance depiction of the old man created a sensation when Rice performed it on the New York stage in 1832.

We have already discussed the phenomenon of blackface that minstrelsy employed. Some of the minstrel companies had lengthy runs in theaters, particularly Ordway's Aeolian group in Boston and E. P. Christy's Minstrels in New York City.

Black minstrels started to appear in the 1850s, but didn't achieve popularity until the 1870s. The most successful of these groups was Callender's Colored Minstrels, which had three different companies working by late 1882.

The black minstrels didn't wear burnt cork, but their show scripts and styles of performance were quite similar to those of the white minstrel companies. The most prolific black songwriter was James Bland, who composed "Carry Me Back to Old Virginny," "In the Evening by the Moonlight," and over seven hundred other songs.

The minstrel shows represented a decent career option for black performers, and Toll reports that by 1881 black minstrels made "pretty good salaries." In the 1870s they even added some religious songs, performed in a folksy style rather than the formal arrangements done by the Fisk Jubilee Singers.

In the 1870s and '80s, the songs of the minstrel show presented a sort of pastoral and nostalgic image of the African American that almost paralleled the way that American Indians were depicted in song. Some songs were in the form of pseudo-spirituals, and some pleaded for racial tolerance. Frank Howard's 1879 song "Pass Down de Centre" contains the lyrics

> Times are hard for de darkie,
> Way down in Tennessee;
> Mister Ku Klux Klan, can't you let me be.

Coon Songs

In the 1880s and '90s, numerous songs used the derogatory term "coon" to refer to African Americans. Ernest Hogan's song "All Coons Look Alike to Me," written in 1896, further perpetuated the stereotype of black people as mildly dangerous, razor-toting and watermelon-eating primitives, and whistling this extremely popular song was regarded as a serious insult by blacks. Ironically, Hogan himself was black. Other black composers of the period like J. Rosamund Johnson and his brother James Weldon Johnson tried to avoid the worst stereotypes, but they still were reduced to writing tunes like "Underneath the Bamboo Tree," with its Zulu motif, to fit white tastes and stereotypes.

By the 1890s the popularity of the minstrel companies had declined, but the grinning Black Sambo image of the happy colored man remained in force, especially in Hollywood. Occasional minstrel shows continued to tour until World War II, and even during the early 1950s.

Black Entertainers

Between 1880 and 1915, black entertainers performed in black theaters all over the country, and even on the Broadway stage. Billy McClain produced a show called *Black America* that had a cast of over five hundred performers and played in Ambrose Park in Brooklyn in 1895. Bob Cole and J. Rosamund Johnson wrote over 150 songs for more than a dozen shows, and Eubie Blake and Noble Sissle wrote several successful Broadway shows, including *Shuffle Along*. By 1922, 360 black theaters employed six hundred acts.

Although the lyrics to these shows did use coon stereotypes, they also covered many other subjects, such as the battle between the sexes, and employed ethnic stereotypes about other groups, especially recent immigrants. This was a common device in all popular music of the period. Nevertheless it was the coon image that seemed most prevalent, and between 1895 and 1900 over six hundred coon songs were written.

Ragtime

In the late nineteenth century the instrumental style known as ragtime emerged. According to music historian Daniel Kingsman, its roots can be found in music published in New York in the 1880s. In its pure form ragtime was always written, not improvised. It involved syncopation, playing on the off-beats, juxtaposed against a steady bass. It was commonly played on the piano, but the banjo, and to a lesser extent the guitar, were also used. Because each piece contained three or four sections and involved key changes and a relatively high level of instrumental facility, the piano was best suited for the style.

A black musician named Scott Joplin became the most famous ragtime composer, and also contributed songs to Tin Pan Alley's derivative "ragtime" genre: pop creations based on simplified versions of ragtime. Joplin as also wrote two ragtime operas that were not publicly performed during his lifetime. Unfortunately, he and other ragtime composers retained in their lyrics some of the same coon and razor-fighting stereotypes purveyed by the minstrels.

Birth and Evolution of the Blues

Blues has a deep connection to black culture. The multi-faceted genre has a lush history.

Country Blues

Alan Lomax believed that the blues originated in the Mississippi Delta, but there is just as much sentiment that the earliest blues were a rural style, found in various parts of the south. The blues is a musical form with specific characteristics, but its appeal easily transcends its rather simple form. Although it is a lament, a music of complaint that expresses dejection and depression, it is also capable of contradicting itself in its expressions of freedom and joy. It can be extremely intense and introspective, as in the tortured inner torment of Robert Johnson, or it can be up-tempo, fun-loving, good-time music, as in Bessie Smith's "Gimme a Pigfoot and a Bottle of Beer."

Scholars date the origins of the blues to the last decades of the nineteenth century. W. C. Handy recalled a group of guitarists playing the song East St. Louis in 1892. Harvard archeologist Charles Peabody informally collected blues in 1901 in Mississippi. Howard Odum was collecting blues stanzas in 1905, and many biographies of jazz or blues artists refer to cousins, fathers, or grandfathers singing blues around the turn of the twentieth century, or even earlier.

Country blues use variations of the blues form, repeating lines either at the beginning or at the end of a verse. Possibly it all started with an AAA form, with a single line repeated three times. For example,

> I'm goin' away, don't you want to go?
> I'm goin' away, don't you want to go?
> I'm goin' away, baby, don't you want to go?

The form could also appear as ABBB:

> I'm goin' away, don't you want to go?
> Never comin' back. Won't be here no more,
> No, I'm never comin' back, won't be here no more,
> Never comin' back, and I won't be here no more.

(Notice the typical slight variations, with words like "baby" slid into the verse in the first version, and the words "no" and "I" slipped into the second version.)

The form could also be modified to include two repeats of a line instead of three. The repeated lines allowed the singer time to think up the following line or verse, which was either improvised on the spot or drawn from the general stock of traditional verses known by many musicians.

The typical blues, as revealed on numerous recordings, contained twelve bars of music (in a piece of music in 4/4 time this would mean that there were forty-eight beats in a verse.) However, recordings by such artists as Blind Lemon Jefferson and Lightnin' Hopkins enable us to understand that soloists varied the form according to their mood and the need to fit more or fewer words into a particular verse. The addition of an extra beat or two did not matter, because only one person was performing. The same notion applied to the concept of rhythm. A metronomic approach was not entirely necessary as long as the singer was the only musician involved in a performance.

Blues Lyrics

In a 1973 publication called *The Country Blues Songbook*, I analyzed the lyrics of over 120 blues by such artists as Robert Johnson, Skip James, and Furry Lewis. Most of the songs were transcribed from recordings of the 1920s and '30s, although some were sung by older blues performers who had been rediscovered by blues aficionados of the 1960s. While a song might touch on a number of the following subjects, I grouped each one according to its one or two dominant themes. Here is the count that emerged:

Woman-man situations: 75
Poor me (self-pity): 34
Violence: 20
Sex: 13
Politics, prisons, commentaries on whites: 12
Boasting songs: 9
Drinking: 6
Hoodoo, magic, and superstition: 5
Floods, storms, and other disasters: 4
Mother: 3
Story songs (not necessarily in precise blues form): 3
Drugs: 1
Rambling: 1
Religion: 1
Sickness: 1
Worried (general concerns): 1

All of the songs in this book were written and performed by male artists; however, since the vast majority of country blues were recorded by men, this imbalance can be viewed as a characteristic of the art form to that point rather than a bias in the sample itself. I did a similar analysis of songs recorded by Bessie Smith, which had somewhat different results, described later in this chapter.

Country blues lyrics differed from the vaudeville-jazz blues, or the urban-oriented predecessors of rhythm and blues songs that were recorded in the late thirties and throughout the fifties. Many country blues songs did not tell a single coherent story, but were more abstract constructs revealing the moods of the singer. For example Blind Lemon Jefferson's "Wartime Blues" begins with the query about what the listener is going to do if they send her man to war, and answers that she will drink muddy water and sleep in a hollow log. The next verse talks about the singer wanting to be like a headlight on a train, and shining his light on Colorado Springs. Many of the country blues are like a novelist's stream of consciousness, where a story makes sense more in terms of mood or ambience than in the elements of a clear narrative. The lack of a specific focus seems to justify the corresponding lack of the chorus we are accustomed to hearing in popular songs.

Blues scholars have a tendency to attribute the deepest meanings of the blues to whatever area of study or belief that they personally favor. Scholars who have a radical-political bent see the blues as an expression of the oppression that African Americans have experienced. Literary scholars are attracted to the abstract elements of the blues and intrigued by the notion of blues as a sort of surrealistic expression. Black scholars who are coming at the blues as a sort of naturalistic expression of theological meaning see the blues as a form of religious expression, kind of a close companion to religious music. Black nationalists enjoy the blues' double meanings, coded messages, and use of the vernacular as a way of resisting white influences. Other writers are intrigued by the voodoo-superstition references in some blues, and they focus on the use of magic, the notion of nonrational meanings and expression, and the African roots of the blues. Analysts with a penchant for the psychological are intrigued by the open sexuality expressed in the blues, which they view as a sort of revolt against bourgeois morality. Each of these authorities justified their views by referring to lyrics that supported their ideas. Since there are hundreds of recorded and even printed blues, written by a variety of artists and professional songwriters, it is possible to make a convincing case for virtually any of these viewpoints. I believe that there a few points that emerge as being central to the themes and fabric of the blues. They are:

1) African Americans have been and remain an oppressed group in the United States. Although there are exceptions, most blues are rooted in pain and loss, and describe loneliness and self-pity. Consequently I see the blues as the music of oppression, though not necessarily in a direct social-political sense. The "politics" of the blues are the very existence of the African American. Blues was one form of temporary or even permanent escape from the prevailing sharecropper–poor farmer society that offered little hope or flexibility to anyone with a black skin. There was indeed much for the blues singer to feel concerned about, and his own life and dreams were certainly a central part of this feeling of hopelessness. Coming from an environment where the family itself had been subject to the whims of the slave owners, stuck in a miserable work environment or unemployed, and with comparatively little hope for the future, is it any wonder that the country blues singer was obsessed with concern about women and prone to feel sorry for himself?

2) The remarkable aspect of the blues is that it represents an artistic solution to a real-life set of dilemmas. The expressiveness of Robert Johnson's desperate quest for love and refuge, Blind Blake playing his good-time rag dance tunes, and Blind Jefferson's abstract musings represent a massive triumph of an oppressed people over an oppressive living environment.

3) As a simple musical form that was easy to understand, and simple to play or sing, the blues were an idiom that any black human being could relate to in late nineteenth and early twentieth centuries. The music and the messages constituted an

ongoing dialogue among African Americans about the conditions of their lives.

Vaudeville and Early Jazz

If the great majority of the country blues musicians were men, the people who performed blues on the stage, particularly in theaters, were mostly women. During the 1920s the Theatre Owners' Booking

Bessie Smith

Association provided opportunities for such artists as Ma Rainey, Alberta Hunter, Bessie Smith, Clara Smith, and many others to perform for periods of a week or two at black theaters in the northern and southern cities of the United States. Ma Rainey and Bessie Smith were the two most famous of the women blues artists. Ma had originally performed with touring vaudeville and medicine shows, and was kind of a bridge between the country blues styles and the more sophisticated sort of songs that lent themselves to presentations on a stage.

Rainey and Smith generally performed with small jazz bands, and their many recordings used some of the same musicians, such as Louis Armstrong and James P. Johnson, who were active in the development of jazz. Almost all of the country blues musicians were credited as the writers of their own songs, although in fact many of the verses used in their songs, and sometimes the entire songs, were actually traditional folk blues. The songs sung by the blues women were more sophisticated, partly because of their association with jazz musicians, and partly because they, unlike the country blues musicians, were playing in cities for large paying audiences.

Based on the *Bessie Smith: Empress of the Blues* songbook, the subject matter of Bessie's songs breaks down as follows. (Of the thirty songs printed in the book, Bessie wrote eighteen and coauthored one other.)

Men: 16
Poor me: 14
Sex: 4
Politics, prison: 3
Dance: 2
Feminism: 2
Flood and storms: 1
Good times: 1
Hoodoo and superstition: 1

While this songbook includes only a sampling of the 160-some songs recorded by Bessie Smith, It is interesting to note that the doings of the opposite sex and the singer's feelings of self-pity parallel the most popular subjects found in the country blues. There is relatively little attention to violence or gambling, although Bessie Smith was by all accounts a very strong woman, who brooked no nonsense from anyone.

Possibly the most interesting song in the Smith songbook is "Young Woman's Blues." The song describes the singer waking up and finding a note from her man, who has decided to leave her. Smith responds with the lyric "I'm a young woman, and I ain't done runnin' 'round." She goes on to defend her reputation and assert that she is as good as any woman in town. Other lyrics celebrate the singer's brown skin, and maintain that she is a good woman who can get plenty of men. This song, composed in 1927, includes the elements of black pride, female independence, a renunciation of marriage, and the proclamation that the singer is perfectly capable of finding as many men as she wishes to. Overall, the song could virtually serve as a feminist anthem of the 1970s, or for that matter as an anti-misogynist rap song of the twenty-first century.

The Blues as Protest Music

There are different kinds of music that protest against social injustice. The most obvious kind of protest song is one written in a deliberate and self-conscious manner by a professional musician. Folksingers Woody Guthrie and Pete Seeger viewed music as a platform for social change. A large number of their songs were written to support specific points of view, such as organizing unions.

In the blues idiom many songs protest against social conditions, but they are usually individual expressions of a singer complaining about specific injustices, rather than calls for political change or offers of support for ideologies. Josh White was really the only blues singer who consistently attempted to use music as a tool for social change. This aspect of his work crystallized during the mid-1940s, largely in collaborations with the black poet Warren Cuney.

Black musicologist Julio Finn sees the blues as being essentially psychological and spiritual, rather than historical and social. Yet the songs of Charley Patton, Blind Lemon Jefferson, and Bessie Smith contain references to floods, wars, escape from an oppressive environment, and prison life. Given that the major record companies were owned and controlled by whites, it hardly seems reasonable to expect that they would have issued a large number of recordings protesting about social conditions. Still, there were numerous recordings made during the Great Depression (1929–1939) that refer to hunger, unemployment, the New Deal, and poverty. Take these verses from Tampa Red's "Things 'Bout Comin' My Way," recorded in 1929:

> Lost all my money, ain't got a dime,
> Givin' up this whole world, leaving it behind,
>   *(Refrain)*
> But after all this hard travelin',
> Things 'bout comin' my way.

Later on in the song Tampa asks his lady friend to take him as he is, even though he "ain't got no money, I'm in a jam."

Tampa went on to record "Depression Blues" in 1931. In this song he tells us that he is returning to Florida, even though people have told him that depression is everywhere.

The Blues and the Preacher

There was often a dichotomy between the moral attitudes presented by black ministers, and their actual behavior. Some blues lyrics satirized the behavior of hypocritical preachers, while the preachers in turn condemned artists whose lifestyles and songs advocated drinking and sexual promiscuity. Black theological academics James H. Cone and especially Jon Michael Spencer see the blues as a sort of earthly counterpart to the expressiveness of the spirituals. Cone maintains that black people know that the body is sacred, and know how to use it in expressing love. Spencer focuses on the fall of man as seen in the myth of Adam and Eve in the garden, and he maintains that this fall explains the cosmology of the blues.

These views are somewhat contradicted by numerous examples of people like Reverend Robert Wilkins, whose notion that one must either sing blues or spirituals, not both, is quoted in another section of one of Spencer's collections. I recall friends of mine coaxing Reverend Gary Davis at great length before he would sing blues songs, departing from his usual "holy blues."

It seems to me that you can't have it both ways. Either Robert Johnson's sinful blues, detailing his inner life and his dealings with the devil, are sacrilegious, or the nature of black religious thought as seen by Spencer is questionable or has drastically changed. It seems more reasonable to regard blues as a protest against formal religion, against the restrictions of both the white governing culture and the black middle class, and in favor of a lifestyle that espoused free choice over constant restrictions and rules. And Robert Johnson's "stones in my passway" represented the price that the bluesman expected to pay in return for asserting these freedoms.

Migration and the Blues

The blues may have been born in the South, but like the African American population they moved north. By the end of 1918 a million blacks had left the South. Northern factories had become desperate to find workers, and the factories employed agents to bring them north.

When blacks migrated to the North or Midwest they found better economic opportunities in the factories, but they were disappointed at the lack of social equality in their new homes. For example, I previously researched the life of Wesley Westbrooks, a black gospel and jazz musician and composer who moved from Arkadelphia, Arkansas to Kansas City, Kansas around 1932. Although Kansas laws passed in the early part of the twentieth century called for equal rights for blacks and whites, movies, nightclubs, and hospitals were segregated. There also was a tri-racial system of school segregation with whites, Mexicans, and African Americans all attending separate schools.

Finding reasonably priced housing was a serious problem for the migrants, and a pattern of restrictions developed. When blacks moved into a particular neighborhood, unscrupulous realtors created a neighborhood panic, followed by the fast exit of whites. Houses were then split up into rental units, and landlords made exorbitant profits by renting small spaces for high fees.

An instance of the African American's lack of economic power can be seen by realizing that in 1931, of the 12,000 retail stores in Harlem, only 391 (172 of which were small grocery stores) were owned by blacks.

Chicago and Early Electric Blues

Chicago became the destination for many migrants from the Mississippi Delta. One of these migrants was Muddy Waters, who was a major influence on the musical direction of the blues. Muddy found that musicians could perform at clubs on the South Side of Chicago. Soon record companies like Chess and Vee Jay emerged. Although most of these companies, with the exception of Vee Jay, were owned by whites, the promotion and sales of the recordings were directed to the black community.

A few black musicians, notably Willie Dixon, became active as songwriters, record producers, and session musicians. Blues grew into rhythm and blues, utilizing bass players, drummers, and horn players. The music was christened "rhythm and blues" by (then) Billboard writer Jerry Wexler, and such artists as harmonica player Little Walter, Big Bill Broonzy, and Muddy Waters found their way on to the R&B charts. The songs became more professional and focused, and electric guitars and basses appeared on most of these records. The electric slide guitar was particularly loud and strong.

In an attempt to compare these songs with the earlier blues songs analyzed, I studied a collection called *Folk Blues*, which contains over a hundred songs of the 1950s and '60s, written by such artists as Chuck Berry, Willie Dixon, Muddy Waters, and Ellis McDaniel (Bo

Diddley). Their subject matter breaks down as follows (the numeral indicates the number of songs):

Romance: 61
Poor me: 13
Boasting: 12
Hoodoo, superstition: 6
Politics: 6
Sex: 6
Rambling: 3
Humor: 2
School: 2
Mother: 1
Violence: 1

Abstraction and stream of consciousness are no longer acceptable in the lyrics of these songs, which tell coherent stories and eschew extra beats. Songs begin to have choruses and "hooks," lyric and musical fragments that are repeated throughout the song.

White Blues and White Audiences

R&B music played a major role in the early years of rock and roll (a style we will discuss in more detail later in the book). Elvis Presley was a huge blues and gospel music fan. And Chuck Berry, Little Richard, and Fats Domino were the earliest black artists to cross over from R&B to rock and roll in a big way.

Before that, quite a few country musicians were influenced by the recordings of Blind Lemon Jefferson, who began recording in 1927. A number of white artists recorded blues in the 1930s, notably Frank Hutchison, the Allen Brothers, and banjoist Dock Boggs. Some of the playing, especially Hutchison's, is excellent, but invariably the white origins of the artists are revealed in their singing style, which is nasal and vocally constricted.

The most famous white blues artist was country superstar Jimmie Rodgers. Rodgers recorded a series of blues yodels—i.e., blues lyrics with yodels thrown into the middle of the songs—starting in 1927. Where and why Rodgers got the idea of combining country blues lyrics, such as "T for Texas, T for Tennessee, and it's T for Thelma, that gal made a fool out of me," with yodeling is an unsolved mystery. It made for a unique and original sound.

During the late 1950s and into the '60s there was a blues revival in the United States. On the one hand, rediscovered blues singers like Skip James and Son House toured the folk coffeehouse scene. Meanwhile, young white blues artists like Dave Van Ronk, Chris Smithers, Stefan Grossman, and John Hammond Jr. toured and recorded. Taj Mahal was virtually the only young black blues artist who had much of an audience, although Larry Johnson and Jerry Ricks did have their adherents.

But it was the sixties British bands that really gave impetus to the blues revival. The Rolling Stones, the Animals, and the Beatles all were enthusiastic fans of both folk blues and R&B music. They recorded some songs by black artists, and the Stones even had Howling Wolf open for their shows. In addition to the rock superstars, there were less commercial British blues bands, like John Mayall's Bluesbreakers or Alexis Korner's groups. Eric Clapton came out of Mayall's band, and to this day is a tremendous blues enthusiast.

Although Chicago continued to be the home of Muddy Waters, Buddy Guy, and other blues artists, the audience for blues music gradually shifted from black patrons in South and West Side clubs, to younger white blues enthusiasts and clubs on the north side of the city. Some of the young white blues musicians of the sixties, like Paul Butterfield, Elvin Bishop, and Michael Bloomfield, had spent many nights at black blues clubs, and they began to perform their own versions of the blues that included some rock influences, and became popular with younger white music fans.

The combination of the British rock invasion and the American folk boom caused the formation of American white blues bands like the Even Dozen Jug Band and Jim Kweskin's Jug Band, and such blues-rock aggregations as the Paul Butterfield Band, Canned Heat, and Janis Joplin's various bands.

A few artists like Sonny Terry and Brownie McGhee developed long-term careers as touring artists, playing at colleges and coffeehouses. Some black artists, like Big Bill Broonzy, John Lee Hooker, and Lightnin' Hopkins, found that there was more interest in their acoustic or folk-roots blues than in the R&B-oriented styles that they had become used to playing. Playing earlier acoustic styles brought these artists a white audience and enabled them to play better venues for more money.

Who Owns the Blues?

The original impetus for the blues was as an expression of what it felt like to be an African American in the period from 1890 to 1940. As the black middle class developed, and the individualistic "rambling" lifestyle became an artifact of an earlier time, to some extent the blues became more of a historical than a contemporary music style.

Over time, outside influence on blues protest lyrics became an issue. Jeff Todd Titon points out that such artists as Leadbelly and Big Bill Broonzy played for increasingly white audiences, and became friendly with white radicals and liberals. These audiences encouraged the artists to write more songs protesting social or racial inequities. As Broonzy did more solo performances, he stopped playing with the small R&B-oriented combos that he had performed with during the late 1940s and the '50s. Some of his songs, like "Black, Brown, and White Blues" ("if you're white you're right, and if you're brown hang around, but if you're black, buddy, get back") were bound to get a positive reaction from white college audiences.

Blues singer J. B. Lenoir started out as a Chicago blues singer, but by the late 1960s he was singing songs about Alabama, Korea, and Vietnam. The CD reissue of Lenoir's work is titled *The Topical Bluesman from Korea to Vietnam*. Lenoir's "Alabama Blues" describes the murder of the protagonist's sister and brother, explaining that his brother was defending his mother when a police officer shot him. He asserts that Alabama has his people behind a barbed wire fence, and is now trying to rob him of his freedom.

The recording of the song "Everybody Crying About Vietnam" is a live recording, done in Germany. It refers to the defeat of a civil rights bill in Congress, and poses the question to the president why black soldiers should be sent to Vietnam when the government does not want to give them their rights.

There is no reason to question the singer's sincerity, but he was certainly aware that these sentiments would be applauded in Europe. By the mid-sixties, as we shall see later, it became difficult to determine whether protest music itself had become something of a commodity.

Authenticity

The question of authenticity is a common one among critics or fans of non-classical music. It has arisen with country and folk singers, with blues artists, and with rap musicians. Charles Keil, in his book

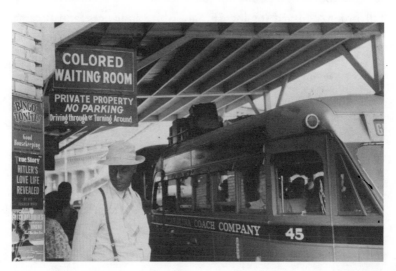

Segregation in the South

Urban Blues, is almost bitter about such singers as Odetta and Josh White "pretending" to do blues. Certainly Josh White's blues pedigree would appear to be more valid than the credentials of a white ethnomusicologist-music critic. Yet the same writer seems to have no such problems with the formulaic patterns in B. B. King's blues performance, or the pageantry of a Bobby Blue Bland concert. I suppose we could say it's simply a matter of taste, and possibly of the fact that the singers Keil preferred at the time had a largely black audience. Odetta's musical training was in art songs and musical comedy. Josh White had become a successful performer playing to largely white audiences. Ironically, in the years since Keil's book was published, this is exactly the transformation that has occurred with B. B. King's audience. All of this highlights how sensitive the issue of authenticity can be.

The relatively young black artist Robert Cray, the recent recordings of white artists Bonnie Raitt and Eric Clapton, and a host of such other artists as Susan Tedeschi or Jonny Lang have brought renewed popularity to the blues idiom, primarily with relatively young white audiences. Johnny Winter and the late Stevie Ray Vaughan are some other white blues artists. A group of white women blues singers has sprung up in Austin around the blues club and record company Antone's. They include Lu Anne Barton, Angela Strehli, and Marcia Ball. Some other blues women include Portland's Mary Flower; Rory Bloch, who grew up around the folk revival in New York City; and Del Rey, who lives in Seattle.

The primary difference between the performances of white blues musicians and black ones is the same one that differentiated the blues of Robert Johnson from the work of white blues-country artist Frank Hutchison. Although many white artists have succeeded in mastering blues instrumental styles, few are able to successfully perform the music's vocal intricacies.

As to the question of who has "the right" to perform the music, perhaps we should be thankful that there are artists who wish to preserve and even develop the blues as a musical style.

Recapturing the Blues

In the last fifteen years such black artists as Eric Bibb, Guy Davis, Ben Harper, Alvin Youngblood Hart, Corey Hart, Keb Mo, and Otis Taylor have emerged to join elder statesman Taj Mahal. One way to look at this is to take our cue from Paul Garan and the surrealists, and to view the contemporary blues as a response to spiritual deprivation on a more abstract basis than the poverty and racism of the culture and time that spawned the blues in the first place. Otis Taylor, however, has written a number of songs that express his feelings about lynchings, slavery, and other aspects of African American history. It is difficult, perhaps impossible, to imagine the white rock-blues artists writing these sorts of songs.

Taylor also made an album called *Recapturing the Banjo*, which attempts to reclaim the banjo as an African instrument. The album also features the work of Harper, Harris, Hart, Mo, and New Orleans jazz player Don Vappe.

World War II to the Sixties

In World War II black soldiers were not truly integrated into the Army, but they did serve in units staffed by white officers. By 1945 soldiers were fighting in integrated units, and in 1951, during the Korean War, Harry Truman totally integrated the armed forces.

The war inspired another round of black migration to the north and the west, and under President Franklin Delano Roosevelt an equal employment act was decreed; African Americans entered government service and were employed in the defense industry. The suburban tract housing boom that followed the war also sowed the seeds of inner-city separation and decay.

When African American soldiers returned home they had trouble readjusting to the racist conditions they had experienced before the war. The NAACP (National Association for the Advancement of Colored People) had been the dominant voice of the struggle for black equality, and had mostly pursued court challenges to racist laws. Some of these were successful, as when in 1946 the U.S. Supreme

Court ruled that segregation in interstate bus trips was illegal, and in 1954 school segregation was outlawed. Now new black leaders emerged who did not accept the "go-slow" tactics of the NAACP or the Urban League. Martin Luther King, a young black minister from Montgomery, Alabama organized the Southern Christian Leadership Conference, which supported the Montgomery bus boycott of 1955.

An even more radical organization, SNCC (Student Non-Violent Coordinating Committee) was organized in 1960, and it initiated a giant voter registration campaign throughout the South.

Civil rights activists injured, imprisoned, and even murdered during this period. NAACP Mississippi leader Medgar Evers was murdered in 1963, and black nationalist leader Malcolm X was killed in 1965. In the ensuing national crisis, 200,000 people of all races rallied in Washington, and President Lyndon Johnson forced civil rights legislation through Congress.

An atmosphere of hopelessness coexisted with this political agitation. Bloody riots took place in the ghettos of the Watts section of Los Angeles, in Newark, and in Philadelphia. A new emphasis on black power, and a desire to exclude whites from key leadership roles in the struggle, led to the creation of the Black Panther Party in Oakland in 1966. At the same time the Black Muslim movement grew in numbers and influence in the black community. The Muslim movement splintered, and in 1978 Louis Farrakhan, who had been a lieutenant of longtime leader Elijah Mohammed, formed his own religious order out of the old Nation of Islam. He continues to be an important and controversial black leader today.

Gospel Music

Gospel music is composed black religious music, usually written down in sheet music form. The first gospel music composer was the Reverend C. Albert Tindley, a Methodist minister. His songs were published in the period from 1899 to 1906.

It was Thomas A. Dorsey who popularized black gospel music. Dorsey was a prolific composer, and he singlehandedly published and promoted the sales of printed versions of his songs at black churches and religious music conventions.

Dorsey had also been a successful blues artist, using the name of Georgia Tom. He felt that the content of the words was the major difference between the two idioms, and that his own ultimate message was salvation in the next world. He wrote catchy tunes and set up his own publishing company, hiring agents throughout the country to help distribute his sheet music. His songs "Take My Hand Precious Lord" and "Peace in the Valley" became "standards" in the gospel field, and were recorded by many white and black religious artists.

A number of stylistic and technical developments fueled the success of gospel music. The use of the microphone aided singers on high falsetto and very low-pitched bass parts, eliminating the need for strain. Male quartets with single and dual lead singers toured the black churches, many performing in a dynamic, emotional style close to screaming. Southern migrants in the big cities related to the music because it was close to the style of Pentecostal church services (which involve parishioners in the service through musical participation and oral exhortations during sermons, and generally have smaller congregations and a less formal character than the worship at churches affiliated with major religious groups), as distinct from the large choirs and slick presentation that many urban churches utilized.

At first gospel music was confined to churches. Sister Rosetta Tharpe and the Golden Gate Singers carried the style to theaters and various venues. The Gates sang a relatively rare topical song called "No Segregation in Heaven," written by white songwriter Ervin Drake. Through the 1950s relatively little gospel music dealt with social concerns, although Otis Jackson wrote about Pearl Harbor, and the Soul Stirrers sang about Korea. Julius Cheeks and Dorothy Love were virtually the only gospel singers to take an anti-segregationist position in their music. Because the focus of the music was not on daily events, but on ultimate redemption in heaven, it simply was not deemed appropriate to discuss contemporary events.

It became obvious that gospel music had a broad appeal that could circulate beyond the black community. A few artists, notably Mahalia Jackson, developed a wide white audience beyond the traditional gospel music venues or fans.

Gospel music was such a dynamic vocal music that it almost inevitably led to the birth of soul. Soul was essentially gospel vocal style married to secular lyrics and rhythm and blues instrumental backgrounds. Sam Cooke, the youthful, handsome, and charismatic lead singer of the Soul Stirrers, was one of the first in a long line of artists who came directly out of the church, like Aretha Franklin and Johnnie Taylor. Other soul artists, like Ray Charles, were not active gospel singers, but their vocals and performing style reflected heavy gospel influences.

At the same time, a movement developed to bring gospel music into a more popular context. The Staples Singers, a family group headed by Roebuck Staples and featuring his daughter Mavis, began to record songs aimed directly at the pop marketplace. Many of these songs coincided with the general ferment going on in the country during the 1960s. Some of these songs alluded either directly or indirectly to the struggles of the civil rights movement. The songs "Respect Yourself" and "Why Am I Treated So Bad?" are examples of this genre.

Today black gospel music comprises a relatively small portion of the market for American music, although such artists as the Mighty Clouds of Joy, the Edwin Hawkins Singers, and Andrae Crouch have experienced some success in the broader music community.

Pop and R&B

In the 1940s Louis Jordan and his Tympany Five sold millions of records to white as well as black audiences. Jordan coauthored many of the songs that he recorded. The lyrics were generally fun-loving and innocuous, as in "Honey Child," a song about a woman who has one brown eye, one blue eye, false hair, and false teeth. Jordan achieved financial success by presenting a more neutral version of the minstrel image.

There were other black pop singers during the forties and fifties, like Nat "King" Cole and Billy Eckstine. They were crooners, whose clear enunciation and conservative style was pleasing to a middle-class, white audience.

A Frank-Zappa-esque extension of the Louis Jordan persona was guitarist-singer Slim Gaillard. Gaillard was a blues-oriented jazz hip-ster who invented meaningless but funny slang phrases that went along with the jive tradition of late swing.

Motown and Stax Records

Two record companies brought black popular music to new heights in the 1960s. Motown Records was started by a black ex-auto worker named Berry Gordy, whose goal was to capture the sound of "young America." Modeling his operation after the practices of his ex-em-ployer, the Ford Motor Company, Gordy created an assembly line of songwriters, studio musicians, record producers, and choreographers to capture the white teenage audience. Between 1964 and 1967 Mo-town had fourteen #1 pop singles, and thirty-one soul music chart toppers. The artists varied from the teen-oriented Supremes to the soulful sound of the Four Tops.

Except for the songs of singer-songwriter Smoky Robinson, al-most all of the early Motown product was written by a stable of staff songwriters, and produced by a similar group of record produc-ers. Sometimes the writers and producers were the same people, and sometimes they were separate entities. Instrumental tracks were cut and then different vocalists or vocal groups were basically auditioned for the final recordings. In other words, the object was to write a hit song, and the producers later decided which artist fit the song.

Meanwhile, Stax, a white-owned record company in Memphis, put together an integrated rhythm section and also gathered a core group of songwriters and musicians to record such acts as Carla Thomas, Otis Redding, and Booker T. and the MG's. Booker T. and the MG's were also the rhythm section on countless recordings by other Stax artists. Most music critics and listeners found the Stax recordings to be closer to black music styles than the Motown offerings were—but then they had never shared Motown's goal of capturing the white teenage market.

Towards the end of the sixties several Motown artists, including Stevie Wonder and Marvin Gaye, grew increasingly restless with the Motown assembly-line method of making records. At the same time a young producer-songwriter named Marvin Whitfield began to write music about social issues. With Barrett Strong he wrote two protest songs, "War" and "Ball of Confusion," in 1970. Originally recorded by the Temptations, "War" was released as a single by Edwin Starr, because Gordy feared that the Temptations' fans might not find a protest song appealing. He soon found that there indeed was a market for protest music. The Temptations then recorded "Ball of Confusion," which complained about a world where drug sales were skyrocketing, segregation in housing remained a problem, and inner-city riots were occurring.

Stevie Wonder, Apollo marquee

In Whitfield's words, with "Unemployment rising fast, the Beatles' new record's a gas" and "the only safe place to live is on an Indian reservation." The production was psychedelic, a new concept for Motown, with wah-wah guitar prominently featured.

Stevie Wonder, born in 1950, had hung around the Motown studios in Detroit from the age of ten. His early hits, beginning before he was a teenager, spotlighted his harmonica playing and his tremendous and contagious enthusiasm. Stevie became restless with his records always reflecting the tastes and values of the Motown production team, and when he came of age he renegotiated his Motown deal with the help of New York lawyer Johanon Vigoda. Wonder became the first Motown artist to control his own productions.

Marvin Gaye was eleven years older than Stevie Wonder, but while he had a successful career as a sort of sex object / matinee idol in the Motown factory system, he began to crave a more artistic career. After a hiatus from performing and a European trip, Gaye played hardball with Motown and insisted on gaining control of his own albums. His 1971 album, *What's Goin' On*, was his artistic breakthrough. The title song, cowritten by Gaye with Al Cleveland and Renaldo Benson, endorsed the peace movement, and even defended the right of young people to have long hair. As an intelligent and thoughtful human being, Gaye realized that Motown had become stuck in the "sound of young America" motto that appeared on all Motown records. Influenced by the civil rights movement, and almost certainly by other conscious soul artists like Curtis Mayfield, and by the work of Motown producer-songwriter Norman Whitfield, Gaye basically forced Gordy to release socially conscious recordings. Berry Gordy can't have been pleased with Gaye's pro-peace, pro-environmental stance. After all, Motown had made its reputation as a company that kept its music out of the political arena. To make things more complicated, Gaye was splitting up with his wife, who was Gordy's sister.

Stevie Wonder was captivated by the *What's Goin' On* album, and he began to write songs that included political issues. His song "Livin' for the City" traced the life of a ghetto child born in Mississippi

Marvin Gaye

to a father who worked fourteen-hour days for very little money. After outlining the hard lives of the entire family, Wonder ends with a plea to change the world. Worse yet, from Gordy's point of view, Wonder followed these ideas up with a virulent anti-Nixon song, "You Haven't Done Nothin'," written in 1974.

By this time Gordy had moved Motown out of Detroit to Los Angeles, where he became more involved in movies and the Broadway show *The Wiz*. The Commodores with Lionel Ritchie and the Jackson Five became the label's featured acts. Politically, it was a return to the old days of selling the sound of young America. Marvin Gaye went through a series of personal crises and died in 1984. Stevie Wonder continued to go his own artistic way, but remained with the label. In 1988 Gordy gave up the record business and sold the label to MCA, which in turn evolved into Universal Records.

Soul

From 1965 until the mid-seventies or so, soul music achieved great general popularity. James Brown, Aretha Franklin, and Otis Redding were among the black artists that crossed over from black music radio into broad popularity. For the most part, soul music, particularly in the beginning, focused on strong, emotional, gospel-influenced vocal performances with a very danceable beat. Only occasionally did soul deal with political issues, although the frequent presence of black solo artists in the world of pop music was something of a statement on its own. James Brown's "Say It Loud, I'm Black and I'm Proud" certainly ties into the themes of black power, even though Brown himself was a conservative Republican.

Many soul songs were written not by the artist, but by songwriters and record producers whose main goal was to spotlight the singer's emotional vocal stylings. The sheer vocal power of an Aretha Franklin brought a whole new dimension to a song like "Respect," which was a hit in its original version by singer and songwriter Otis Redding. Aretha's version not only highlighted the very notion of respecting African Americans, but brought the added dimension of respect for women.

By the early to mid-seventies, soul songwriters and recording artists began to explore political and social issues in their music. Norman Whitfield and Marvin Gaye, as mentioned earlier, had pioneered this genre with Gaye's brilliant 1971 album *What's Goin' On*. The Chi-lites' "For God's Sake Give More Power to the People" and "We Need Order" were somewhat political, if a bit more vague and formulaic in the issues that they raised. Kenneth Gamble and Leon Huff wrote a number of songs for the Ojays for the *Survival* and *Ship Ahoy* albums. *Ship Ahoy* is a lengthy and passionate re-creation of a voyage on a slave-trading ship bound from Africa to the New World. The lyrics—"Somebody got to be your master," and "Me and you, sister, crack the whip"—are about as explicit as any of these songs got. If anyone didn't respond to the lyrics as such, the emotional nature of the vocals drove the politics home.

Other socially conscious black artists kept one foot in soul, and another in various aspects of pop music. Stevie Wonder recorded "Music from My Mind" in 1972, and Sly and the Family Stone recorded

"Don't Call Me Nigger, Whitey" in 1969, and the brilliant "Family Affair" in 1971. The latter included the lyric "One child grows up to be somebody that loves to learn, / The other child grows up to be someone you'd love to burn." Sly's group was integrated, both racially and gender-wise. This constituted a political statement of its own.

The Isley Brothers began their careers as a gospel group, but George Lipsitz, in his book *Footsteps In the Dark: The Hidden History of Popular Music*, includes a detailed discussion of their pop music career, melding personal concerns with political issues. Their 1977 song "Footsteps in the Dark" was later used by Ice Cube in his 1992 song "It Was a Good Day." The latter song presents a day in the Los Angeles ghetto as being good because there were no gang murders, overdoses, etc. Oddly, Anne Murray recorded a hit song in 1983 called "A Little Good News" that loosely covers some of the same terrain that Ice Cube did, ten years later. The theme of Murray's song, written by Tommy Rocco, Rory Bourke, and Charlie Black, is that the singer "sure could use a little good news today." The song then refers to wars, hostages, assassinations, and the economy. The verse that is closer to Ice Cube's song starts out by saying that nobody "robbed a liquor store on the lower part of town, / Nobody OD'd, nobody burned a single building down."

Many of the soul music masterpieces of the sixties and seventies were written and produced by white musicians like Rick Hall, Dan Penn, Spencer Oldham, Barry Beckett, and two members of the integrated Stax Records' rhythm section, white guitarist Steve Cropper and black keyboard ace Booker T. Jones. Their content was often more romantic than political, but the very notion that southern "redneck" musicians had a high level of commitment and the ability to write and record soul music was a political statement of its own.

By the late seventies soul music had pretty much diminished in importance on the pop charts, replaced by a disco inferno. Disco was dance-oriented rather than lyric-directed. There was a strong emphasis on costumes, dances, and good times. The keyboard often replaced the guitar, at least temporarily, as the primary instrument in American popular music. Few lyrics had anything to do with the real world of the ghetto, or any other political issues. It was all about dancing and "shaking your booty."

Disco was associated with the homosexual world, particularly the New York gay dance club scene. The Village People were an integrated quartet with each person in the group representing a different homosexual role—the cop, the intellectual, etc. The R&B group the Coasters had pioneered this concept of assigning each member a different stereotype (minus the homosexual overtones) with their entertaining stage shows.

One of the intriguing aspects of disco is that numerous people turned against it in an almost vitriolic manner. Many musicians resented it, because it was essentially a production-driven music involving what these days has become conventional—studio tricks, electronic drums, samples, etc. Songwriters felt that the "ooh-ooh baby" lyrics violated the rules of songcraft. And in the public mind, disco was identified with wild dancing, drugs, sexual promiscuity, and sexual ambiguity. Although not all disco groups were black, K.C. and the Sunshine Band and that particular period of the Bee Gees' career being examples, there was a racist element to this perception.

The reaction against disco culminated in a Chicago ballpark "disco sucks" rally. Baseball fans were invited to show up, see the game for ninety-nine cents, and bring a disco record for demolition. Chicago disc jockey Steve Dahl, who had lost his job at a radio station that had changed its format to disco, dynamited thousands of disco records while ninety thousand fans stormed the field. Many music critics have pointed to the rally as the beginning of the end for disco music.

Jazz

Of all of the African American musical forms, jazz is undoubtedly the most complex, and from the standpoint of musicians the most rewarding. Although there are numerous fine jazz vocalists, jazz is primarily an instrumental style. Jazz developed alongside ragtime music, but while ragtime was essentially formal, and relied on music notation, jazz was a combination of written and improvised music.

Although it is not clear *where* jazz began, certainly its development owed a good deal to New Orleans and the Storyville entertainment area. (Storyville was a section of town where houses of prostitution were rampant. Many of these bordellos featured musical entertainment as part of their offerings.) The early jazz players in New Orleans were blacks and Creoles. Creoles were of mixed blood, and often came from a more middle-class background than their black colleagues, which had afforded them more formal musical training. Admittedly this is a generalization, and does not hold true in all instances for either group. However, lighter skin color did allow the Creole musicians to spread the jazz doctrine to white audiences that the black musicians were unable to reach because of the social restrictions of that era.

There were some white jazz players in New Orleans, but they were overshadowed by the talents of such musicians as King Oliver and Louis Armstrong. Storyville was shut down in 1917, and the music largely gravitated to Chicago. When jazz left New Orleans the term "Dixieland" replaced the appellation "New Orleans jazz." (Some music critics regard Dixieland as a more commercial form of "authentic" New Orleans jazz, but in general the terms have become virtually synonymous.) In the early 1920s a large group of young white musicians, including Benny Goodman, became totally hooked on jazz. By the 1930s Dixieland had evolved into swing bands that utilized twelve to fifteen musicians. Dixieland combos had typically used five to seven players. The swing bands necessitated the use of music arrangers, which in turn required the musicians to be able to read music. Swing bands also often added one or two singers to the mix.

The most famous Dixieland musicians were black. Louis Armstrong, King Oliver, Johnny Dodds, Kid Ory, and many others were among them. In contrast, though there were quite a number of black swing bands, like those of Don Redman, Jimmy

Lunceford, Andy Kirk, and Count Basie, it was the white swing bands led by Artie Shaw, Benny Goodman, Gene Krupa, the Dorsey Brothers, and Harry James that got the best gigs and sold the most records. These bands were not closed to black musicians, however—Shaw employed the great black singer Billie Holiday for a time, and Goodman hired the incredible jazz guitarist Charlie Christian and pianist Teddy Wilson. (I have not mentioned Duke Ellington in this list, because he was first and foremost a composer, not the leader of a swing band. This is not to say that his band didn't swing!)

By 1940 a movement among younger black jazz musicians, including Charlie Christian, Thelonious Monk, Charlie Parker, and Dizzy Gillespie led to the development of a much more complex form of jazz, called bebop. Bebop had several effects. It restored control of jazz to black musicians, because virtually all of the pioneers of the idiom were black. It also created many problems for the older black and white jazz musicians of the time. Some were unable to adjust to the more complex musical aspects of bebop, including the use of more difficult chords. Many of them, including Louis Armstrong, denounced bebop as being non-melodic nonsense. In addition, bebop was part of a social scene marked by the use of hard drugs, a sort of surrealist attitude, and new clothing styles that didn't appeal to more traditional jazz musicians, who did not like to use heroin and did not share the beboppers' intellectual preoccupations. Bebop also had problems in creating a mass audience. What vocal styles were associated with it did not tend to lead to hit songs, and the music was often not danceable and required the listener to concentrate. Although Dizzy Gillespie briefly experimented with a big band, most bebop was played in small combos, with anywhere from three to eight musicians. Many of the tunes were structured in a way that didn't make sense to older musicians or listeners, because often the players departed almost violently from the melody of a song.

Jazz as Political Music

During the 1920s jazz was associated with alcohol, wild parties, wild dancing, and sexual promiscuity. To some white people these were attractive alternatives to their stodgy, business-driven lives, but to the great middle class jazz represented immorality and licentiousness. The reactions to early jazz on the part of music critics tended to be violent, and even racist. Critics made references to "jungle music," tom-toms, and other comments that attempted to relate the music to "primitive" African music. These attitudes were not found among music critics and composers, but the American Federation of Musicians, the musicians' union, even *ordered* its members not to play jazz in 1901.

Apart from a few songs during the swing era, like "Strange Fruit," a song sung by Billie Holiday and written by composer Lewis Allen about a lynching, the jazz of the 1930s was generally apolitical. Many of the bebop musicians, however, were literate and politically aware, and became caught up in the political turmoil of the 1960s involving the civil rights movement. Bebop drummer Max Roach wrote and recorded an album called *Freedom Now!*, featuring his then wife Abbey Lincoln on vocals. Bass player Charles Mingus wrote a tune called "The Faubus Fables," making fun of racist Arkansas Governor Orval Faubus. Pianist Randy Weston became fascinated by African music, writing suites based on it and settling in Ghana for a while. Saxophonist-composer-arranger Oliver Nelson wrote several extended pieces that were expressions of the history of black music, such as his *Afro American Sketches*, and saxophone giant Sonny Rollins contributed his *Freedom Suite*.

Music Collectives

In a number of cities jazz musicians formed cooperative organizations, designed to assist one another in obtaining decently paid gigs, but also exploring artistic collaborations with dancers, visual artists, and writers. In New York there was the Jazz Composers Guild; in

Los Angeles Horace Tapscott gave up an international performing career to create and nurture UGMAA, the Union of God's Musicians and Artists Ascension. In St. Louis the Black Artists Group (BAG) was formed around a federal government grant program in 1968.

The longest-lived and most successful of all of these groups was the AACM (Association for the Advancement of Creative Musicians) The AACM was based in Chicago and still is active today, focusing on music education for ghetto kids. The AACM sponsored many concerts, and their members made numerous recordings. The political aspect of their music was the playing of numerous African instruments, some performances that involved Africanisms such painting their faces. There was always an emphasis on black pride in their work.

The other collectives eventually disintegrated due to lack of funding, internal disputes, or the departure of key figures for other cities.

Later Developments

Jazz became more and more of a specialized genre with a limited audience. Miles Davis experimented with fusing jazz and rock during the late 1960s, adding electric guitar and bass to his group. Following the commercial success of Davis's fusion, pianist Herbie Hancock and Donald Byrd pursued the idiom with subsequent hit records.

Sony Records' attempts to turn trumpet player Wynton Marsalis into a superstar, casting him as a modernist who was equally capable of playing classical music and contemporary, almost avant-garde jazz, helped Marsalis create a career, although it did not bring the hoped-for record sales. In 1999, Sony released him from his contract; now, as artistic director of the Lincoln Center, Marsalis focuses on the preservation and performance of the entire jazz repertoire. In 2001 Ken Burns broadcast his multi-program *Jazz* documentary on public television, celebrating certain figures, including Marsalis, and gave experimental or political music short shrift. George Lipsitz sees Burns's work as a bourgeois embodiment of jazz history, one that regards jazz as an elitist intellectual art form, rather than one tied to "the street."

Whether one agrees with Lipsitz or not, today the highest sales of jazz recordings go to Kenny G., a white, long-haired saxophone player who writes short, accessible tunes that fit the soft-jazz radio format. Music schools turn out an increasing number of technically qualified musicians, and although many of these musicians are black, the audience remains mostly white. Many of today's jazz-oriented singers are also fluent in various commercial music styles, incorporating rock, soul, folk, and pop elements in an often bloodless but commercially pleasing music.

Jazz remains a fascinating, vital musical form, but it has strayed farther and farther away from its roots in African American music. Periodically these roots reemerge in the sampling of jazz recordings by a few of the more conscious and intelligent rap artists.

Rap

Historically American popular music has revitalized itself just when critics think that its creative impulses have finally run their course. Rap became the new black music style that revolutionized American music, just as the blues, gospel, and soul music had done before. Rap music was part of the hip-hop culture that by the mid-1980s had begun to dominate the urban black scene.

It all started in the Bronx section of New York. Several Jamaican disc jockeys started organizing dances that featured boom boxes with gigantic speakers. In addition to music, the hip-hop scene included break dancing and graffiti painting. All three of these cultural forms represented a rebellion against the bourgeois world of urban America. Graffiti painters sprayed their designs on subway cars, billboards, railroad overpasses, and anywhere their spray cans could reach. Their activities were illegal, but this in itself proved fascinating to the downtown New York art community. In break dancing, each dancer got a turn to be in the center of the ring, and to demonstrate his or her mastery of acrobatics.

DJ Kool Herc, one of the first and most influential of the disc jockeys, was Jamaican, and many of the other DJs were Jamaican or from other countries in the Caribbean. Herc is usually mentioned by rap historians as the person who pioneered talking over records, and then taking two turntables and mixing from one record onto another. The sound of the needle moving across the record, known as "scratching," became part of the sound of rap.

In effect, the DJs were producing records on the spot in these dance club performances. Herc began doing this in the early 1970s. Some DJs, like Jellybean Benitez, went on to become noted record producers. Afrika Bambaataa, another early DJ, was a founding member of a Bronx gang. Upon his return from a trip to Africa he formed a group called the Universal Zulu Nation, which was intended to draw kids away from gangs and into the music.

Early Rap

Some of the early rap records, like the 1979 Sugar Hill Gang's "Rapper's Delight," were friendly, ultra-danceable, humorous if egomaniacal boasts about the virtues of the singer. Historically there is a tradition of toasting in the black community, where two men test one another in a competition that consists of insults directed at the other person's mother. Blues and boogie-woogie piano players adapted this tradition, and even recorded some slightly cleansed versions of what they called "the dirty dozens." Folklorist Roger Abrahams collected and published many of these boasts while studying folklore at the University of Pennsylvania, and living in South Philadelphia.

Another historical stream of rap came from black comedians and jokester musicians, like Pigmeat Markham or Slim Galliard. Markham was a comedian, and Galliard was a musician who invented his own para-bebop verbal language, inserting it into his jazz tunes.

Grandmaster Flash's single "The Message," featuring Melle Mel, came out in 1982. It foreshadowed much of the political aspect of

Grandmaster Flash

rap, and has been sampled on subsequent rap records by other artists. The song describes a ghetto scene, replete with broken glass, urine in the halls, rats and roaches, cars being repossessed, hanging out, stealing, bill collectors, and a kid who doesn't want to go to school. The refrain asks that the speaker not be pushed, because "I'm close to the edge, tryin' not to lose my head." He then proclaims that his life is like living in the jungle and he doesn't know what keeps him afloat. After a few references to violence and death the recording ends with the police coming and arresting the singers.

The song was a creation of Sugar Hill Records songwriter Ed "Duke Bootee" Fletcher, who at first failed to interest Grandmaster Flash and his group, the Furious Five, in recording it. The Five viewed themselves as a party band, not a political one. In the end, the label's owners, Sylvia Robinson and her husband Joseph, successfully pressured the group to record the song.

Over twenty-five years have passed since "The Message" was re-leased, yet the song mentions virtually every socially conscious sub-ject found in rap lyrics to date. Notice the difference in the level of bluntness between this recording and previous message songs by such writers as Gamble and Huff, Stevie Wonder, Norman Whitfield, and Curtis Mayfield. Although many of these earlier songs complained about racial inequities, they did not use four-letter words, and their pleas for social change did not involve direct and aggressive attacks on the white power structure.

The initial impact of rap records was limited by a lack of airplay, especially on white radio stations. In its early years MTV barely played black pop music, and it certainly wasn't going to play any-thing as incendiary as "The Message" at that time. Furthermore, the independent record companies behind early rap records did not have the financial resources to make slick, glossy videos that could com-pete with those coming from the major labels.

Rap and Naturalism

Ever since rap has begun, critics have seen it in a variety of ways, de-pending upon their own political ideology. Some, like Chuck D., see it as the "black CNN," bringing information about social conditions in the inner city to the attention of everyone. Others are outraged by the violence, the continual harping upon smoking marijuana and the treatment of women as sex toys to be used at the discretion of men. More negative criticism has emerged around the obvious emphasis on wealth and its acquisition.

The problem of presenting violence on a surface level harks back to the naturalist movement in nineteenth-century American litera-ture. Novelists Frank Norris and Stephen Crane seemed to feel that everything in life was predetermined, or that human beings were simply creatures defined by heredity and environment, without the power to change their lives.

One can also regard rap's depiction of violence in light of the difference between a photographer who makes a statement by sim-ply revealing an image without staging or editing it, and one who essentially sets the picture up in a preconceived way that is designed to get a specific reaction. For example, a photo showing a clear-cut forest could present the picture in such a way that it is absolutely appalling, or it could be shown in a somewhat more benign way that focuses on the lighting shining through the barren landscape. More sensational than enlightening to the listener, rap's graphic depictions of ghetto life—including police violence and the seeking out of African Americans as scapegoats, bad housing, rats, corrupt politicians, and government oppression of blacks—often seem to be more for artistic than political effect.

On the other hand, some rappers, like the group Arrested Development, offer instruction in black history to young people who are generally not aware of that history. Their songs may refer to slave revolts or to black scientists, inventors, cultural figures, and sports heroes. As I read and listened to hundreds of rap lyrics for this book, for example, Chuck D. of Public Enemy seemed to me to be outstanding in the sense that although his lyrics are always quite masculine and powerful, he never seems to feel the need to trumpet illegal behavior as though breaking the law is in itself a triumph over oppression. Nor do his songs degrade women.

Gangster Rap

Rap groups fall into various camps. Some groups recite innocuous dance lyrics, while some boast of their powers to defeat other rappers in verbal or literal battles. As the political messages espoused by N.W.A. escalated into shrill if accurate critiques of the police, gangster rap emerged as a dominant force.

The reasons for the dominance of gangster rap are complicated. Initially there were bizarre censorship issues, largely coming out of the clash between Miami's Two Live Crew, led by Luther Campbell, and outraged parents. The parents formed a group called the PRMC, the Parents Music Resource Center. Its goal was to label records in order to warn parents about obscene material, much as the movies offer NC-17 or PG-13 guidelines.

Record companies did not like the idea of stickering records, because they were afraid that it would discourage stores from carrying them and radio stations from playing them. Several states passed anti-obscenity laws that threatened record store owners with prosecution if they sold "obscene" records to minors. The record labels then shifted their focus from an opposition to stickering to opposing the right of store owners to sell whatever product that they deemed suitable. The fundamental legal question regarding the possible obscenity of rap records has to do with whether the records violate community standards or appeal to prurient interests.

Amusingly, Luther Campbell had no problem with the stickering of his records. In fact, he even made two versions of some of his recordings, one a so-called clean version, the other a "dirty" one.

In the early days, the only black critics who were willing to challenge violence and misogyny in rap were a handful of ministers and a woman named C. Delores Tucker, who actually harbored ambitions of taking over a rap label. More recently, such perceptive social critics as Bakari Kitwana, Tricia Rose, and T. Denean Sharpley-White have objected to various aspects of rap that relate to women's issues. For example, producer Jermaine Dupri brings his recordings to burlesque clubs to see whether strippers can easily dance to the records. If they can do so, he feels that the record will be successful.

In fact, many gangster records are really pornographic efforts, with constant references to sexual parts and sexual acts. In all fairness, very few social critics, outside of a few feminist scholars, have taken on the pornography industry itself, a multibillion-dollar industry that no one has ever accused of being run by African Americans.

Sampling

One of the issues that surfaced early in the history of rap is the right to use small portions of material previously written and recorded by other artists. This use can vary from a complete bass track to a single James Brown scream or a short instrumental solo.

There are actually two sets of rights at stake. First, there is the performance on the original recording; then there is the ownership of the publishing rights to a song. Although the courts have never definitively ruled on sampling, today most rap artists and record companies who use samples make arrangements with the creators of the sample. Usually the copyright is shared in some fashion, and there are a handful of lawyers who are experts in negotiating these rights.

In general rappers have not received much in the way of artistic credit for coming up with the notion of combining these musical elements into a new work. It is one of the most creative developments that has occurred in contemporary record making.

Current Issues

When rap music first arose it functioned as a spontaneous and unplanned revolt against the control of black music forms by white music producers and record companies. One could say the same thing about heavy metal music or punk rock for that matter, or the folk song revival. In each of these cases the music was recaptured by those who had originated it. Now a handful of producers, many of whom double as artists (Russell Simmons, Sean Combs—a.k.a. P. Diddy or Puff Daddy— Prince Paul, and Jay Z, among others) and triple as business entrepreneurs, have been able to greatly exceed what black

Kanye West

record entrepreneurs were making when black music started to cross over to broad popularity in the sixties and seventies. Although no black entrepreneurs own companies the size of Motown, or even Philadelphia-International, many have deals with major labels that basically amount to partnerships. Jay Z, for example, recently signed a $150 million "360 deal" with Live Nation, whereby they will own a percentage of his various enterprises, including concerts, in return for guaranteeing him huge amounts of money.

Music trade papers and many books have stressed that the majority of the market for rap consists of white suburban kids, although these figures refer to the actual sales of records. It is not a measurement of the radio audience. For rap music, most of the airplay is still limited to black radio stations where presumably the listening audience is mostly black. So there may be a higher percentage of African Americans actually listening to the music, if we include radio and the sharing of tapes and CDRs.

It seems to me that this white audience for rap represents something significant. Rap reveals a violent world where the police threaten one's everyday life, and where gangs carry similar threats. Poverty is an everyday phenomenon in the ghetto, with the rats and roaches disclosed so long ago in "The Message." For rap to play a more aggressive political role in the black community, let alone the culture at large, it must become more issue-oriented, and less obsessed with sex, violence, and bling. Such matters as ghetto unemployment, black-on-black crime, delinquency, meaningless violence, poor schools, bad housing, unemployment and under-employment, and disappearing fathers should be added to the litany of white injustices against African Americans that preoccupy rappers. It is also surprising that rap doesn't really call for much in the way of specific political action, except for its generalized support of black nationalism and in some instances for the Muslim movement. George Lipsitz has pointed out that Russell Simmons and Sean Combs have been active in voter registration drives and, in Simmons' case, agitation for better schools. Yet he also points out that the fashion wings of these producers' companies deal with sweatshops in Africa and Los Angeles that do not pay decent wages to their workers.

Lyrics by Category

I recently examined two books of rap lyrics. *Rap: The Lyrics* was edited by Lawrence A. Stanley, and published by Penguin Books in 1992. *Hip-Hop and Rap Lyrics* has no credited editor, and was published by Hal Leonard in 2003. Each book contains lyrics for 175 songs.

There is some overlap between the two books, because some of the artists covered in the Stanley book also appear in the Hal Leonard book, although the bulk of the material in the latter appeared after the Stanley book was published.

Placing the songs into single categories was sometimes difficult, because one song might be about a protagonist who is smoking weed, looking for women, and also rapping on the microphone (making self-references). What I tried to do was to focus on the central subject of each lyric. Here are the categories I arrived at:

> **Boasting:** The lyrics assert that the rapper is the greatest artist, the best lover, etc. For example, Big Daddy Kane says in "Smooth Operator,"

> I'm good 'n' plenty,
> Servin' many—
> I give nightmares to those who compete—

> **Politics:** Songs like Ice T's "Freedom of Speech" emphasize great African American historical figures changing or shaking up the social system:

> I want the right to speak
> I want the right to walk where I wanna—
> Talk and rebel every time—

Some specifically promote unity and aim to leave the listener with a positive message, as in the Disposable Heroes of Hiphoprisy's "Language of Violence":

Don't take I for granted
When you hear man ranting
Don't just read the lips
Be more sublime than this.

Violence: The image presented is of a dog-eat-dog world in which you must hurt, kill, or maim the opposition before they can do the same to you. Some songs in this category, like N.W.A.'s "100 Miles and Runnin'," present violence as a reality of community life, and of interaction with whitey, rather than being an enjoyable or desirable choice, e.g., "I'm stereotyped to kill and destruct / Is one of the main reasons I don't give a fuck." Pure gangster rap, on the other hand, offers no explanation for the violence, though racial hostility is often implied or stated. Naughty by Nature's "Ghetto Bastard" challenges, "I don't do jack but fight and lighten up the street at night / Play hide and seek wit a machete, sexin' Freddy's wife."

Misogyny: Sex is demanded; women are referred to as "bitches" and treated as inferior objects. The lyrics contain constant, often intentionally shocking references to sexual intercourse and present the rapper as an incredible sexual athlete, as in Two Live Crew's "Me So Horny" (quoted here in a "clean" version): "I'm like a dog in heat / A freak without warnin'."

Party music: This category includes raps about school, everyday life, dances, humor, and rap music itself. DJ Jazzy Jeff & the Fresh Prince complain in "Parents Don't Understand," "The next half hour was the same old thing / My mother buying me clothes from 1963."

The boasting model can be and is combined with all of the other types except for the political category. Some artists who are essentially politically oriented unite this with violence as being two sides of the same coin. N.W.A. in particular frequently did this.

The lyrical content in the two books broke down as follows:

	Stanley	Hal Leonard
Boasting:	31 songs	45 songs
Politics:	27 songs	10 songs
Violence:	20 songs	26 songs
Misogyny:	18 songs	21 songs
Party music:	17 songs	27 songs
Romance:	11 songs	24 songs

There were also a handful of songs about history, humor, misandry (all men are pigs), parents, and school. Only eight songs in the first group focused on drugs, and only two in the second group.

This survey is useful, but of somewhat limited value because certain artists' songs, such as Lauryn Hill's, were not included, probably because their publishing companies did not permit them to be used—and, as I have already mentioned, many songs had multiple subjects. For example *dozens* of the songs contained drug references, but they simply weren't mostly about drugs.

The most interesting thing about this survey is the great reduction in the number of political songs apparent between the 1992 and 2003 collections. It is even more dramatic than the numbers indicate, because four of the political songs in the Hal Leonard book— three by Ice T and one by Ice Cube—actually date from the period covered in the Stanley book.

If rap artists are serious about their critiques of contemporary culture and not just conducting an exercise in rhyme, they need to be willing to work to change that culture. The difficulty is that the more aggressive forms of rap are often the ones that sell the best.

Many rappers seem to feel that they need to live the gangster role in order to maintain their credibility as macho rappers. For Tupac and others, this was done at the cost of their lives. Others, like producer Suge Knight, have served or are serving jail terms, or seem to be in constant trouble with the law. This can be seen as another bizarre instance of life imitating art, or it can be viewed as certain artists' lack of insight into just what it is that rappers are trying to change in the culture.

- That said, it fascinates me that rappers receive little or no credit for the imagination of their rhymes, their ability to bend with musical beats, or their colorful use of words. Aren't these the sorts of things that we should be trying to encourage children to do in our schools? Professor Adam Bradley has written an entire book about the sophistication and value of rap poetry titled *Book of Rhymes: The Poetics of Hip Hop*. Bradley details such matters as inner rhymes, wordplay, rhythm, and storytelling in arguing that some rap artists are indeed serious poets. Since so much of rap criticism focuses on the content of the lyrics, rather than its structure, these stylistic contributions tend to be devalued. They also contradict the view of rap music as a thuggish device used by gangsters. One might say this lack of appreciation is another example of racism.

White Rappers

There have been comparatively few white rappers who have made much impact on the idiom. The Beastie Boys drift in and out of a sort of punk rap. The idea of fighting for their right to party seems a bit pale next to the frightening worlds of Ice T and Ice Cube. Vanilla Ice achieved tremendous but short-lived popularity with his fake ghetto pose, but subsequently has disappeared into the one-hit wonder pile. Eminem, or his alter ego Slim Shady (his real name is Marshall Mathers), has been the only white rapper to make any lasting impact. Mathers shares much of the dysfunctional family background of some of the ghetto rappers, and was endorsed and introduced by Dr. Dre. Not only has he never pretended to be anything other than white, but he makes a point of acknowledging his race. He is also prone to violence and misogyny in his raps, so he fits into that segment of rap culture without too much difficulty.

Rap is now a viable international musical form, and is well-known among both Native American and Latino young people. The beauty of rap is that it requires no real musical training, just a fascination with words and an interest in technology that is sufficient to enable the artist to develop original beats. As such the ability to create this music is accessible to anyone with an interest in creating it. So rap has become international, with rapping in Japanese, French, Spanish, Arabic, and Hebrew.

Rap music has been excoriated, denounced, censored, and praised. Professor Tricia Rose has presented an intelligent and balanced view of the idiom in her book *The Hip Hop Wars: What We Talk About When We Talk About Hip-Hop and Why It Matters*. While not overlooking the positive messages presented by such groups as Mos Def, Talib Kweli, and the Roots, she is troubled by the way that gangster images and sentiments have encouraged violence against youth and disrespect for women. She questions the meaning of "keeping it real" when gangster rappers never get around to mentioning the many women supporting their families with two and three jobs while their male partners languish in jail or on the unemployment lines. Or is that *too* real for the gangster rappers?

Authenticity: Songwriters, Artists, and Record Producers

When artists record songs, it is easy to impute motives to them based on the lyrics of the song or the passion of a performance. However, songs get recorded for a number of reasons that may not leap immediately to mind. An artist might record a song simply because a particular style or point of view happens to be popular at the time. For example, when Glen Campbell recorded Buffy Sainte-Marie's song "Universal Soldier," he was pressured by the media to explain why he had recorded an antiwar song. Campbell, who never recorded another protest song—his subsequent major hits tended to be romantic

songs or songs about less controversial subjects—had no clear answer
to give. The song might have been suggested by his record producer
or by the record company, solicited by a music publisher, or simply
occurred to Campbell as a potential hit. The song was released in
1965, at the height of civil rights agitation and the birth of mass sentiment against the war in Vietnam. Similarly, after Dylan hit it big,
a wave of Dylan clones arose, trying to reproduce first his political
sentiments, and later his writing style.

In terms of rap, the "authenticity" problem concerns the authority of the singer. Or, as record people like to say, does a song have
"street credibility?" Many of the more socially concerned rap artists,
like N.W.A., Common, Nas, or Kanye West, seem to feel that they
must earn their rap credentials by throwing in gratuitous references
to violence, derogatory comments about women, boasts about mate-
rialistic excess, and details about drugs or romantic conquests. This
is possibly the most pathetic legacy of gangster rap—the artists must
prove himself, so to speak, by including this material. Very few artists can resist this particular device, and so we find such female artists
as Missy Elliot, Lil' Kim, and Da Brat asserting *their* super-sexual
skills, and performing their own versions of the macho posturing
of so many male rappers. Some artists, like Queen Latifah and Salt
'N Pepa, have avoided this trap. When Lauryn Hill questioned the
entire hit-making process in rap in her song *Superstar*, it was like a
blast of fresh air in a smoke-filled room.

It is also difficult to deny that there is a definite double standard
working in regard to songs about violence. Compare the attention
that rap got, and is still getting, to the somewhat aimlessly rebellious
violence and hostility presented in quite a bit of hard rock and heavy
metal music. When Eminem, the premiere white rapper, turned out
to have some talent as an actor as well as a songwriter and performer,
suddenly it became acceptable for him to rant against women and
insult the past and present members of his own family. (Apparently
an angry and talented actor has privileges that an angry and talented
rapper does not—even if that rapper happens to be white.) And what

about the misogynist lyrics of such heavy crowd favorites as the Rolling Stones?

Songs by White People About African Americans

Some songs of this type will be covered later in the book. The section on songs written for the purpose of bringing about social change will include songs by such composers as Pete Seeger, Woody Guthrie, Tom Paxton, and Utah Phillips.

Another category of songs will be covered in the chapter on the music of hate. Various segregationist groups recorded songs that were intended to make fun of African Americans and the civil rights movement, and there are a few record companies that currently release music that expresses anti-African American sentiments.

What this section concerns is music by white artists or songwriters who are not especially involved with the genre of protest songs, but who have written or recorded songs that express positive sentiments about African Americans.

Cole Porter is best known as a sophisticated Broadway songwriter, whose songs like "Night and Day," or "I've Got You Under My Skin," are generally ranked with those of Jerome Kern or the Gershwin Brothers as "standards," songs known and performed by cabaret artists and many jazz singers.

In 1934 Porter wrote the song "Miss Otis Regrets (She's Unable to Lunch Today)." The song is about a woman who has an affair with a man, and then shoots him. A mob comes and drags her out of jail and lynches her. Therefore, Miss Otis is "unable to lunch today."

Although Porter makes no racial attribution to the characters in the song, the fact that the woman shot the man after she "strayed" in lover's lane, and the "mob" then strings her up on a willow tree, indicates the singer is the black servant of the heroine.

While Porter's songs were generally praised for their wordplay and lyric subtlety, they were not particularly known for expressing political or social viewpoints. Yet this song is one of the earliest examples in pop music of songs protesting racism. This song was recorded by Ella Fitzgerald, and later by Rosemary Clooney and Bette Midler.

By the 1960s many of the rock bands had begun to take political positions in favor of the civil rights movement. The Young Rascals were a group of young New York singers who performed in a style that was obviously influenced by black singers. In 1968 they wrote and recorded the hit song "People Got to Be Free." The lyric simply says that people should all help one another, and want to be free. The last verse refers to the "train of freedom" that has been "long overdue." This is almost a direct reference to Curtis Mayfield's song "People Get Ready."

Another pop singer whose work had previously consisted of songs from the doo-wop era was Dion, previously known for his work with the group Dion and the Belmonts. In 1968 he recorded the song "Abraham, Martin and John," a celebration of three great Americans, all of whom were assassinated. A key portion of the lyric points out that "the good die young." The song also goes on to say that we all will be free someday. Supposedly Dion did not originally want to record the song, but it transformed his career, making him into a credible solo artist.

Although Laura Nyro is identified with the peace, love, and flowers era of the late sixties, most of her songs are about love, dancing, or good times. In 1969 she wrote the song "Save the Country." Written in a black gospel style, the song refers to the dream of the two young brothers, the Kennedys, and mentions a precious king "who loved his people to sing 'We Shall Overcome.'"

Tony Joe White is associated with the Memphis white soul musicians. His 1971 song "Willie and Laura Mae Jones" is about the singer's black neighbors, and how his family and theirs worked the fields together. White talks about taking his guitar over to the Joneses' house and how he and Willie would play together through the night while the children danced. As the song continues, both families have to move off the land to make a living, a dilemma faced by so many poor farmers, white and black. At the end of the song,

the singer meets Willie downtown and suggests that they all get together, but Willie "Shook his head real slow and his eyes were kind, /
This is another place and another time." Waylon Jennings and Dusty
Springfield are among the artists who also recorded this song about
the closeness born of shared experiences in the South that had disappeared with "progress."

Another 1971 recording is "Long Way to Hollywood," composed
and recorded by Steve Young, and later covered by Hank Williams
Jr. Young was born and raised in Alabama, and the song refers to his
family's heritage of hard work and privation. The third verse of the
song makes common cause with African Americans:

> I've got another song about the south
> It's white and it's black
> There ain't no banjo on my knee
> But that song is on my back.

Another odd addition to this genre is the song "Black and White,"
written in 1956 by radical activists David Arkin and Earl Robinson.
The song, almost childlike in its construction, supports the notion of
black and white children going to school together. Nineteen-fifty-six
was still early in the civil rights struggle, but the song became a huge
hit in 1972—by which time U.S. schools had been integrated—as
recorded by the decidedly nonpolitical rock band Three Dog Night.

This brings us to Elvis Presley's recording of Mac Davis's song "In
the Ghetto (Vicious Circle)." Elvis always acknowledged his love for
gospel music and blues, but it wasn't until 1978 that he recorded a
socially conscious song. The song tells the life story of a child born in
the Chicago ghetto. As he grows up he "learns how to steal and how
to fight." As a young man the protagonist of the song buys a gun,
steals a car, and is killed. It is easy to compare this song—by a white
songwriter, sung by one of the biggest rock artists of all time—with
later rap songs that paint a similar picture. It's a far cry from "Love
Me Tender!"

Bruce Hornsby is an excellent pianist and songwriter who had an enormous hit in 1986 with his song "The Way It Is." Hornsby is a white southerner from Charlottesville, Virginia. Hornsby's song contrasts the lives of those on welfare with a man in a silk suit who makes fun of them. The song then refers to civil rights legislation, and the difficulties that African Americans have in obtaining decent jobs. In the chorus of the song Hornsby says that people say that some things will never change, but he asserts, "Don't you believe them."

Our final example in this section is a 1989 song written by country songwriter Bobby Braddock and recorded by Tanya Tucker. The song was called "I Believe the South Is Gonna Rise Again."

It starts off with a portrait of the singer's family. Her father never took a vacation and died at age forty-four. The family lived in a sharecropper shack. Braddock then contrasts this family with a black family living down the road. The key phrase to the song, "I believe the South is gonna rise again," is followed by an explanation that Braddock doesn't mean that it will be the way that people thought "back then." He then in effect makes a plea for racial unity, with everyone walking hand in hand, with a "brand new kind of brotherhood."

Music About Interracial Romances

Interracial romances have long been a highly sensitive subject in America. In 1966 fourteen-year-old Janis Ian wrote a song called "Society's Child," about a romance between a black high school student and his white girlfriend. The girl's parents, schoolmates, and teachers combine forces to denounce the relationship, and the girl's mother forbids her to see her boyfriend, referring to him as "boy" rather than using his name. Ian grew up in a black neighborhood in East Orange, New Jersey, and the song was a composite of situations that she had observed.

In the song the girl capitulates, because she is "society's child," unable to resist society's pressures. She does hope for a future time when such relationships will be possible. The refrain to the song is "I can't see you anymore."

"Society's Child" initially did not get much airplay or attention, except in Flint, Michigan. However, Leonard Bernstein used Ian in a television special, praising the song and criticizing radio for being too cowardly to play it. As a result both Ian and the song received some critical attention and airplay, although it never became a hit.

Bill Medley had been one of the two Righteous Brothers, known as blue-eyed soul singers. In 1968 he had a romance with a black session singer and recording artist named Darlene Love, and wrote the song "Brown-Eyed Woman" about that love affair. In the song the man is unable to get his woman friend to see him without an awareness of the trappings of hundreds of years of white oppression against African Americans. Despite his continual pleading, she breaks up with him. The song got to #46 on the *Billboard* charts, but did not achieve anywhere near the hit status that several of the Righteous Brothers' duets had enjoyed. Shortly after the record was released, the relationship came to an end.

Country music is often regarded as being politically conservative, and often it is. Merle Haggard's songs have included such patriotic pleas as "Okie from Muskogee" and songs about hard times, like "If We Could Make It Through December." In 1972 he wrote a song called "Irma Jackson" about an interracial romance. The song daringly proclaims the singer's love for his black girlfriend, and protests against the world's narrow views.

Haggard traces the history of the relationship, which started out when the two were friends in childhood. They then fall in love, but Irma decides to go away, and the singer accepts her decision. He concludes by asserting that he will love Irma Jackson until he dies.

One can only guess what country disc jockeys and man country fans thought about this song. Haggard has marched to his own drummer from the beginning, and clearly understood the risk that he was taking in recording such a song during the Nixon era.

To give the reader some perspective on Haggard's song, I had a black friend named Wesley Westbrooks who grew up in Arkadelphia, Arkansas, during the 1920s. In 1931, when he was about eleven years old, he was delivering milk for a white dairy owner. Wesley became friendly with a young white girl who was the daughter of the dairy owner, and occasionally she would give him an ice cream cone and chat with him after he got through with his deliveries.

One night Wesley's parents were warned that word had gotten around that the two were having a love affair. The person who delivered the message made it clear that Wesley needed to leave town as quickly as possible.

The very next day Wesley's parents put him on a train to Kansas City, Kansas, where he had an uncle. They did not tell Wesley why this was necessary for many years. Instead they simply told him that he could get a better education in Kansas City.

Remember, Wesley was eleven years old at the time, and the relationship was entirely innocent. The force of America's interracial sex taboo has never been entirely overcome, although interracial romances and marriages are more common today. After all, the president of the United States is the product of such a romance.

Race: An Ongoing Issue

Race has been a critical issue in this country practically since the United States was founded. It is interesting to see country, rock, and even a Broadway-oriented songwriter like Cole Porter exposing some of the issues that finally came out in the open in the civil rights movement. It would be interesting to know how much attention Tanya Tucker's or Merle Haggard's fans paid to the lyrics of these songs. Several researchers have established that many listeners do not pay close attention to the lyrics of songs and often misunderstand their meanings. For example, many people who heard Bruce Springsteen's song "Born in the USA," released in 1984, thought that it was a super-patriotic song. In fact, conservative columnist George Will suggested to the Reagan campaign that it try to use the song in Reagan's re-election campaign. Knowing very little about Springsteen's views, they unsuccessfully requested permission to use the song at political rallies.

Social scientists have studied listeners' responses to song lyrics, and discovered that often they not only didn't pay much attention to lyrics, but frequently misunderstood their meaning. No matter how broad interpretations can be, if we look closely at the music that addresses race issues over decades, we can see the struggles that persist, as well as some resolution and growth in our societal understanding of such issues.

4

WOMEN'S LIVES AND SONGS

Women are not a minority group from a numerical standpoint. They also constitute a portion of every other group discussed in this book. Nevertheless, the issues that confront women in our society deserve a separate discussion in any examination of the music and culture of America.

Outside of protest singers, performers do not generally sing songs about minority groups that they do not belong to. On the other hand, songs *about* women constitute a large portion of the repertoire of songwriters and musical performers. Because of this, whether the performer is a man or a woman, there are some unusual problems in attempting to analyze the role of women through an examination of "their" music. Because of the sheer volume of material available, it is virtually impossible to do a thorough survey of attitudes toward women revealed through songs. Instead we will touch upon some key social issues, and relate them to songs by and about women. This will necessarily cover a variety of musical styles and genres.

The Role of Women

Historically women have fulfilled certain roles as the inevitable result of biology. Women bear children, and in most societies they assume the responsibility of caretaking in the child's early years. Other roles that women fulfill depend upon the social organization of each particular tribe, nation, and social or ethnic group. Anthropology teaches us that in some tribes women are the heads of the family, and descent is reckoned in the matrilineal line. In other groups husbands take multiple wives, and in some cases wives have multiple husbands.

Generalizations about the alleged differences between men and women are therefore dangerous. Some scholars are dedicated to declaring one gender mentally or physically superior, and others are taken with the idea that there are no fundamental differences between men and women. Part of men's frequent domination of women is certainly based upon the fact that in general men are physically stronger than women. This parallels the oppression of slaves by slaveholders who used guns to eliminate rebellious acts.

The leaders of the American Revolution were not especially interested in women's rights. Although freed slaves gained the right to vote in 1866, women were not afforded that right until 1920. At the end of nineteenth century only 7 percent of Americans had completed high school, but 60 percent of the graduates were women. This was because men were expected to join the work force as quickly as possible. In 1880 14.7 percent of women were in the labor force, but that number had grown to 24.8 percent by 1910. The jobs available to women were limited, and they were often employed in domestic service. In 1910, 17 percent of employees in clerical and sales positions were women; this rose to 30 percent by 1920. Certain professions became consigned to women such as nursing, working as librarians, or teaching in preschool or grade schools.

In the music world, certain instruments were deemed suitably feminine for women. Piano, flute, and harp were considered ladylike, although the great majority of piano recitalists were, and continue to be, men. There are hundreds of stories of women who have been discouraged from playing brass instruments by their parents or music teachers because of the antediluvian notion that women lack the strength to produce a good sound on these instruments, and that playing a horn doesn't look feminine.

Music and Romantic Love

By 1900 the treatment of women in American songs had become somewhat ritualized. Popular music, usually written by men, considered women in terms of romantic love. Women were "placed on a pedestal," representing purity and grace, and their goal was assumed to be marriage to an appropriate husband. Occasionally, an aggressive or suggestive woman would be treated with some interest in such songs as "The Sunshine of Paradise Alley." By and large, however, women were portrayed as somewhat helpless objects that needed to be protected by men.

Folk songs portrayed women on a somewhat broader canvas. The traditional ballad "The Devil and the Farmer's Wife" has been reported with a variety of tunes and texts. The basic story is that the

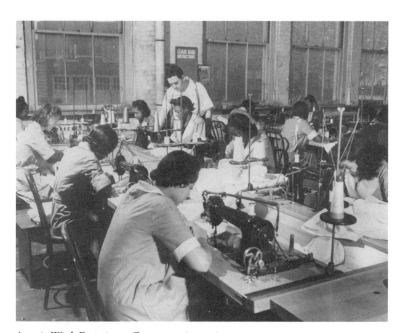

Astoria Work Experience Center, sewing unit

devil returns to earth in order to find a wife. He visits a farm where the farmer-husband happily relinquishes his spouse, saying, "Take her then with all of my heart / And I hope from hell that she never does part." The devil proceeds to cart her off below, where she immediately kills two little devils. The third little devil begs his father to return her to earth, so the devil makes the long trek back, prompting the farmer to wonder: "The old man went a-climbing up the side of the hill. / If the devil won't have her, then who the hell will?" The final verse offers the moral: "This shows that the women are worse than the men / They can go down to hell, but they'll come back again." Another version sees this ability as an asset: "There's one advantage women have over men / They can go down to hell and come back again." Both versions indicate that the woman in the song is the powerful figure, dominating not only her husband, but the devil as well.

"The Devil and the Farmer's Wife" paints a picture of women as being powerful, willful, and shrewish. Other American folk songs take the woman's part and complain about the drudgery of women's lives and their subordination within the family. One example is the traditional song "The Wagoner's Lad":

> Hard is the fortune of all womankind,
> They're always controlled, they're always confined;
> Controlled by their parents, until they are wives,
> Then slaves to their husbands, the rest of their lives.

Single and Married Women

The Southern mountain song "I Wish I Was a Single Girl Again" contains a whole litany of complaints against marriage, including the lines "Dishes to wash, spring to go to, when you are married, Lord, you got it all to do. / Two little children, lyin' all in the bed, both of them so hungry, Lord, they can't raise up their head." The woman's husband is denounced as a drunkard who doesn't provide well for the family. The chorus says: "Lord, I wish I was a single girl again."

The opposite point of view is taken in the folk song that Burl Ives often sang, "When I was Single." The husband in this song complains that he had plenty of money until he got married.

Folksinger Harry Tuft sings a song called "Across the Blue Mountains." In this song a young girl falls in love with a married man who invites her to go with him "across the Blue Mountains, to the Allegheny." Her parents disapprove, suggesting that the man take his own wife on the trip. The girl protests, saying that he is the man of her own heart.

In the song "The Wagoner's Lad," the heroine seems to be between a rock and a hard place. Her love wants her to come with him, but her parents oppose it, because he is poor. The song doesn't resolve the choice, but clearly the woman feels that either way she loses—it is simply a question of whether she will be controlled by her parents or by her husband.

World War I and Women's Suffrage

The United States entered World War I in 1917. On the one hand this had a positive effect on women's expanding role in American life. Women joined the labor force, sold war bonds, or organized benefits for the troops. Some worked as nurses, even serving overseas with the Red Cross.

The National Woman's Suffrage Association (NWSA), founded in 1870, initially took a pacifist opposition to World War I. In fact, the only member of Congress to vote against America's entering the war was also the first woman to be elected to the House of Representatives, Jeannette Rankin. She had worked to win the vote for Montana women, who gained that right in 1914, voting her into office in April 1917.

Eventually, pressure to support the war drove the NWSA into abandoning its antiwar position. Its membership doubled, rising to two million by 1919. The role of women in the war effort coupled with increased militancy by women resulted in the passage of a federal amendment for women's suffrage in 1919, and by August 1920, thirty states had ratified it. American women had gained the right to vote.

Another of the groups that had supported suffrage was the Women's Christian Temperance Union (WCTU). The WCTU had its own songbook, and several songs supporting suffrage were included. One called "I Am a Suffragette," dated from 1912. The ending of the song stated:

> Yes, papa votes, but mama can't,
> Oh no, not yet, not yet
> And I'll not marry any man,
> 'Til I my suffrage get.

Suffrage Parade, New York City

The alcohol industry had opposed women's suffrage, because it feared that women would spearhead opposition to alcohol. True to their fears, the Women's Christian Temperance Union (WCTU) led the charge, and Prohibition was enacted, lasting from 1920 to 1933.

Two organizations led the fight for temperance. The Women's Christian Temperance Union (WCTU) was active from 1870 until 1930. The Anti-Saloon League, organized before 1900, actually spearheaded Prohibition, the banning of alcohol sales in the United States.

The Hutchinson family, previously mentioned in the section on the Mexican War, were among those who used their performances as a platform to advocate temperance. Songs that denounced the use of alcohol painted pitiful and dramatic scenes of men abandoning their families in times of need, or ignoring critical family events such as the serious illness of a child. Ewing cites temperance songs that sold in the hundreds and songbooks that circulated in the thousands, dating from the 1860s.

The archetypical temperance song was Henry C. Work's "Father, Dear Father, Come Home to Me Now," published in 1864. The lyric is delivered by the drunkard's child, who asks the father to come home from work to tend to the singer's poor, sick brother. As the song progresses, the sick child's condition deteriorates, and he calls out for his father. The song concludes with the child dying at three o'clock in the morning. The child's last wish, which goes unfulfilled, is "I want to kiss Papa goodbye."

The temperance movement was closely identified with the living situation of women, and even with the women's suffrage movement. It was also intertwined with the preaching of a number of religious leaders. In the chapter on women and music I will return to some of these issues.

Between the World Wars

If men had feared that the right to vote would lead to more widespread demand for women's rights, they turned out to be wrong.

Many women retreated from the workplace after the war. On the other hand, the twenties were a period where the social structure loosened up. The Roaring Twenties images of bathtub booze, gangsters, roadsters, and flapper girls became a part of American folklore, if not a typical scene in American life.

By the end of the twenties the depression set in. As unemployment rose, women, especially minorities, tried to take up the slack by working in service occupations. Through the first half of the twentieth century, many middle-class women were able to hire a domestic to perform household tasks and to take care of their children.

Women in Popular Music and Jazz

During the period between the two world wars, there was a huge difference between the treatment of women in popular music and in the blues. One of the differences was that in popular music artists did not write their own songs. The songs were composed by professional songwriters. With a few exceptions, notably lyricist Dorothy Fields, these songwriters were men.

In popular music, the female singers of the 1930s and early 1940s—such singers as Rosemary Clooney, Peggy Lee, Patti Page, Dinah Shore, Jo Stafford, and Kay Starr—came out of the big bands. These singers performed tunes by Tin Pan Alley songwriters, except for Lee, who wrote a number of songs with Dave Barbour. Even in Lee's songs at that time there was nothing that was particularly representative of women's issues. Later Lee recorded some songs by Jerry Leiber and Mike Stoller that took on a more aggressive and independent stance in discussing female roles.

The twenties saw an explosion of female blues singers, many of whom wrote their own songs. The late Rosetta Reitz, who owned a blues reissue label called Rosetta Records, pointed out that some of the titles of these twenties songs included "I Ain't No Man's Slave" (Rosa Henderson, 1923), "Ain't Much Good in the Best of Men Nowadays" (Bessie Brown, 1926), "Trust No Man" (Ma Rainey, 1926),

"Women Don't Need No Man" (Lucille Bogan, 1927), and "You Can't Sleep in My Bed" (Mary Dixon, 1929).

In "Wild Women Don't Have the Blues," Ida Cox asserts that wild women are the only ones who ever get by, and proclaims that she'll put her man out if he doesn't act right.

According to her biographer, Sandra Leib, Ma Rainey, one of the most important blues singers, wrote three-quarters of her songs about what a woman does when her man "does her wrong." Some of these songs frankly depict a life of sexual freedom and promiscuity, involving homosexual women, men, and prostitutes. Ma's rivals in the song included transvestites, "sissy men," etc. It is interesting to note that the songs of the female blues singers did not generally concern themselves with racial discrimination.

Not all blues songs reflected these attitudes. Poet, folksinger, and historian Carl Sandburg collected a song in the 1920s in Texas called "When a Woman Blue." The song asserts that when a woman gets blue she hangs her head and cries, but when a man gets blue he grabs a train and rides.

Women in Country and Folk Music

A similar image of independence and self-worth was surfacing in country and folk music. Bufwack and Oermann report numerous references to "banjo pickin' girls" in southern folk and country records of the 1920s and '30s. Banjoist Lily Mae Ledford of the country band the Coon Creek Gals sang about the banjo pickin' gal who went from Cuba to Chattanooga, and asserted that if "you haven't got the money, better get you another honey."

Sturdy mountain women like Liza Jane and Black Eyed Susie appear alongside strong women of the West like Calamity Jane, Poker Alice, and Peg Leg Annie.

Because a good deal of early country music was recorded "on location" in such Southern mountain areas as Bristol, Virginia, there was very little distinction in the 1920s between folk and country music. Some of the references to sex in these songs were pretty straightforward, although rarely as blunt as in the blues. The songs "Streets of Laredo" and "Who Stole the Lock on the Henhouse Door" were about prostitutes and prostitution, and "My Love Is a Rider" is an outright sexy song about a cowboy, allegedly written by outlaw queen Belle Starr.

An early country music group called the Blue Ridge Mountain Singers recorded only ten songs, but six of them dealt with betrayal, adultery, and two-timing. These were new issues for country music in the twenties and thirties, although they became a staple of Nashville songwriters in later years.

Women and Labor Songs

Another sort of country-folk song dealt with social issues, especially labor conditions. "The Southern Cotton Mill Rhyme," a song collected at the Textile Union Hall in 1929, makes common cause with men and women mill workers against the bosses. One verse accuses, "'Cause we go walking down the street, all covered with lint and strings, / They call us fools and factory trash and other lowdown things."

Florence Reece's "Which Side Are You On?," written during a 1931 coal mining strike in Harlan County, Kentucky, uses the refrain, "Which side are you on? Which side are you on?" Oddly, Reece wrote the song from a man's point of view ("My daddy was a miner, and I'm a miner's son . . .").

The song "Cotton Mill Girls" seems to date back from the 1920s and has the chorus

> Hard times, cotton mill girls *(repeated three times)*
> Hard times everywhere.

Other verses refer to low wages and poor working conditions. One of the oddest footnotes to the treatment of women in song was recorded by the late Gene Autry, a movie cowboy actor and singer who later became very active in the conservative community. He sang the song "The Death of Mother Jones," shortly after the death of that radical unionist in 1930. No composer credits are given on the reissue of this recording, which attributes the song to "Anonymous," but the song concludes with a sentiment that Autry would probably not have endorsed in later life: "May the workers get together to carry out her plan, / And bring back better conditions for every laboring man."

In 1925 Mary Howe wrote a piece for chorus and orchestra called "Chain Gang Song." It appears to be the first treatment of prison life by a white woman. In 1939 Julia Smith wrote "Cynthia Parker," an opera about a white girl who was raised by Comanche Indians and then forcibly repatriated by whites.

The Fifties and Sixties

World War II duplicated some of the social changes that occurred during World War I. Women worked in many jobs that had previously been closed to them. For example, before the war a number of school districts and insurance companies had actually banned the hiring of married women, but because of the labor shortage, these bans were lifted. In addition, many women took on factory jobs, though these "Rosie the Riveters," as they were called, knew from the beginning that they would be replaced at the end of the war.

After the soldiers came home, many of the women in the labor force were indeed replaced. The new paradigm that arose starting in the mid-forties dictated that women would finish their education, then enter the labor force until the birth of their first child. When the youngest child was in school it became common for women to return to work.

Many people moved to the suburbs, and most people owned washing machines, cars and television sets. The depiction of women in movies began to focus on sex and submissiveness. The independent, thinking women actresses like Katherine Hepburn or Rosalind Russell were replaced by sex symbols like Marilyn Monroe or Jayne Mansfield, or women depicted as airheads, like Sandra Dee and Doris Day. Underneath this suburban serenity was a pattern of family instability. Divorce rates climbed to their present level of 50 percent.

A teenage culture developed, as teenagers had some discretionary income from working or from allowances. Many went to great length to purchase cars. By the mid-fifties rock and roll had become a significant part of American musical life, and many teenagers could listen to music on their car radios, safe from parental supervision. A pattern took shape of teenagers enjoying music that was deliberately antithetical to the taste of their parents. With this shift in popular music came a wave of music artists who evoked fresh energy and expressesed new perspectives.

Music of the Fifties

The first rock and roll records (discussed later in the chapter on rock and roll) derived from a sort of shotgun marriage between country music and the blues. In the mid-fifties there was a move towards more innocent musical styles that had fewer black influences. These songs avoided the sort of salacious and dance-oriented recordings that middle-class parents found so dangerous. Artists like Conway Twitty and Connie Francis really didn't sing songs that had the traditional, somewhat literary sort of romantic messages that earlier pop songs had contained. The subject matter was still romantic love, but now the viewpoint of the songs shifted towards the attitudes and interests of teenagers.

The Sixties and the Folk Boom

While the chapter on protest music will cover the folk boom in more detail, it is worth noting here that while many of the first popular groups in the folk revival consisted of three or four men, like the Brothers Four, the Limeliters, and the Chad Mitchell Trio, this boys' club was shattered by a number of female singers, especially Odetta, Joan Baez, and Judy Collins. Baez became an overnight star with her appearance at the Newport Folk Festival in 1959, and Peter, Paul & Mary reached the heights of folk-pop stardom with their 1962 first album.

The image of the successful male and female performers in the folk revival differed. The Kingston Trio and the other groups dressed in Ivy League button-down shirts and slacks, and used a good deal of often-scripted humor in their performances. The female performers tended to have long, straight hair and to use little or no makeup. This was a different image of women in pop music than anything that had previously been promoted.

Bob Dylan arrived in New York in January, 1961. After a period of paying dues in Greenwich Village, Dylan acquired a big-time manager (Al Grossman), and a record deal (Columbia Records. Two of his songs, "Blowing in the Wind" and "Don't Think Twice," became hit songs through the performances of Peter, Paul & Mary. Many of the artists mentioned here, including Dylan, Seeger and Woody Guthrie will appear in more detail in the next chapter of this book.

Although Dylan ignored the traditional aspects of conventional lyric-writing, women in his songs remained a vehicle for male convenience. In that respect, Dylan was adopting the most macho and backward poses of pop music, as well as country and blues songs. Dylan was always the one that was leaving for another freight train ride, another relationship, or a new way of life. At his most extreme ("If I had To Do It Again, I'd Do It All Over You"), Dylan was an archetypal male chauvinist pig.

The British Invasion, the 1650 Broadway Songwriters, and Motown

By 1964 the folk revival had run out of steam. There was an overabundance of folk-pop trios, quartets and even nine person groups, all of whom were recording and performing college concerts. The revival would have probably slowly expired, but the British music invasion put the nail in the coffin.

I have generally not dealt with artists who are not Americans in this book. However, the Beatles had such an overwhelming presence and influence on the American music scene that it is impossible to ignore them. As was the case with Dylan, the Beatles started out performing other people's songs, and gradually began to perform their own music. By the time they got to the United States in February, 1964, the four "mop tops" with their cereal-bowl haircuts had virtually taken control of the American music industry. In their wake came a raft of British groups, including the Dave Clark Five, the Hollies, Gerry and the Pacemakers, etc. Later came Herman's Hermits, the Who, Led Zeppelin and others.

In 1958 a young Don Kirshner partnered with music business veteran Al Nevins to form Aldon Music. The two headquartered their operation at 1650 Broadway, rather than in the nearby Brill Building, which had been the home of many music publishing companies and aspiring songwriters and record producers.

In a period of a few years, the two signed songwriters and sometime performers Jeff Barry, Neil Diamond, Gerry Goffin, Howard Greenfield, Ellie Greenwich, Jerry Keller, Carole King, Barry Mann, Neil Sedaka, and Cynthia Weil. All of these writers were in their early twenties, and brought a new sensibility to pop songwriting. As songwriters and performers they had countless hits—though it is interesting to note that the women's cowriters (Barry, Goffin, and Mann) were always named first in their published songs. King's piano work was so sought after that many of the artists who recorded her songs either used her to play the piano, or had others play the parts that she had created for demonstration records. We will have more to say about King later in this chapter.

Meanwhile, on the West Coast Jackie DeShannon and Sharon Sheeley were writing many successful songs. Although there had been successful woman songwriters before, this was the first time there were so many of them—and so many women active behind the scenes in production, arranging, studio playing, and background singing.

The content of the tunes certainly owed little to any women's rights movements. There were dance tunes like "Who Put the Bomp in the Bomp, Bomp, Bomp" by Mann and Weil, teenage laments like "Run to Him" by Goffin and King, and wordplay songs like "Do Wah Diddy" by Barry and Greenwich. Many of these songs were performed by teenaged "girl groups" like the Shangri-Las, mistresses of motorcycle angst, and the Phil Spector–produced Crystals, Ronettes, and others. There is some controversy about how the Goffin and King song "The Loco-Motion" became a hit. The traditional story is that Little Eva, the artist, was babysitting for the Goffin-King family, and they decided to have her sing on the demo of the song. The demo came out so well that it ended up being a hit record. A conflicting version of the saga has the contact with Little Eva being made by the vocal group the Cookies, who introduced her to the songwriters.

Motown Records, begun in 1960 in Detroit, also focused on teen-oriented love songs, which female acts like the Supremes recorded along with male artists like Smoky Robinson and the Miracles, Stevie Wonder, and the Four Tops. But Motown's producers, songwriters, and studio musicians were almost invariably male, until songwriter, producer, and singer Valerie Simpson entered the picture and was signed as a producer for Motown Records in 1966.

Feminism and the Women's Movement

In 1963 Betty Friedan ignited the feminist revolution with her book *The Feminine Mystique*. She brought to the fore many issues that were of vital concern to (mostly) middle-class white women. These issues included male domination of females and the need for women to have careers outside the home. In Friedan's view these careers fulfilled a number of functions. They kept women mentally alert; they brought in income to families and inferentially provided some financial independence for women. Above all, careers enabled women to assume their correct place as equals rather than inferior beings.

The book effectively led to the formation of the National Organization for Women (N.O.W.), the founding of *Ms.* magazine, and the popularity of women's friendship and discussion groups called consciousness-raising sessions. For the first time women were asserting their need for same-sex friendships in the same way that men played cards or went bowling together. The subject matter at these consciousness-raising meetings was generally dissatisfaction with spouses, a feeling of depression at the amount of child care and housework that they were expected to do, and an incipient political-social consciousness that dictated that women should lobby for reproductive rights, an Equal Rights Amendment, and childcare facilities.

Forty-five years later it is striking how tame Friedan's book seems, and how class-based most of her observations and conclusions are. It was not news to most African American women that they needed to pursue a career. Their financial situation, more than any longing for self-respect, demanded that they work. Class distinctions made issues of equality or consciousness-raising seem less relevant not only to African American women but to Native Americans and Hispanics as well.

Friedan's book was only the opening wedge in the new gender warfare. Radical feminist organizations like Women's International Terrorist Conspiracy from Hell (W.I.T.C.H.) and Redstockings came forth with much more comprehensive agendas and proposals. To writers like Germaine Greer and Robin Morgan, men in effect became the enemy. Women began to question not only the structure of the middle-class family, but heterosexuality as well. To some of the radical feminists, man's "on top" position was symbolic of male domination in the world at large. "Sisterhood is powerful" became one of the important slogans of the new movement. Women began experimenting with same-sex relationships, and in some cases with sexual abstinence. If man was the enemy, why sleep with him? These thoughts emerged as investigations by such sex researchers as Kinsey revealed that many women never had achieved an orgasm, often as a result of ignorance, disinterest, or a lack of sensitivity on the part of their male partners.

Women also began to resist the intellectual sovereignty of the male species. Males were by far the dominant intellectual force in the culture: they were the full professors at the Ivy League colleges, they constituted the vast majority of elected politicians, and they ran the corporations that paid women less money for doing the same jobs as their male colleagues. Women were hired in at lower salaries, and they were generally promoted more slowly than men. Women were kept out of certain jobs, such as skilled labor trades.

In the midst of this feminist ferment, Lyndon Johnson took office as president of the United States. Women regarded him as an archetypal male sexist figurehead (not that Kennedy had exactly been a women's libber.) Yet Johnson demonstrated a progressive commitment by virtually forcing civil rights legislation through Congress. At the same time, however, he escalated the presence of American troops in Vietnam, bringing the United States into a virtual civil war with itself. Some of the same forces that had been mobilized in the civil rights movement began to resist the war in Vietnam. Feminists encouraged women to protest the war by resisting the sexual advances of soldiers. Suddenly the country experienced thousands of young people growing their hair long, resisting military service (in some cases immigrating to Canada to avoid being drafted), and living in hippie communes. The hippie lifestyle espoused communal living and the notion of living off the land. Sexual mores were relaxed and relatively free, and chores were supposed to be shared by the residents.

For all their ideals, both the civil rights movement and the communes relegated women to the same demeaning roles imposed on them in the middle-class societies that had been painted as the enemies of feminism. Black SNCC leader Stokely Carmichael—one of the more dramatic radicals in the movement who drew media attention while such leaders as Ella Baker and Fannie Lou Hamer were virtually ignored—was quoted as saying that the only correct position for women in the movement was the prone position. On the communes women did the cooking, cleaning, and child care. Probably the leading mode of liberation that they were able to pursue was a choice of multiple sex partners.

For better or for worse, the American family is still reeling from the many broken marriages and the psychological confusion that accompanied these experiments in quasi-utopian socialism. Virtually none of the original communes remain.

The Singer-Songwriters

By 1964 the popularity of the Beatles had brought the folk revival to a rapid halt. The next wave of performers, male and female, were primarily singer-songwriters, like Laura Nyro, Joni Mitchell, James Taylor, and Carly Simon. The singer-songwriters broke with the original socially conscious aspect of folk music by writing an ever-increasing number of songs about personal issues.

Laura Nyro expressed a uniquely personal vision in her songs. She restructured the English language in a way that made her work different from anybody else's, her invented phrases, like "stoned soul

Laura Nyro

picnic" and "surry on down," conveying meaning even though they were not in general use. Many of her songs became hits for other artists, notably the 5th Dimension; Blood, Sweat & Tears; Three Dog Night; and Barbra Streisand. Nyro's first album was released in 1967, but she never achieved the level of popularity as an artist that she enjoyed as a songwriter. Of all of the singer-songwriters, Nyro's musical sensibility was closest to rhythm and blues and doo-wop music.

Of the ninety-eight lyrics printed in the songbook celebrating her career, only a handful deal with political or social causes, and yet there is a socially conscious sensibility in her work that is clearly her own individual voice. Only Nyro would write a lyric like

> Bleed a little
> Bleed a little
> Till your freedom calls you.

Her 1969 song "Save the Country" refers to Martin Luther King ("the precious king") and the Kennedys ("the two young brothers") and concludes with the plea to

> Save the people
> Save the children
> Save the country.

Although Nyro continued to write and record after her successes of the late sixties and early seventies, she became a bit reclusive. She had a child, moved to Connecticut, and began a lengthy relationship with a woman. None of her later songs were turned into hits, and Nyro became a songwriter's songwriter, someone whose work was far more appreciated and understood by her peers than by the general public.

Joni Mitchell has been an enormously influential songwriter, musician, and performer. Her first album, *Song to a Seagull*, released in 1968, covered a wide range of subjects, ranging from pictorial descriptions like "Night in the City" to portraits of offbeat acquaintances, such as the snarling cabdriver Nathan La Freneer in the song she named for him:

> He asked me for a dollar more
> He cursed me to my face
> He hated everyone who paid to ride
> And share his common space.

Mitchell's work coincided with the feminist movement in that she demanded the right to do whatever men did, to fall in love with as many people as she chose. In the song "Cactus Tree," on the same album, Mitchell delineates a catalogue of various men that she has been involved with, and says that she will love them when they are around, but that if they follow her she will leave them because

> . . . her heart is full and hollow
> Like a cactus tree
> While she's so busy being free.

This first Mitchell album is primarily a solo album, with only minimal instrumental support from others. Mitchell was one of the first female musicians who gained the respect of both male and female musicians and fans. Her innovative use of alternate guitar tunings, her relatively simple but effective piano playing, and her occasional later use of the dulcimer all stamped her as an exceptionally talented musician. But most of all it was the songs, unusually thoughtful and mature for someone in her early twenties.

Perhaps the creative landmark of Mitchell's career was the 1972 album *Blue*. The subject matter includes the unhappy tale of a child put up for adoption by her mother ("Little Green"). Many years later Mitchell revealed that this was a true story from her own life, and she was able to find and be reunited with her daughter. There is the bright dance tune "California," about returning home, and the album's final tormented song, "The Last Time I Saw Richard," which describes a meeting with her ex-husband, who has subordinated his dreams to a middle-class existence.

Mitchell's mass exposure in the marketplace began with her writing the hit song "Both Sides, Now)" for Judy Collins. Joni went on to write "Woodstock" for Crosby, Stills and Nash, and to have hits of her own with "Help Me" and "Free Man in Paris." She became increasingly entranced with jazz and jazz musicians, using Jaco Pastorius, Tom Scott, and John Guerin on her later albums. Experiments with jazz musician Charles Mingus followed, and Mitchell recorded an album of songs in 1979 where she wrote lyrics to Mingus's tunes.

The Mingus album was a risky artistic venture that lost Mitchell some of her audience; in turn she went into a semi-retirement from the music business. She continues to occasionally release albums, and the 1994 album *Turbulent Indigo* includes songs about AIDS and battered women.

Joni Mitchell has experienced something similar to the career path of Laura Nyro. Some of her earliest songs—"The Circle Game," "The Urge for Going," and "Clouds (Both Sides Now)"—are reflective and philosophical, like poet Jacques Prevert's lyrics in the best French café music. As Mitchell's career developed she employed more consciously sophisticated allusions to poets and painters as she shared the continuing saga of her own personal life. She seems abundantly aware of the contradictions of her life, as when she goes to Memphis in search of the blues and pays a visit to songwriter and guitarist Furry Lewis—who makes no bones about the fact that he does not like her. She notes the contradiction between his poverty and her limo parked outside his house, but somehow fails to anticipate his hostility.

In her 1970 album *Ladies of the Canyon* Mitchell celebrated a New York street clarinet player in the song "For Free." My friend Israel Young had a music store called the Folklore Center near the corner where the street musician played. He told me that Mitchell had come back to visit the clarinetist after the record came out. When he

Joni Mitchell

complained that she had made thousands of dollars from the song and he'd gotten nothing, she bought him a new clarinet. Since he was a junkie, he immediately pawned it.

These sorts of contradictions between the social sensibilities of a financially successful artist and the realities of everyday life for the struggling artist, or for that matter worker, are what make it so difficult for the person at the top of the pyramid to understand the dilemmas of the people at the bottom of the structure. Mitchell's work, however, reflects an understanding of such complexities.

Other artists still cover Joni Mitchell's earlier songs, but for some thirty-five years her audience has continued to contract, and her bitterness about her inability to get airplay and sell records has made her a historical rather than a contemporary figure.

Other Sixties Women

Although there were some important female performers in the folk-rock movement of the sixties, like Terry Garthwaite or Tracy Nelson, a performer like Grace Slick of the Jefferson Airplane was regarded as a "chick singer"—in the jargon of musicians, a woman who sings with the band, but has no say in the group's musical direction, and whose talent is often impugned by the other, male performers—as absurd as this may seem. At times this impression may have been concocted deliberately by managers or record companies, or sometimes by individual singers.

Similar reactions have plagued even some of the finest female jazz singers, as well as country artists like Tammy Wynette, whose physical ailments and spats with her sometimes husband George Jones seemed to command great attention from the media. The initial reaction to Dolly Parton tended to similarly focus on her appearance, her physical attributes, and her beehive hairdo—especially during her days working with Porter Wagoner. Parton was able to partially reverse this attitude through her acting work in the movie *9 to 5*, where she played a sexy secretary turned liberated woman. She also became known as a prolific and successful songwriter.

Enduring Women's Issues, from the Seventies On

The feminist movement became somewhat isolated from the mainstream of the average American woman. Abortion was legalized in 1973, women were granted a more equitable chance to play collegiate sports, and many women seemed to feel that they had gotten what they wanted. The Equal Rights Amendment was defeated, because it was not ratified in enough states to become a successful constitutional amendment, and a sort of counterreaction to the feminist movement developed.

A new emphasis on female fashion and a celebration of glamour eroded much of the progress of the women's movement. However, many of the issues raised in the movement remain today.

The abortion issue has been particularly fraught. The Catholic Church is strongly opposed to abortion, and various Christian groups see it as a legalized form of murder. Family planning clinics have been bombed or torched. Women's right to abortion eroded under the Bush administration in the first decade of this century, and doctors who perform abortions continue to be threatened, injured, and even killed.

Another ongoing concern has been the breast implants that became popular. In 2008 alone, over 300,000 women and teenagers had breast augmentation surgery, according to the National Research Center for Women and Families. Aside from the philosophical objections many feminists raise to cosmetic surgery generally, implants have drawn the attention of the women's movement as a health threat: women with implants have been shown to have an increased risk for cancer. Dow-Corning, which manufactured many of these implants, has gone into bankruptcy to avoid the financial burden of settling claims on these cases.

Many women today still cannot count on equal pay and promotion for equal work. In 2008 a woman named Lilly Ledbetter was denied the opportunity to sue her employer, Goodyear Tires, for wage inequality, because the U.S. Supreme Court determined that she had waited too long. Since the 180 days they set as the statute of limitations was far less time than it took Ms. Ledbetter to discover that she was being paid less than her male coworkers, the case became a cause célèbre. Since President Obama signed a law invalidating this decision, a March 1, 2009 report in the *New York Times* indicated that women in 2008 still were receiving about three-fourths of the average wage that men enjoyed. The percentage varied, according to the specifics of the occupation, but the median difference was a weekly wage of $600 vs. the man's wage of $800.

As we have seen, a segment of contemporary rap music encourages violence, or at least a lack of respect toward women. So does the work of heavy metal misogynists like Axl Rose or various comedians. Black critics have often been reluctant to attack gangster rap, and if they do are careful to cite similar attitudes by white rock artists. As previously discussed, however, Tricia Rose has made a number of critical comments about the treatment of women in gangster rap music.

Whether or not women facing these issues today accept, reject, or champion the freighted term "feminist," the words of British author and scholar Rebecca West, writing in 1913, may provide at least a basis for agreement: "I myself have never been able to find out precisely what feminism is. I only know that people call me a feminist whenever I express sentiments that differentiate me from a doormat."

The Women's Music Movement

In 1973 Judy Dlugacz cofounded Olivia Records as a women's music record company. The original concept was to provide an outlet for female artists who played primarily for female audiences. The goal of the company was to use women in every possible role—as engineers, record producers, and studio backup musicians and vocalists. Many Olivia records were sold at women's bookstores, and at concerts by the performers.

Meg Christian was the first artist for the label, and her initial album sold over seventy thousand copies. This album was followed by Olivia's all-time best-seller, Chris Williamson's *The Changer and the Changed.*

I analyzed the fifty-seven songs in the Chris Williamson songbook, and found that seven of the songs referred to male chauvinists, one was about a relationship with a man, twenty-one of the songs were not gender specific, four concerned politics, five had a feminist perspective, seven were about same-sex relationships, seven had

spiritual or New Age connotations, and eleven were about miscella-
neous subjects. Of course, to much of her audience, the twenty-one
non-gendered songs would probably be interpreted as concerning
female relationships.

Olivia Records, a primarily lesbian label, no longer exists, and
many would make the case that with a number of major artists coming out as lesbians, its functions have filtered into the mainstream
culture.

Another important artist in the women's music movement was
(and is) Holly Near, founder of Redwood Records. Although many
of the Olivia artists celebrated the women's movement, they did not
tend to focus on other political issues. Near not only writes and sings
feminist songs, but she has gone to El Salvador and Nicaragua in
support of radical political struggles in these countries.

Another thing that sets Near apart from the Olivia artists is that
she is openly bisexual, often cowrites with men, and has often used
a male pianist as her accompanist. Her song "Singer in the Storm,"
which is also the title of her autobiography, makes common cause
with many. It contains the lyric "She does not fear the pouring rains,
that drench her to the bone, / She only fears the consequences, of
living all alone."

Near has also used both men and women to sing and play on her
records, and has released a number of Redwood recordings by male
artists who focused on political issues rather than gender struggles.

Carole King

Although Carole King achieved early fame as a songwriter, after her
marriage to fellow songwriter Gerry Goffin broke up she moved
from New York to Los Angeles and started a career as a recording
artist. Her 1971 album *Tapestry* has now sold over twenty-two million
copies worldwide.

Of the seventy songs in the book, fifty include a man in the song,
nineteen are about love, nine have spiritual connotations, and an

additional fourteen songs treat various other subjects. As is often the case, some songs fall into more than one category.

Many of the songs were cowritten with other writers, including her ex-husband, Gerry Goffin. As a New York songwriter, King had usually composed music and left the lyrics to someone else. However, on the *Tapestry* album she wrote both the words and music to most of the songs.

The predominance of men and relationships in King's songs might suggest that she finds it difficult to leave these themes out of her songwriting. The title song from the *Tapestry* album, written almost like a medieval fantasy, is one of the most suggestive of self-subordination. The hero goes on a lengthy and fruitless quest, finally returning to his beloved at a much later date. The song ends with the phrase, "Now my tapestry's unraveling, he's come to take me back." It is as if King is telling us that a woman's patience and passivity will ultimately be rewarded by a man's love and approval.

Male songwriters of the same period, like Bruce Springsteen or Neil Young, obviously write some romantic songs. However, they also may write about world peace, cars, baseball, or abstract subjects. Seemingly they do not feel a similar pressure to include women in such a disproportionate number of their songs. Nor can one imagine them placing their lives in a holding pattern pending the approval of a lover or wife.

Eighties and Nineties Ladies

By the 1980s America was entering a post-feminist period. Although there was still some music being marketed under the title "women's music," the feminist movement had succeeded in bringing many women's issues to a broader public.

Country Artists

K. T. Oslin is a Texas singer-songwriter with experience in Broadway shows and television commercials. Her song "80s Ladies" was a women's anthem of its own, delineating how women had developed the strength to go beyond broken marriages: "We've burned our bras and we've burned our dinners / And we've burned our candles at both ends." She goes on to say that "there ain't much these ladies ain't tried."

Other country artists emerged who sounded more folk-influenced than most of the seventies female country artists. Nanci Griffith is a country-folksinger who is widely respected as a songwriter, and who has developed a loyal audience without becoming a superstar. Some of her songs are introspective and personal, and others are story songs, like her hit song "Love at the Five and Dime." This is a song about a girl and her romance with a part-time local musician whose dream of stardom turns into love and marriage, but not financial success.

Mary Chapin Carpenter achieved enormous success with several of her dance-oriented country songs, like "Down at the Twist and Shout" and "I Got Lucky." Her more expressive songs were on some of the best-selling albums that featured the dance tunes. Her song "He Thinks He'll Keep Her," cowritten with Don Schlitz, outlines a marriage that deteriorates from a sedate middle-class existence to the woman's giving her husband his walking papers because, she says, "I'm sorry, I don't love you anymore."

On the same album, *Come On, Come On,* released in 1992, the song "I Am a Town" presents the singer in the persona of a town. It is not about any specific person, but relates the history of a town from the viewpoint of the town itself. Compare this to the more common female country fare of complaints about men's drinking habits or unfaithfulness.

On her 1994 album *Stones in the Road,* Carpenter addresses more social-political concerns. In the title song, she writes, "The starving children have been replaced by souls out on the street, / We give a dollar every time we pass and hope our eyes don't meet."

On the same album, her song "John Doe No. 14" is taken from a newspaper article about an unknown man who dies in a mental hospital, where he has lived for some years. She constructs her story around the newspaper story: "My spirit so wild so I let the river take it / On a barge and a prayer upstream."

As more and more intelligent and assertive women writers and performers have emerged on the Nashville scene, some of the attitudes expressed by male singers and performers have begun to change. Mac MacAnally's song "All These Years" is about a man who comes home early from work and realizes that his wife is having an affair with another man. The couple examine their lives thoughtfully before agreeing to stay together. She sings, "All these years, what have I done, / Made your supper and your daughter and your son."

She decides to stay because "I can finally see how much I stand to lose." The song became a #3 country by the country-rock band Sawyer Brown in 1993.

Other country songs have given voice to women's attitudes toward divorce and domestic abuse. "Independence Day," written by Gretchen Peters and recorded by McBride & the Ride, was an enormous hit in 1993. The song concerns a battered woman who leaves her husband and burns down her house. A year later Reba McEntyre had a hit with the song "She Thinks His Name Was John." The song is about a one-night stand that leads to the singer getting AIDS. It was written by Sandy Knox, a woman whose brother died of the disease, and Steve Rosen. In 2000, the Dixie Chicks scored a hit with the song "Goodbye Earl," written by Dennis Linde in the late nineties. Earl is a wife batterer, and the singers arrange for his demise.

Folk Artists

As though in answer to the synthesizer-disco oriented sound, a group of female folk-oriented singers emerged in the eighties who continue to be popular today. Their ranks include Tracy Chapman, the Indigo Girls, Michelle Shocked, and Suzanne Vega.

Vega's song "Luka" imagined the life of a battered child: "They only hit you until you cry / And after that you don't ask why."

Some of Vega's other songs are more in a spiritual/philosophical vein and make reference to environmental issues. Other songs are

New York vignettes, like "Neighborhood Girls," a song about a prostitute who hangs out in front of a bar.

Tracy Chapman's 1990 album contained two enormously popular songs, "Talkin' 'Bout a Revolution" and "Fast Car." "Revolution" refers to poor people rising up and transforming the world, while "Fast Car" is a more reflective song, about ghetto children dreaming of leaving the inner city. Chapman is a black artist whose songs do not get played on black "urban contemporary" radio, because musically they are in a folk-rock groove, and their messages are more on the controversial side than anthems to bling.

The Indigo Girls each write songs and play guitar. Their songs rang from love songs, which are fairly explicitly written about women's relationships with women, to environmental and politically oriented songs. Amy Ray's song "World Falls" refers to the beauty of the natural world. On the 1999 *Come On Now Social* album, Ray's song "I, Go" says that grandmother was a suffragette and was blacklisted for what she wrote. She goes on to incite her audience to "fan the flames"—presumably the flames of rebellion. On the same album her musical partner Emily Saliers wrote the song "Trouble," about poverty and American intervention in the Dominican Republic, which ends with the lines

> I pledge my allegiance to the dollar
> And when the clergy takes a vote
> All the gays will pay again.

The Indigo Girls are also strong supporters of Indian rights, and on the double album *1200 Curfew,* released in 1995, they recorded Buffy Ste. Marie's bitter song "Bury My Heart at Wounded Knee" twice, once live and once in the studio. Obviously they feel strongly about the song and the issues that it raises.

Other folk-oriented women artists not covered here include the late Kate Wolf, Chicana artist Tish Hinojosa, Lui Collins, Katie Curtis, Sally Fingerett, Julie Gold, Patty Griffin, Tracy Grammer, Patty Larkin, Natalie Merchant, Claudia Schmidt and Dar Williams.

Many of the older folksingers, like Joan Baez and Judy Collins, continue to record and do concerts. Both of them write quite a few of their own songs, particularly Collins.

The Nineties and Beyond

In the eighties and nineties women assumed new roles and attitudes in rock and roll. L7, Babes in Toyland, and Hole are women's bands (only Hole includes one man) that have achieved some measure of respect and sales in the rock community. Courtney Love, the leader of Hole, first achieved notoriety as the wife of the late Kurt Cobain. Kim Gordon is the female singer and bass player in the band Sonic Youth. None of the other people in these bands

Sonic Youth

have any strong association with past or present rock stars. They are simply women who have worked hard to write songs, sing, and play in a very competitive field. They represent something of a contrast to the rare female rock bands of earlier times, like Fanny, the Bangles, or the Go Gos, who were, rightly or wrongly, treated as novelty musicians, dismissed as cute or as sex objects before being judged as musical artists. Other rock bands that included men but were led by women, like the late sixties San Francisco folk-rock band the Joy of Cooking and the seventies and eighties band Heart, were not strongly identified with feminist views, other than by implication.

Riot Grrrls

In the early 1990s a movement of female musical agitators arose that became known as the riot grrrl movement. This musical style was also associated with feminist fan zines. The artists asserted their right to scream and to play loud, in the same way that male rock bands had been doing for years. The music was basically female punk rock. The bands often addressed such issues as rape, domestic abuse, sexuality of all kinds, and female empowerment. The movement was focused in Olympia, Washington, at Evergreen State College, and in Washington, D.C.; musical and feminist ideas were regularly exchanged between the two cities. The most popular group emerging from the scene was Sleater-Kinney, which formed near the end of the riot grrrl movement, in 1994, and stayed together until 2006. They were one of the hardest rocking "girl bands" that ever existed, and in 2001 music critic Greil Marcus called them the best rock band in America. Although riot grrrl as a style has peaked in popularity in America, the movement has become international, and has led to a number of Lady Fest musical gatherings, especially in England.

Feminist-Oriented Solo Artists

Melissa Etheridge is an out lesbian but many of the songs on her albums are gender-neutral and sufficiently open-ended that they any listener can identify with them. On her multiplatinum 1993 album, *Yes I Am,* the closest she gets to a political statement is in the song "All American Girl," where she sings about "an All-American girl— And she will live and die in this man's world."

Liz Phair is an indie rock artist from Chicago who has taken a sort of bawdy, nineties, Joni Mitchell-esque attitude towards men. In her song "Fuck and Run" she exults that she takes full advantage of every man that she meets. Yet she is seduced and abandoned in the song.

In "Chopsticks," on her second album, *Exile in Guyville,* Phair sings,

> He said he liked to do it backwards
> I said that's alright with me
> Then we can fuck and watch TV.

This combination of running over men while at the same time showing vulnerability bears some resemblance to the song "Cactus Tree" on Joni Mitchell's first album.

The queen of role reversal is Madonna. Ever-fascinating to the media with her blatant affairs and her interest an obscure Jewish rituals, Madonna is the subject of numerous books, critical analyses, and even entire college courses. Suffice it to say that she has exercised a tight rein over her career. Complex analyses of her persona and music are difficult, because it is hard to tell where Madonna the singer-artist leaves off and Madonna the business-savvy media manipulator begins.

While some of her biggest hits, such as "Like a Virgin," were composed by men, she is not a creature cowed or created by male producers or songwriters. In fact virtually every album has been produced by a different record producer. Madonna has a tremendous feel for what is hot, and what is not, and any video or movie images of her represent what *she* wants us to see.

What Madonna seems to require, more than anything else, is that she be on the borderline of shocking behavior. She steps across the line just far enough for people to remain fascinated by her—to continue to see her movies, to buy her books and albums, and to purchase tickets to her many sold-out performances—but somehow it's never outrageous enough for her to receive open censure from religious or political figures. It is difficult to imagine Tipper Gore or the current crop of conservative senators taking Madonna to task in the same way that they feel comfortable criticizing rap artists. Her feminist contribution, to the extent that there is one, is to refuse to allow anyone to tell her what to do.

Tori Amos has made some strong statements in song about personal and political issues. Many of her songs refer to conflicts about religion that reflect her strongly Christian background. Her 1991 song "Me and a Gun" is an emotional and harrowing description of her own rape. She recorded it without any musical accompaniment. The lyrics include: "It was me and a gun and a man on my back . . . yes I wore a slinky red thing does that mean I should spread for you. . . ."

Alanis Morissette played a major role in the music industry in the mid to late nineties. She signed with Madonna's label, Maverick, and her first album, released in 1995, sold over thirty million copies around the world. The album easily eclipsed the sales of *Tapestry,* or any other album by a female artist. Listening to this album reveals a contradiction between the numerous expressions of self-pity and hurt and the dynamic and angry nature of the vocals. In much of Morissette's work there is a strong element of bitterness expressed about men who used her, abandoned her, or lied to her. Morissette's second album, *Supposed Former Infatuation Junkie*, tempers some of the anger with reflections on her trip to India. Compared to fellow Canadian-born artist Joni Mitchell, who seems to enjoy her former lovers, no matter whether they left her or she left them, Morissette addresses her former companions in a more strident, sexual, and bitter way. Clearly, there were many women who shared her anger in the middle and late nineties, at least enough to make her into a major star.

Canadian pop star Shania Twain appears in these pages because she has sold over forty-six million copies of her recordings in the United States. Her songs were all cowritten with her ex-husband, Robert "Mutt" Lange. Lange's previous calling card was that he produced Def Leppard.

Twain's most successful recordings were made between 1993 and 2000. The songs have an attitude quite opposite to Morissette's. They portray a powerful and self-confident woman who is not going to let any man take advantage of her. This doesn't constitute a rejection of relationships with men; in fact, every single selection in the songbook *Shania Twain's Greatest Hits* is about romance. The feminist aspect is that the woman in these songs is portrayed as in control and sure of herself.

The Conciliators

Artists like Janet Jackson, Whitney Houston, Gloria Estefan, Paula Abdul, and Mariah Carey represent forceful images, but not ones that threaten the establishment. All of these artists are dependent upon teams of writers, and/or producers, who are invariably men. When Jackson and Carey do write songs about social issues, their sentiments are laudable, but anemic and somewhat vacuous.

Jackson's song "Rhythm Nation," cowritten with her producers Jimmy Jam and Terry Lewis in 1989, tells us to "Lend a hand to help / Your brother do his best."

The song also tells us that we are "in a race between education and catastrophe." These are difficult sentiments to argue with, but are not exactly at the cutting edge of rebellion.

Mariah Carey's 1990 coauthored song "There's Got to Be a Way" appeals to the listener's conscience with a pitiful description of a homeless man and informs us that

> There's got to be a way
> To unite this human race.
> And together we'll bring on a change.

But exactly what changes does Ms. Carey have in mind? It seems as though many women artists feel some pressure to make social statements, but not all of them have insights to contribute.

Lilith Fair

In 1997 Canadian singer-songwriter Sarah McLachlan became frustrated with concert promoters who seemed to invariably limit the number of female acts that they would book at a club or concert. For the next three years she organized a touring show called Lilith Fair. Each year she booked more acts, until in 1999 there were so many acts that it required three different stages to present them all. Although McLachlan took some criticism for using too many folk or soft-rock artists, over the years such acts as Meredith Brooks, Erykah Badu, Sheryl Crow, Missy Elliott, Sinead O'Connor, Bonnie Raitt, Meshell Ndegeocello, Christina Aguilera, and Nelly Furtado appeared. All of the acts were either solo female acts or bands led by women. Terry McBride, who is Sarah McLachlan's manager, announced in late 2009 that Lilith Fair would return in summer 2010.

Alicia Keys

Current Artists

The first decade of the twenty-first century has featured a number of women artists who have become successful through television and film exposure. Among these artists are Hilary Duff, Britney Spears, Christine Aguilera, Jennifer Lopez, Miley Cyrus, and Jessica Simpson. It would be fair to say that most of the work of these relatively young artists is focused on romantic topics, as opposed to social issues. Other popular artists of the day, like Alicia Keys, Beyoncé Knowles, and country artists Faith Hill and Taylor Swift, also focus on personal rather than social issues. Sheryl Crow has taken some activist political positions, but they remain separate from her catchy musical offerings.

Women in Jazz

In the world of jazz, there is a long tradition of female piano players and singers. Kansas City pianist, composer, and arranger Mary Lou Williams was a respected figure in jazz in the 1940s and '50s, but she was one of the few women who was accepted into the boys' club of jazz. Trombonist-arranger Melba Liston achieved a similar status in the fifties and sixties.

Sherrie Tucker's book *Swing Shift* uncovers dozens of female big bands that traveled all over the United States. The most famous of these bands was the International Sweethearts of Rhythm. Tucker unveils all sorts of fascinating details. There were black bands that had white members who were "passing" for black, and even had to apply burnt cork and makeup for trips through the South. No white female bands hired black members, although male band leaders did.

Phil Spitalny seems to have been a relatively fair band leader for his all-girl orchestra, but he observed the bizarre custom of auditioning new players while dressed in his underwear. As we could almost expect, the women in the all-girl orchestras were paid less than the men were making in their bands. One informant told Tucker that the typical male sideman was making $125 to $150 a week, while female musicians were being paid $45 to $85.

During World War II women had access to many more musical jobs than before, not only in bands but even in radio orchestras and recording studios. When the war ended, here as in the factories, women were expected to surrender these jobs to returning soldiers.

The Hormel Meat Company hired white female returning soldiers in the 1950s to travel around the country, promote Hormel meat products at grocery stores, and perform concerts in the towns they visited.

Because the company couldn't find enough female musician war veterans, they later hired some women who had not been in the service.

In their book *Jazzwomen: Conversations with Twenty-one Musicians,* Wayne Enstice and Janis Stockhouse questioned all of the musicians they interviewed about gender problems. Their answers often included prejudices against women playing brass instruments, the typical comment "You play well, for a girl," and a reluctance of male musicians to hire women. One of the oddest portions of the book is the section on singer-songwriter-actress Abbey Lincoln. Lincoln tells how she resented her husband Max Roach's insistence that she scream on his *Freedom Now!* album, and she also was disgusted that people would come to see her sing in clubs and expect her to scream.

Women have begun to make inroads as composers and arrangers. *Jazzwomen* cites Toshiko Akiyoshi, Carla Bley, and Maria Schneider as composer-arrangers who have gained some respect in the jazz community. There are also female saxophone players like Jane Ira Bloom and Virginia Mayhew, but they are clearly outnumbered by the many male jazz musicians. The bulk of women's identity as jazz musicians comes from the great singers, like Billie Holiday, Ella Fitzgerald, and Sarah Vaughan (today's most popular vocalists include Diana Krall and Diane Reeves, as well as Norah Jones, who is not universally regarded as a jazz singer but is the most popular vocalist in anything resembling the form), along with such piano players as Joanne Brackeen, Barbara Carroll, Marilyn Crispell, Hazel Scott, and Marian McPartland.

Women's Roles in Music

The role of women in today's music is full of ambivalence. Positive-image rapper Queen Latifah is quoted as saying that no one ever slams her: "I think the people who they're referring to are females who play themselves like that." Oddly, this sounds almost exactly what that great philosopher Luther Campbell says about women: they are mothers or daughters or hos. It also sounds like something I have heard many young women students say, something to the effect of "I'm not a feminist, but . . . ," indicating an aversion to the term or an ambivolence about assuming a feminist identity.

Women assume a multiplicity of roles and attitudes. They are writers, singers, and composers. Some of them sing about issues that are germane to women's experiences, or to anyone's life. Others choose to ignore this level of consciousness and to sing the old romantic love ballads, most of them written by men. Some female artists sing about sex, some about taking control of sex; some sing about men or women that they love, or men that they hate.

Certainly women's attitudes as expressed in song tend to be more frank and open than they have ever been in this culture. Women who want to sing about women have that option. It is only the size and nature of the audience that is not under the control of the artists. That is still the function of the star-maker machinery that controls American popular music.

Songbook Analysis

I analyzed two fakebooks to try to break down the songs about women. There are over seven hundred songs in *The Legal Fakebook*, and hundreds more in the *Giant Book of Rock*. In the Legal book I only did songs starting with the letters A and N, and for the rock book I took the first five songs from the fifties, sixties, seventies, and eighties. I did not include songs by English songwriters, and I did not include more than one song by any one songwriter.

In *The Legal Fakebook*, twenty-two and two-thirds of the twenty-four songs were written by men, with one and one-third by women. Seventeen songs were about love, one was somewhat pro-feminist, and the other twelve were about various subjects, such as locales, scenery, etc. In the rock fakebook, all twenty songs were written by men. They broke down as follows:

Fifties: 4 songs about love, 1 about a dance
Sixties: 1 about love, 4 about various subjects
Seventies: 3 about love, 2 about various subjects
Eighties: 3 about love, 2 about various subjects

None of the songs expressed any spiritual interests, or had any New Age orientation.

I then did a survey of two feminist songbooks in order to compare the subjects of these songs to those not classified as feminist.

The two books were *All Our Lives: A Women's Songbook,* edited by Cheyney, Diehl, and Silverstein (1976), and *Here's to the Women,* by Wenner and Freilacher (1987). I have designated the books as CH and WE in the table below. The subjects broke down as follows:

	Male Chauvinism	Love	Sex	Politics	Feminism
CH	141	0	15	29	6
WE	6	2	1	47	41

Because the second book was written eleven years after the first, it contains many more songs by Olivia Records artists. Note that "political" songs do not necessarily concern women specifically.

The Music Industry and Women's Music

Although there are more women working in the music industry than there used to be, the heads of all the major labels remain white males. Sylvia Rhone is one of two outstanding women record executives. Formerly the head of Elektra, she now is the president of Motown, one of the many divisions of Universal Records. Julie Greenwald is the president of Atlantic Records.

There are women music publishing executives, and a handful of women record producers, notably Linda Perry, Sylvia Massey Shivey, and Missy Elliott. None of the major record companies are active in women's music, although from time to time they sign feminist artists like Melissa Etheridge or Bonnie Raitt. There are a number of women that own or co-own smaller independent labels, but by and large the music business remains a boys' club. As long as this is the case, there will be a need and a market for women's music.

5

PROTEST SONGS: MUSIC AS A TOOL FOR SOCIAL CHANGE

There is a difference between songs that weigh in on social issues and songs that are written in a deliberate attempt to bring about social change. Throughout the history of American folk and popular music, songs have commented upon social conditions. Some of the subjects of these songs have included the plight of minority groups, Robin Hood heroes who reputedly steal from the rich and give to the poor, historical events, and contemporary issues. In the earlier portions of this book we have dealt with some of these matters, like the issue of women's suffrage or battles between American Indians and whites.

Songs that describe working conditions turn up in various collections of American folk music. John Lomax collected thousands of songs for the Library of Congress, traveling widely throughout the United States and introducing his son Alan to the genre. Together they traveled not only to cotton fields and the Southern Appalachian Mountains, where the people's geographic and cultural isolation had allowed them to preserve archaic English musical traditions, but to prison farms and chain gangs, previously untapped for musical material. Lomax's collection of cowboy songs, published in 1916, helped set the stage for the introduction of folk music to the broader public through a national workers' movement.

The song "The Farmer Is the Man" complains about the lot of the farmer, who "lives on credit till the fall." In the song the farmer ends up losing his farm to the "mortgage man." "The Buffalo Skinners" spins the odyssey of an unfortunate trail drive. At the end of the drive the head drover hires the cowboys, claiming that they all owe him money because they drank his whiskey. The cowboys respond by killing him, leaving his "bones to bleach, on the trail of the buffalo."

Clark Halker has uncovered hundreds of labor song-poems from the nineteenth century. Most of the composer-authors were white males, which is an interesting contrast with the songs of miners and textile workers that we will discuss later in this chapter. Most of them also, according to Halker, "earned their livelihoods in working-class occupations." That is, these worker poets or songwriters were not professional poets or musicians writing about things that they had learned about on a secondhand basis, but actual workers.

Halker describes the song-poems as espousing various points of view, from the relatively conservative supporters of the Knights of Labor all the way to anarchism. Many used existing tunes that were well-known to the average person. The gospel hymns of Dwight Moody and Ira Sankey were particularly favored for these parodies. Some of the tunes, like "In the Sweet Bye and Bye," were used by more than one poet.

After 1900 the popularity of song-poems declined sharply, although a few radical or populist papers continued to print them. The late Philip Foner found 277 known composers of protest songs in the labor press before the inception of the Industrial Workers of the World (IWW) in the early twentieth century, and an early anthology of socialist songs appeared in 1901. But it was the IWW who put songs to use as an aggressive organizing tool.

IWW members, known as "Wobblies," were different from any other American labor union, before or since. They were basically anarchists, and yet they believed in the general strike, that is, a strike by workers against an entire city, where workers from all trades would come out to support a particular striking group in its demands of city government. The Wobblies were anti-capitalist, but more anarchist than socialist. They organized groups like apple pickers that no other unions had the slightest interest in recruiting.

The IWW began using street bands in 1908 in Seattle, when they found that their street corner speeches were being drowned out by Salvation Army brass bands. The function of the songs was not only to attract attention and gain an audience for Wobbly speakers, but to deal with political issues as well. The songs were sold as song sheets, and later in a pocket collection called *The Little Red Songbook: Songs to Fan the Flames of Discontent*. This songbook first appeared in 1909. In Joyce Kornbluh's book about the IWW, there is a 1908 report of a meeting where "the literature sales are slow, the collection fair, and the songs sell like hotcakes."

The Lawrence, Massachusetts strike in 1912 was considered to be the first singing strike, with songs used on the streets and at soup kitchens that served the strikers.

Among the composers represented in the *Little Red Songbook* were T Bone Slim, Dan McGann, G. G. Allen, Joe Hill, and Ralph Chaplin. Chaplin's song "Solidarity Forever," written in 1915, is probably the single most popular American labor song, with its rousing chorus: "Solidarity forever, solidarity forever, solidarity forever, / For the union makes us strong." *based on - - - (*

The rather formal nature of the verses, such as "When the union's inspiration through the workers' blood shall run," makes them less memorable than the chorus. To this day this song is used to open numerous union meetings.

In World War I the IWW took a pacifist position, which resulted in the destruction of their influence and the jailing of many of their leaders. The Wobblies were the first union to utilize songs as an integral part of their organizing and agitation. Technically the IWW still exists, but it has only a small number of members. The songbook, now greatly expanded, is still in print.

Joe Hill

The most famous of all the Wobbly minstrels was Joe Hill, a Swedish immigrant who became a hobo/songster and organizer. He ran afoul of the law in Salt Lake City when, the night a grocer was murdered in a holdup and shot his assailant, he turned up at a local hospital with a gunshot wound. He claimed the wound was a result of a crime of passion but refused to reveal any details.

Historians and labor agitators have debated the facts of this case ever since Hill's execution in November 1915. The indisputable fact is that Joe Hill became a powerful symbol for the labor movement, not only in the United States, but in his native Sweden, and in many other parts of the world. Some of Hill's songs, especially "The Preacher and the Slave," are still sung today. It used the tune of "In the Sweet Bye and Bye." Below are a few verses of the song, together with the chorus.

> Long-haired preachers come out every night,
> Try to tell you what's wrong and what's right;
> But when asked about something to eat
> They will answer with voices so sweet.
>   *(Chorus)*
> You will eat, bye and bye
> In that glorious land above the sky;
> Work and pray, live on hay.
> You'll get pie in the sky when you die.
> Workingmen of all countries unite,
> Side by side we for freedom will fight;
> When the world and its wealth we have gained,
> To the rafters we'll sing this refrain.

Many of Hill's songs are forgotten today, because their subject matter was too specific, like the song "Where the Fraser River Flows." In other cases the language is either too stilted or dated. Wayne Hampton points out that the outstanding characteristic of

Hill's songs was his use of humor. He was convinced that a good song could be learned and remembered, while a pamphlet would be read once and thrown away.

The single strongest part of Hill's musical legacy is a song about him that he did not write. Poet Alfred Hayes and composer Earl Robinson wrote the song "Joe Hill" in 1938, and it has been instrumental in spreading Hill's image and fame around the globe. It starts out: "I dreamed I saw Joe Hill last night, / Alive as you and me." The singer tells Joe that he's been dead for ten years, but Joe responds that he never really died. The song tells some of the history of Joe's death, arranged, according to the song, by the copper bosses. Joe reports that his spirit went on to organize the workers. The song ends with the vision that wherever men are striking or organizing, that's where you will find Joe Hill.

Songs of the Miners and Textile Workers

In the 1920s, the Communist Party became involved in organizing alternative radical unions that included miners and textile workers in the South. Out of this political agitation, and out of the dreadful working conditions that these workers were compelled to endure, two separate families of protest songs emerged.

The first of these was created by the local people who had grown up working in the coal mines or textile mills, in a community with an active musical tradition. Many country and folk musicians lived in the cotton mill areas of the Carolinas and the coal mines of Kentucky, and their songs represented actual events in their lives and the lives of their friends and families.

The union leaders, some communists and some not, soon realized that songs could provide glue for their organizational efforts. In a technique that was used later to organize the auto industry, the mill workers created mobile squadrons of workers who would go from one mill to another without notice, attempting to organize the workers. In the case of the cotton mills, the squadrons included singing musicians.

Southwestern musicians, circa 1940

In Kentucky, one family was lionized by the party: Aunt Molly Jackson, and her half-brother and sister Jim Garland and Sarah Ogan Gunning, were groomed by party operatives not only to work with the coal miners, but to fund-raise at large rallies in New York. Their songs began to use rhetoric that was straight out of Marxist manuals, like Gunning's song about how she hated the capitalist system.

Heber points out that the majority of the song-makers in the cotton mills were women or teenage girls. In North Carolina a ballad maker named Ella Mae Wiggins emerged as a songwriter who wrote about life in the cotton mills. She was murdered in Gastonia, North Carolina while organizing textile workers. Her union brothers and sisters believed that she had been deliberately targeted by thugs employed by the mill owner because of the popularity of her songs. New York radical and writer Margaret Larkin carried Wiggins' song "Mill Mother's Lament" back to New York. A performer herself, who had become interested in folk music while growing up in New Mexico, Larkin later wrote two articles about Wiggins. One appeared in the communist paper *The Daily Worker*, and the appeared in the non-communist but radical-supporting magazine *The Nation*. In the coal mines Florence Reece (though not herself a mine worker; women were considered bad luck in the mines) became famous on the basis of a single song, "Which Side Are You On?," which is still sung today.

based on - - -

Conservative Songs

Not all of the music of the nineteenth and early twentieth century that included social commentary supported radical causes. We have previously mentioned the many minstrel-derived coon songs, and the numerous songs that disparaged virtually every racial, religious, or ethnic group. There is no evidence that conservatives used songs as part of an organized political movement, in the way that the Wobblies did. However, certain events galvanized conservative sentiments in songs.

The Scopes evolution trial of 1926 made a strong impact in the South. This trial involved the prosecution of a Tennessee school-teacher for teaching that man, in the words of the state's 1922 Butler Act, had "descended from a lower order of animals." The act made it illegal to teach Darwin's theory of evolution in Tennessee. A number of country songs praised prosecution attorney William Jennings Bryan for his attacks on Scopes and the theory of evolution. Country songwriter Carson Robison wrote a song about the trial that was recorded by country star Vernon Dalhart. Other songs in this genre included Reverend Andrew Jenkins' "Evolution—Bryan's Last Great Fight." An odd recording by Charles J. Oaks entitled "The Death of William Jennings Bryan" celebrated Bryan's role in the trial, along with his somewhat contradictory populist advocacy of free silver during his presidential campaign of 1896. Perhaps this combination of conservative religion and populist economics was not all that unusual in the South—as in the case of the numerous pro-farmer politicians who were strongly racist. In a separate chapter we will consider the more extreme versions of racist songs under the rubric of "the music of hate."

Music and the Communist Party

Initially the American Communist Party did not see the value of folk music in their political struggles—though some members were familiar with the older socialist or Wobbly songs, like "Solidarity Forever." Many of the early members of the party were immigrants whose musical background involved choral singing. Consequently revolutionary choruses were formed, some of which sang songs in Eastern European languages or in Yiddish. No English-language chorus was formed until 1933. The repertoire of these choruses was bombastic and doctrinaire, and decidedly not oriented to American folk music.

In 1931, the Workers Music League was founded as an offshoot of the Communist Party of New York. It had as many as twenty affiliates with chapters in major cities, the strongest of which was in New York. Many prestigious American composers of the day, including Aaron Copland, Henry Cowell, and Elie Siegmeister, were members of this organization, and composer and pioneer ethnomusicologist Charles Seeger (Pete's father) was its theoretical godfather.

The most influential communist in the area of music used for political purposes was the German refugee Hans Eisler, a choral conductor and composer of film scores and songs. Eisler wrote contemporary dissonant music in the then-popular twelve-tone style derived from composer Arnold Schoenberg. One of his songs, written in 1934, proclaims:

> From Atlantic to Pacific
> Sounds the warning
> Workers beware!
> Guns are trained on the Soviet Union
> Proletarians prepare!

Eisler was contemptuous of folk music, and even publicly berated Alan Lomax for "foisting these damn songs" on the working class. In communist circles the Russian Association of Proletarian Music

(RAPM) established the party line, according to which folk music won credit for originating with the exploited but was also felt to be contaminated with patriotic and religious values that derived from feudal and capitalist states.

Yet the gap between the communist anti-folk aesthetic and the use of traditional music as a tool for social change was slowly closing. In 1935, Georgi Dimitrov, a Bulgarian Marxist theoretician, introduced the concept of the Communist Party joining with liberal and socialist groups in a United Front movement. In earlier days party leaders had felt that acceptance of the Communist Party was the only real way to initiate viable social change. Liberals and other non-communist left-wingers were seen as enemies of the people. The new concept was to open the party's arms to these people as allies—embracing their tactics and aesthetics in the process—and to convert them eventually into loyal communists.

Margaret Larkin, who had come back from Kentucky and North Carolina enthusiastic about the new generation of politically conscious working class ballad-makers, developed an ally in *Daily Worker* columnist Mike Gold. He felt that the Workers Music League was writing pretentious music that was unsuitable for the working class. Gold delivered a ringing endorsement of the music of Ray and Lita Auville, West Virginia radicals who played fiddle and guitar. The "serious" composers had been contemptuous of the Auvilles, but Gold felt that they represented something new and exciting in protest music.

Eighty years later, what songs of the Auvilles have been printed seem almost as stilted and pretentious as the music Gold was criticizing. For example, their song "I'm a Civilized Man" contained the lines "I'm a civilized man, I'm a Red, / I have advanced thought in my head." However lame these lyrics may have been, Gold perceived the music, rooted in Southern mountain music, was closer to the lives of the actual working people than the efforts of the League's composers.

Charles Seeger, who initially had little interest in folk music, was among those who had disliked the Auvilles' songs. Like Eisler,

Copland, and Cowell he felt that new and exciting music could be written by "serious" composers for the working people. But he was greatly affected by hearing Aunt Molly Jackson and Jim Garland, who had been blacklisted in the mines for their organizing activities and moved to New York. Seeger also became friendly with the song collector Alan Lomax, who felt that folk music could be a valuable tool for promoting social change.

Now interested in and even intrigued by American folk music, Seeger accepted a job collecting folk songs for the Farm Resettlement Administration. Soon Charles was collecting folk songs, his wife Ruth (Crawford) Seeger was transcribing and arranging them, and he had introduced his son Peter to the five-string banjo and American folk songs.

The Radical Schools of the Thirties and Black Protest Music

During the 1930s a group of socially oriented schools that promoted radical causes opened up in the South. Commonwealth College in Arkansas, the Kentucky Workers Alliance, and the Southern and Highlander Folk Schools in Tennessee were all active. At Commonwealth, Reverend Claude Williams, "the red preacher," combined Marxist humanism, a grassroots approach to the gospel, and music in a single package. He also taught a young singer named Lee Hays how to adapt Negro spirituals to contemporary social issues.

Not all of the singing was led by communists. In the Southern Farmers Tenant Union, a rural labor adjunct to the Socialist Party, a black sharecropper and organizer named John Handcox wrote a series of songs that became famous in the radical movement. Handcox's song "Raggedy, Raggedy" is an example of a "zipper song," into which local figures or timely issues could be inserted into a repeating pattern. It started with the phrase, "Raggedy, raggedy are we," and then other phrases, such as "homeless, homeless," were plugged into the song. Professor Ronald Cohen's authoritative survey, *Work and Sing: A History of Occupational and Labor Union Songs in the United*

States, also lists a number of songbooks published by non-communist radical associations. They include socialist Harvey Moyer's 1905 *Songs of Socialism,* and songbooks published in the 1940s by various unions,

We mentioned Lawrence Gellert briefly in the section on African American music. Gellert was a committed radical who left New York City in the early 1920s and moved to Tryon, North Carolina. Living with a black woman there, he became fascinated with African American music and storytelling, and developed a unique access to black protest songs that went for beyond what any folklorist had ever perceived or encountered. He collected over two hundred such songs, along with numerous other songs and stories, recording them on a wire recorder. Two books of his songs were published, one in 1936 and the other in 1939. A small independent record company called Timely Records pressed about hundred copies of Gellert's material. Josh White also rearranged some of the songs and recorded them on his *Chain Gang* album.

Although Gellert's material was initially received with some interest by communist and radial sources, folklorists objected to the fact that he had not used standard field methods in collecting the music. To protect his informants, Gellert did not list their names, but only the towns where he had collected the songs. Gellert also alienated some of his radical peers by printing uncensored lyrics. If a song used the word "nigger," then Gellert printed it that way. Some folklorists claimed that Gellert was a fraud, and had really written the material himself. But when Rounder Records issued two of the songs Gellert had collected in the early 1980s, after decades of obscurity, it became apparent that Gellert had indeed collected the songs, as he had claimed.

Today several scholars are working on books about Gellert, and his collection is housed at Indiana University.

The Spanish Civil War and Protest Music

During the early 1930s, the specter of fascism hung over the entire world. Hitler came to power in 1933, and in 1935 the Spanish

Civil War erupted. Hundreds of American radicals joined Europeans fighting against the fascist dictatorship of Francisco Franco. Though folk music was definitely becoming the dominant vehicle for spreading liberal social messages, this European war generated one last stand for the Hanns Eisler–led school of using formal music as the mechanism for generating protest songs. Richard Reuss, an American scholar whose specialty was political music, pointed out that such songs as "Freigheit" ("Freedom") and "The Peatbog Soldiers" became the ones most identified with the anti-Franco cause. These songs were originally written in German. Although they actually antedated the Spanish conflict or did not specifically mention it, they were sung at the many rallies that were intended to support the Loyalist (anti-Franco) cause. Some other songs from the choral tradition did specifically deal with Spain, such as "No Pasaran (They Shall Not Pass)." The radical record company Timely Records issued a record of Eisler-oriented material in 1940. The songs were sung by Ernest Busch and some veterans of the actual war in formal choral arrangements. The record was called *Six Songs for Democracy*.

American labor organizer-performer-songwriter Ray Auville was the only American using folk songs as his platform who wrote any songs dealing with the war, and his songs were not widely circulated or sung.

An odd coda to the Eisler-Seeger controversy is that after the end of the Spanish Civil War the Seeger group in effect reclaimed the war as a platform for writing protest songs in a folk vein. A number of songs, most notably "Vive la Quince Brigada" ("Viva the 15th Brigade") were written and recorded in 1943 by various members of the Almanac Singers, including Pete Seeger and Tom Glazer.

Changes in American Life and the Union Movement

Although America was in almost constant turmoil through the entire decade of the 1930s, it was an exciting time for the radical movement. As a result of the Great Depression many important changes took

Picket at a textile mill in Greensboro, Georgia

place in the way that the federal government operated. The social security system was created for retirees. The government established work programs that built roads, bridges, and post offices, and employed many Americans in the National Park and Forest Services. Other federal programs employed writers, musicians, artists, and actors to do everything from collecting folk songs to painting murals in post offices.

In 1935, eight international labor unions created the Congress of Industrial Organizations (CIO). America's traditional unions were organized into the American Federation of Labor (AFL), founded in 1886. The AFL believed in organizing workers on a craft basis, so that one group of workers at a factory might belong to the carpenters' union, another to the electrical workers' union, and so forth. The CIO believed in organizing an entire factory into a single union that would represent all of the workers in a particular factory.

The CIO unions were much more militant than the AFL had ever been. They were also more favorably inclined (in general) to the

notion of integrating black and white workers in the same union local. The older AFL unions maintained a pattern of separate white and
black locals. Oddly, one of the last unions to achieve complete inte-
gration was the American Federation of Musicians, an AFL union.

In general, the union-agitating singers described below fit more
comfortably into the CIO model. Such unions as the United Mine
Workers (UMW) and the United Automobile Workers (UAW) were
enthusiastic about the possibility of using music as an organizing
tool. Meanwhile, the average worker scrabbled for an economic foot-
hold in this period of high unemployment and poverty.

The Almanac Singers

A group of New York–based folksingers became the first organized
troupe to attempt to use folk music as a vehicle for social change. They
worked as the Almanac Singers, but it was never really a set line-up
of people. Pete Seeger was the anchor, the guiding force and the one
who was most consistently involved in labor music and causes. Lee
Hays moved up from Arkansas to join the crew, and Woody Guthrie was active, especially as a songwriter. Future screenwriter Millard
Lampell was also involved in the songwriting end of things; other
sometime members include Peter Hawes and his brother Butch; Bess
Lomax, Alan's sister; Arthur Stern; Sis Cunningham; Brownie Mc-
Ghee; Sonny Terry; Josh White; Leadbelly; and Tom Glazer.

The goal of the Almanac was to make the union movement a
singing one. This was especially true of Seeger, as revealed in David Dunaway's biography, and Pete's own book, *Where Have All the
Flowers Gone.* Instead of using parodies of popular tunes, hymns,
or vaudeville songs, the Almanacs adapted traditional folk songs or
wrote new tunes.

There were some intrinsic problems with these goals. Most American workers had little or no interest in folk music. The cotton mill
workers and coal miners hardly needed help from New York radicals
to invent their own music, and assembly line workers in Detroit, for
example, had little interest. By the late 1930s workers were interested

in pop music, swing, and some country music. It was the Almanacs' concept to force-feed the workers with the music that *they* thought was appropriate.

The reasons why the Almanacs chose this path were complicated. For Hays and Guthrie folk music was a logical choice, because that was what they had played or sung before they joined the Almanacs. A number of the others, especially Seeger, were entranced with the music that they had recently discovered and sustained an idealistic pastoral bias in favor of traditional music as opposed to, say, Broadway songs. Seeger himself has been quoted as saying that the Almanacs dressed in what they considered to be appropriate garb for proletarians—jeans and overalls. It didn't occur to them that workers only dressed that way on the job, and expected entertainers to dress in stage costumes, in the same way that they dressed up when they went out to hear them.

The flaw in the Almanacs' thinking was that they had extrapolated that what had worked in the South, the traditional songs of miners and textile workers, would work everywhere. They assumed that with a bit of energy and effort the music would carry the day. They didn't take into account that the Almanacs, unlike Aunt Molly Jackson or John Handcox, had no ties to the communities that they were working in. No one knew them, and their familiarity with specific local issues was more ideological than personal. An amusing example of this lack of understanding was when the Almanacs performed for the West Coast Longshoreman's Union (ILWU), a committed radical union. The reaction of the members was expressed succinctly in the comment "What do we need these hillbillies for? We've got work to do."

Professional Protest

During this period a New York songwriter, publisher, and entrepreneur named Bob Miller was discovering a quiet gold mine with ballads depicting the plight of the poor and the unemployed. Picking up on the custom of commemorating disasters or tragedies with songs about them, he found a quick and ready audience, though the popularity of individual songs in the genre was short-lived. Sometimes he recorded under his own name, and sometimes he used pseudonyms. Other artists also recorded some of his songs. Among these songs were "Farm Land Blues," "Farmer's Letter to the President," and "11 Cent Cotton and 40 Cent Meat." All of these songs were recorded around 1930 and have been reproduced on a multi-CD set by the German company Bear Family Records. A typical Miller lyric from the 1931 song "Bank Failure" was, "We've got to break our backs, and continue payin' tax."

Earl Robinson was an unusual member of the radical folksong movement. He was a classically trained composer who wrote formal music, but he also performed as a singer-guitarist. In 1939 he and John La Touche wrote a cantata called *Ballad for Americans*. Through the influence of radical supporter and prominent record producer John Hammond, Columbia Records recorded the cantata with the famous singer-actor Paul Robeson. It sold thirty thousand copies during the first year, and was even used as the theme for the 1940 Republican Party convention. (Wendell Willkie, the party's candidate for president at the time, was an anti-racism activist and more progressive than many of his fellow Republicans.) It advocated racial equality in a direct manner with such lines as "Man in white skin can never be free, / While his black brother is in slavery."

The Hitler-Stalin Peace Pact

In August 1939, Hitler and Stalin signed a non-aggression pact, pledging not to interfere in each other's affairs. Prior to this event, radical folksingers, like most Americans, had anticipated that the Spanish Civil War was simply a rehearsal for an impending World War II between the fascist government of Germany and the Western democracies. The United States had a somewhat uneasy relationship with Russia, based on mutual paranoia and a negative American reception of the early communists' desire to spread their revolutionary doctrines throughout the world. Nevertheless, most radicals, and

Pete Seeger

certainly communists, envisaged that if there was gong to be a war, the United States and Russia would unite against Germany.

The Hitler-Stalin pact threw the radical music community into a state of confusion. Prior to the pact, protest songs had glorified the brave Spanish people and the radical volunteer soldiers who had risked their lives against Francisco Franco's German-supported fascist regime. Now the Communist Party advocated moderating this hawkish anti-fascist sentiment in favor of one advocating peace. The communists and their supporters suddenly found themselves in the same camp as the American isolationists, opposing any impetus toward mobilizing for a war against Germany. The decision to soft-pedal anti-fascist sentiment required a certain amount of mental retooling that made some radicals uncomfortable.

By 1940 Pete Seeger, Millard Lampell, Lee Hays, Bess Lomax, and (sometimes) Woody Guthrie were living together in a communal house in Greenwich Village. In response to the non-aggression pact, they started writing antiwar songs. Eric Bernay, who had issued the *Six Songs for Democracy* album on the Keynote label, also released an antiwar album, entitled *Songs for John Doe,* in the spring of 1941. He used another name for the record label, General Records, because he was aware of how much controversy these songs would stir up, with their objections to military conscription, and unflattering references to the president and his administration. Not even Eleanor Roosevelt was spared some barbs. In the song "The Ballad of October 16th," sung to the tune of the old folk song "Jesse James," the chorus stated:

> Franklin Roosevelt told the people how he felt,
> And they damned near believed what he said,
> He said I hate war, and so does Eleanor,
> But we won't be safe till everybody's dead.

Another verse asserted:

> Nothing can be wrong, if it makes our country strong,
> We've got to get tough to save democracy,
> And although it may mean war, we must defend Singapore,
> This don't hurt you half as much as it hurts me.

Another song referred to the Agricultural Adjustment Administration (AAA) killing three million hogs a day, and compares that to the impending slaughter of troops in a war. The folk song "The Young Man Who Wouldn't Hoe Corn" is turned into an antiwar song about a young man who dies suddenly one day: "Only one clue to why he died / A bayonet sticking in his side."

The timing of the release of the John Doe album was something less than ideal for the Almanacs. In June 1941, Germany invaded Russia, ending the period of peaceful coexistence between the U.S.S.R. and Germany. Suddenly the Almanacs, along with the entire pro-communist movement in America, had to gear up to support Russia, whether in song or politics. The peaceniks shifted over to virtually proselytize for American entry into the war.

Alan Lomax and Woody Guthrie

Alan Lomax played a unique role in the development of the protest songs. Alan was a sort of godfather and facilitator of the entire American folk song revival. He was a song collector, a record producer, a concert organizer, a radio program producer, an author, and a sort of overall guru of American folk music.

Although Lomax had always loved and promoted the most roots-oriented music that he could find, he was also aware that some of the more authentic singers were not necessarily great entertainers in a commercial sense. It was partly through Lomax's encyclopedic knowledge of folk music that such "commercial" folksingers as Burl Ives and the Weavers achieved fame and fortune. Lomax was certainly aware that the demands of a mass audience and its gatekeepers—the concert promoters, recording companies, and booking agents who promote music—inevitably create fundamental changes in the style of the music's presentation. In a certain sense, by promoting the music that he loved, Lomax was creating a whole set of commercial and aesthetic influences on it that were somewhat opposed to his own musical and social values.

One of the most colorful of Lomax's protégés was Woodrow Wilson Guthrie, known to audiences and historians alike as Woody. Guthrie was the son of an Oklahoma realtor and politician of fluctuating fortunes. He left Oklahoma in the Dust Bowl period and drifted out to California, where he found employment as a singer on the radio.

Although Woody was looked on as one of the few non-urban folk in the radical folk song movement, he was nevertheless sophisticated and intelligent. Joe Klein, who wrote the first serious biography of Woody, explained: "Although Woody paid lip service to the idea of simplicity, he was burdened by the constant pressure to produce greatness."

Despite being married with children, Woody couldn't seem to stay in one place. His pro-communist positions ultimately led to the loss of his radio job, when he and the liberal station owner had serious political disagreements. When Woody left his family and moved to New York in 1940, Alan Lomax became his major supporter, helping him land radio shows and a recording contract with RCA Victor Records, and in general trying to assist his career. Woody had a very ambivalent attitude toward commercial success. On the one hand, he rewrote his song "So Long It's Been Good to Know You" as a commercial for a radio show that was sponsored by a tobacco company. On the other, when commercial success meant dressing the part of a hillbilly, doing consistent performances and showing up on time, Woody balked.

RCA recorded two three-disc collections called *Dust Bowl Ballads* for RCA. Some of them were inspired by the movie version of John Steinbeck's novel *The Grapes of Wrath*. Although the records were well received by critics, they were a commercial failure. A few of the songs survive in the repertoire of contemporary folksingers.

In May of 1941 Guthrie was hired by the Bonneville Power Administration to write a series of songs about the construction of the Grand Coulee Dam. Woody was at the height of his creative powers, and wrote twenty-six songs in a month: historical songs about the Oregon Trail, songs that propagandized for the dam, humorous talking blues, and songs about work. The song "Roll On Columbia" is virtually the state song in Washington, and it is still widely sung in the Pacific Northwest. Its idealistic vision of the building project's economic value is characteristic of this song series. The chorus lyric is:

> Roll on, Columbia, roll on.
> Roll on, Columbia, roll on.
> Your power is turning our darkness to dawn,
> So roll on, Columbia, roll on.

Woody's other major patron was Moses Asch, the owner of Disc records, and later Folkways. Asch allowed Woody to record whatever

Woody Guthrie

he wanted to record, pretty much whenever he wanted to record it. Usually Woody wandered into the studio with Cisco Houston, Sonny Terry, or some of his other musical friends. Periodically Asch would issue an album of the songs, a process that is still going on today. Although neither Asch nor Guthrie is alive today, the company has been acquired by the Smithsonian Institution.

Many of Guthrie's songs, like his ode to a female Russian tank commander, took very specific subjects. Two of his most powerful protest songs that are still in circulation among professional folksingers are "The 1913 Massacre" and "The Ludlow Massacre." The 1913 song is about a strike in the copper mines of upper Michigan, and "Ludlow" describes a coal miners' strike in Colorado the following year. The "Ludlow" verses tell of miners being kicked out of company housing and digging a cave to hide "thirteen children and a pregnant woman." The governor of Colorado calls out the National Guard, and the guards torch the miners' tent town, suffocating the children in the cave. This attack is verified by historical record; however, Guthrie used poetic license to have the miners fight back and defeat the troopers. In fact, the strike was lost, and the union was broken.

Around 1980 my friend Harry Tuft and I were invited to do a performance of Western songs by the Trinidad, Colorado historical society. This is exactly the area that Woody wrote about in his song about Ludlow, and I sang the song at the show. A woman came up to me after the show and asked why I called the event a massacre. Put on the spot to speak for Guthrie, I asked her whether the children had indeed died there. She acknowledged that this was so. I asked her, "What would you have called it?" She did not answer, but it was obvious that some seventy years after the fact the memory of this event was still a bitter topic in the mining country of Colorado.

One of Woody's most enduring compositions is the song "This Land Is Your Land." The song was written in 1940, and intended as a sort of antidote to Irving Berlin's song "God Bless America." "This Land" was written at the tail end of the Great Depression, and right in the middle of the Hitler-Stalin non-aggression pact. This may help to explain Woody's original concept of a sort of anti-patriotic patriotic song. The original last line of the chorus was "but God blessed America for me." The reader may find this puzzling, but the original verses of the song included two less idyllic verses than the ones that are generally sung in schools and at Boy or Girl Scout camps. One verse refers to a wall that tries to stop the singer from walking, with a sign that says "Private Property." The other verses state that

> One bright sunny morning, in the shadow of the steeple,
> By the relief office I saw my people.
> As they stood there hungry,

I stood there wondering if
God blessed America for me.

Pete Seeger has told me that he believes that these verses became
obscure because they were not printed in the scout songbooks that
provided the initial mass exposure of the song. In another piece of
irony, the song has been used as a commercial by Kaiser Hospitals
and United Air Lines.

Woody was never a great singer, and he was far too disorganized a
personality to have pursued a long-term successful career as a professional folksinger-entertainer. His influence has permeated America's
musical life through the work of Bob Dylan, and more recently
Bruce Springsteen. Both of them acknowledge his influence. In fact
when Bob Dylan came to New York, he immediately sought out
an ailing Guthrie, who was slowly deteriorating from Huntington's
chorea. Clearly Dylan, at least initially, wanted to *be* Woody Guthrie.

In Lee Hays's collected writings, he pointed out that Woody represented absolute freedom, unlimited by any sense of responsibility.
One might call him the original beatnik or hippie. He scattered three
wives and eight children in various parts of the country. He lived the
antithesis of a middle-class life, and in that way he is undoubtedly
appealing to any young people (or older ones) who can't imagine
themselves settling down, or envy those who do not do so.

British punk/folk rocker Billy Bragg has written melodies for a
number of Woody's lyrics that were never put to music, and there are
several tribute albums that include reminiscences or performances by
such artists as Bruce Springsteen and Ani DiFranco.

Leadbelly

Huddie (Leadbelly) Ledbetter's writing and performing career included some protest songs and many Southern prison songs. If
Woody's legend formed itself around his devil-may-care, rambling man persona, Leadbelly's was more on the order of the African American folk hero John Henry. Twice jailed for murder, and

Leadbelly

released partly because of his ballad-singing prowess, Leadbelly briefly traveled as a chauffeur, valet, and folk performer with John and Alan Lomax.

Leadbelly was hard to categorize. He played piano, concertina, and, most of all, the twelve-string guitar. The Almanacs all liked and respected Leadbelly, and Woody even lived with Huddie and his wife Martha in New York for a while.

Because Leadbelly was a Southern black man with a strong accent, he was not as well suited for union agitation or liberal labor audiences as a more polished performer with better diction. Today he is best known for his song "Good Night Irene," popularized by the folk-singing quartet the Weavers but subsequently recorded by many other artists. The weaving together of the verses and the use of the chorus are Leadbelly's contribution to the evolution of this song. Some of Leadbelly's verses appeared in Odum and Johnson's 1929 collection.

Leadbelly's best-known protest song was "The Bourgeois Blues," a song about an incident in Washington, D.C., where Leadbelly and his wife Martha spent an evening with Alan Lomax and his fellow folklorist Mary Elizabeth Barnacle. They tried to eat together in a white restaurant, and then in a "colored" one, but neither would serve the integrated party. Leadbelly then wrote a song about the incident, condemning Washington as a bourgeois town. In lines like the following, he varied his performance, sometimes using the word "nigger" and sometimes "colored folks": "Me and my sweet wife Martha, we was standin' upstairs, / I heard a white say I don't want no colored people (niggers) up there."

Leadbelly's choice of the name "bourgeois" for this complacent racism probably reflects his exposure to the radical politics of Alan Lomax and his friends in the Almanacs.

Thanks to Judy Bell, of the Richmond Organization, the publisher of Leadbelly's music, I was able to obtain some lead sheets of topical songs that Leadbelly wrote on other subjects. "The Roosevelt Song," probably from the period of the Hitler-Stalin pact, says that Roosevelt is trying to get England and Germany to "hesitate about that war." This is a kinder interpretation of Roosevelt's behavior than is found in the Almanacs' *Death of John Doe* album.

Leadbelly also wrote a song about the Scottsboro Boys, a group of black men falsely accused of raping a white woman on a train. The song uses a technique that Leadbelly developed of delivering a recitation while playing guitar chords at the beginning of a song. The lyric asserts that in Alabama, if a white woman said that a thousand blacks had harmed her, then all of them would be killed.

Another Leadbelly song that includes social commentary is "Nobody in the World Is Better Than Us." The song describes the sacrifices made by African Americans in the military, and complains that this hasn't seemed to help bring about equality.

Like Woody Guthrie, Leadbelly dreamed of achieving commercial success. Shortly before he died he made an abortive trip to Hollywood, vainly hoping to get into the movies. As was the case with Woody, Leadbelly's work lives on in the recordings and performances of other folksingers. His songs "Cotton Fields," "Rock Island Line," and "Goodnight Irene" have all been pop hits, and some of his other songs, like "Midnight Special," are in the repertoire of many current performers. He didn't necessarily write all of these songs, but it is generally his arrangements that have kept the songs alive.

Protest Music and Audiences

By the early 1940s the communist attitude about the use of folk music had come full circle. The "discovery" of such agitator-songwriters as Jim Garland and Aunt Molly Jackson made it clear that folk music could be enlisted in the cause of social change. Radical composers and songwriters scrambled to establish their credibility in the folk arena. Trained composer-musicians like Earl Robinson and Pete Seeger adopted the styles and mannerisms of folksingers. In turn, by the beginning of World War II radicals' attitudes toward folk music influenced such singers as Aunt Molly Jackson and Leadbelly to adopt radical jargon in their songs. On a certain level it had become fashionable and useful for singers to use the medium of protest music to enhance their careers and build their audiences. It was a lesson that Bob Dylan thoroughly understood and effectively refined twenty years down the road.

World War II and the Almanacs

A number of the Almanacs served in the armed forces in World War II. Pete Seeger was in the Army in the South Pacific, and Woody Guthrie enlisted in the Merchant Marine before enduring a brief stint in the Army. The first topical war song that achieved any circulation was Woody's "Reuben James," written in 1941. The song concerned the first American ship downed in World War II, torpedoed while escorting the delivery of British war weapons. This occurred just before our formal entry into the war on December 7, 1941.

Some other songs written and performed by the Almanacs included "Deliver the Goods," "Round and Round Hitler's Grave," and "UAW-CIO." In the early part of the war, the Almanacs began to achieve some popularity. Alan Lomax arranged for them to appear on some radio shows, and the William Morris Agency, a major booking agency, became interested in signing them. They arranged a now legendary audition at the Rainbow Room in Rockefeller Center. The group, spearheaded by the unpredictable Woody Guthrie, improvised an increasingly radical set of verses about the Rockefellers, who owned the complex. The managers of the venue thought that this was hilarious, and wanted to "book the act." When they started to discuss dressing Woody in hillbilly regalia, he and the others walked out.

Some early interest on the part of Decca Records turned sour when a series of articles in New York newspapers pointed out that the Almanacs were the same folks who had recorded *The Death of John Doe* a few short months before. When Seeger and Guthrie left to join the service, the group essentially broke up. A sort of subsidiary group including Bess Lomax and Butch Hawes went to Detroit. Between June and November of 1942 the Detroit performers snagged 107 bookings, but eventually the radical movement and the unions became tired of them.

Spin-offs of the Almanacs, like the Union Boys, with Tom Glazer and Josh White, and the Washington, D.C.–based Priority Ramblers, made some recordings during the war. By the end of the war the Almanacs had disappeared, but the stage was set for the postwar era and the start of People's Songs.

Pete Seeger and People's Songs

Although we have mentioned Pete Seeger in passing, his long and distinguished career requires a more detailed discussion. During the early years of the Almanacs Seeger served as an organizer and stabilizing force. His role as a performer, songwriter, and banjoist was less important initially. Seeger came back from the war charged with energy, and immediately set out to organize a larger and more comprehensive version of the Almanacs. He envisioned the new group as a force that would galvanize the working class. He felt that if the workers could be taught to sing together, it would promote their fight for better wages and working conditions. David Dunaway, Seeger's biographer, says that in later years Seeger would "painfully discover, the chain linking song to action is not so direct."

The original group that started People's Songs included Seeger, Alan Lomax, Woody Guthrie, Lee Hays, Boots Casetta from Los Angeles, and other performers, folklorists, songwriters, and composers. The goal was to broaden the base of "people's culture" that the Almanacs had tapped.

According to Richard Reuss, Lomax and Guthrie wanted new songs to be close to folk-rural patterns, but Seeger and Lee Hays were more tolerant of other musical forms. Some of the members were composers and even Broadway-oriented songwriters. The peak year for People's Songs was 1948, when there were two thousand members.

I did an analysis of the two largest collections of songs by Guthrie and Seeger: the *Almost Complete Songs of Woody Guthrie* and Seeger's songbook *Where Have All the Flowers Gone?*

I only included songs written or rewritten by the performers (since both artists sang songs by other composers as well as their own). What stands out in Seeger's works is his idealism, and an emphasis on peace and ecology. Guthrie was much more prone to search for heroes in his songs, and he loved to write about farmers and workers who had tough lives. However, Guthrie died in 1967, and did not write songs for some years before his death, while Seeger's book was published in 1993. If Guthrie had continued to live, he probably would have latched onto environmental subjects. Another difference between the two is that Guthrie rarely wrote original melodies. He was basically a lyricist who grafted his poems onto existing tunes, especially those he had picked up from Carter Family recordings. Seeger's strength was in writing melodies. Most of his lyrics come from collaborators, or were settings of poems or inspired by novels or the Bible.

The primary difference between their song lyrics reflects a fundamental difference in their personalities, with Seeger's outlook and songs both demonstrating more optimism than Guthrie's. Guthrie's general vision, perhaps based on the tragedy of his own illness and the many deaths by fire that decimated his family as he was growing up, was inevitably a more negative viewpoint. He had trouble understanding Seeger's personality, claiming that he couldn't comprehend anyone who didn't drink or smoke or chase women. The point I am trying to make is that Seeger certainly understood that our culture had many inequities, and that many people had to struggle to make a decent living. Instead of translating his restlessness into personal disorganization, as Guthrie did, he channeled it into building his own house, exploring many facets of music, and even making films.

Josh White

Josh White had a dual musical career in his teenage years, recording both religious music and blues. He came to New York just prior to the start of the Almanacs, and did occasional jobs with Pete Seeger or other members of the group. His distinctive guitar work can also be heard on recordings with some of the Almanac spin-offs.

Working with black poet Waring Cuney, White wrote a number of brilliant songs that bitterly complained about the racial situation in the United States. After the war, black servicemen had come home to find conditions unchanged. There were still lynchings, it was still difficult or impossible for African Americans to vote in the South, and segregation in Southern schools and buses prevailed. Many hotels and restaurants continued to resist serving black patrons.

Some recordings of White's songs were issued by Keynote, and another set called *Chain Gang* was put out by Columbia. On the Keynote recording the last verse of the song "Uncle Sam" complains that:

> If you ask me, I think democracy is fine,
> I mean democracy, without a color line;
> Uncle Sam says, "We'll live the American way,"
> Let's get together and kill Jim Crow today.

Some of the other songs on the album complain about black Air Force personnel not being permitted to fly, and Navy personnel being restricted to mess boy positions. The song "Southern Exposure" complains about being treated "no better than a mountain goat. Boss takes my crop and the poll tax takes my vote."

The songs on the *Chain Gang* album are even more powerful. They were almost like musically organized, semi-commercial versions of the Gellert collection, which in fact was the source of some of the songs. The songs not only protested discrimination, but told stories of black men beating up unjust bosses or escaping from the chain gang.

Josh White was a very different sort of performer from Leadbelly. He was handsome and articulate, an excellent guitar player who sang with impeccable diction. He became a popular performer at New York's Village Vanguard club. He seemed headed toward the realization of the dreams of success that Leadbelly had unsuccessfully harbored.

The Red Scares, the Election of 1948, and the End of People's Songs

No sooner had Germany and Japan been defeated than friction between America and Russia openly emerged. The two rivals were now the world's only superpowers, and they immediately carved up different parts of the world into spheres of influence under their control. Both sides increased the size of their armed forces, and Russia began a crash course in building its own atomic and hydrogen bombs. Each country employed extensive networks of spies to ferret out each other's secrets.

In 1948 former Vice President Henry Wallace decided to run for president as the candidate of the brand new Progressive Party. While Harry Truman was avowedly anticommunist, Wallace ran on a "make peace with Russia" platform that was very appealing to American radicals.

The Wallace campaign enlisted a number of People's Songs' stalwarts, especially Pete Seeger. Seeger sang at the national convention and toured with Wallace. Here was a chance for radical songsters to directly enter the political process, using their songs as a tool for social change. In return the Progressive Party financed People's Songs, paying half the salary of Boots Casetta. No one really expected Wallace to win the election, but the goal was to get at least five million votes and to build a political base for later elections.

People's Songs members turned out dozens of songs for Wallace, including Ray Glazer and Bill Wolff's "The Same Old Merry-Go-Round," which contained the lyric "The donkey and elephant, ride up and down, / On the same merry-go-round."

Alan Lomax wrote some lyrics to the old English song "I've Got Sixpence":

> The Republicans, they grieve me,
> The Democrats only deceive me,
> I've got a brand new party, believe me,
> As we go rolling up the vote.

Despite all of this effort, Wallace ended up as the fourth-place finisher. Dixiecrat J. Strom Thurmond polled about 20,000 more votes than Wallace's 1,155,608 total. Thurmond also carried four Southern states, while Wallace failed to carry a single state.

As more and more pressure was placed on entertainers and other Americans to assert and demonstrate their loyalty to the United States, and to declare opposition to Russia and communist ideology, some of the supporters of People's Songs withdrew from the organization.

Committees in the Senate and House of Representatives began to hold hearings questioning the loyalty of various artists. These witnesses were asked if they had ever been members of the Communist Party. Those who acknowledged membership were then asked to name other members of the party.

At this point folksinger Burl Ives admitted his association with the party, and named other members. His defense was simple naïveté. Josh White, who had been one of the most outspoken of all the protest singers, claimed before the House committee that he had been duped by the communists. His biographer Elijah Wald says that White claimed that his dealings with the party were motivated by opportunities to get gigs and to make romantic conquests. Because White was black, he was treated with kid gloves by the House Un-American Activities Committee, because they did not wish to be accused of being racists. White also continued to perform songs advocating racial equality and blasting Jim Crow. Tom Glazer and Oscar Brand were non-communists, who disassociated themselves from People's Songs and soft-pedaled their political views.

People's Songs collapsed after the Wallace campaign. Without the financial support of the Progressive Party it could not pay its bills. The organization re-formed under the name People's Artists, and became a talent agency for various left-wing causes. Naturally this work was not offered to any of the singers who had testified before Congress, or who had denounced the communist movement.

The Weavers

In the midst of all of this turmoil Pete Seeger and Lee Hays had begun to sing with two younger musicians, Ronnie Gilbert and Fred Hellerman. Seeger turned what was supposed to be a solo gig at New York's Village Vanguard into a booking for the quartet. A two-week booking ended up as a six-month residency, and the group attracted considerable interest in the music industry. Gordon Jenkins, an arranger-producer at Decca Records, loved the group and signed them to the label. Between 1950 and 1952 they sold over four million records. One of their major hits was Leadbelly's song "Goodnight Irene." The group shared composer credits with Huddie Ledbetter on "Kisses Sweeter Than Wine," reworking his adaptation of an Irish melody into the song. Woody Guthrie shared in the festivities when the group had him rewrite the song "So Long It's Been Good to Know You."

So at the same time that the federal government was "cleansing" communists from the entertainment business, People's Songs' favorite sons and daughters were making hit records, reaching far more people than they had during their propagandizing days. The Weavers' managers tried to keep them from performing at radical rallies, or having any direct associations with radical movements. This meant that at the hootenannies, or group concerts, held by People's Songs and later People's Artists, the people who had initiated the events now could not participate.

When the Weavers first got together they did sing for radical causes, and they even recorded some protest songs for the Hootenanny Records label. However, it would have been difficult for conservatives to object to the content of the Weavers' Decca recordings. "On Top of Old Smokey" was a traditional English-American love ballad, "Goodnight Irene" was a sad song about an unfortunate love affair, and the rewrite of Guthrie's "So Long, It's Been Good to Know You" made the song into a sort of innocent reminiscence of the Dust Bowl years. The closest the Decca offerings got to radicalism was that the song "Kisses Sweeter Than Wine" covered the life cycle of an average working man and his wife. Instead, the Weavers were scolded by the left; Irwin Silber, who was now running People's Artists, criticized the group in the magazine *Sing Out* for not having any black members when they performed so much African American music.*

---

* At a conference about the folk music revival in Bloomington, Indiana in 1992, Lou Gottlieb told an interesting story. He had organized a group on the West Coast called the Gateway Singers. In those days he too was involved with the Communist Party, and the party successfully pressured the group to fire their white female singer and replace her with a black woman.

The Weavers and the Blacklist

It was inevitable that someone would figure out that these healthy, upbeat folksingers bringing a fresh new sound to the world of pop music were some of the same radicals who had performed at hundreds of radical meetings since the 1930s. Sure enough, the Weavers were listed as communists in *Counterattack* and *Red Channels*, two publications run by three ex-FBI agents. Both of these publications were dedicated to ferreting out communists.

As a result of these listings, the Weavers began to lose bookings, a prospective television show disappeared, and Decca Records cancelled their record deal. Pete Seeger was summoned by the House Un-American Activities Committee. Most of the unfriendly witnesses had taken the protection of the Fifth Amendment, which states that a witness cannot be required to incriminate himself. Seeger invoked the First Amendment, which questioned the right of the committee to inquire into his beliefs. He was cited for contempt, but in 1961, after numerous delays and appeals, the charge was dismissed because of a technicality.

The Effects of the Blacklist on Political Music

In 1949 and 1950 the CIO expelled eleven allegedly communist-led unions from the organization. People's Artists was now forced to realize that their fantasy that music could make a difference in the American union movement had come to an end.

From 1950 to 1953, the United States was engaged in the Korean War, which further incited anticommunist feeling in the country. The Weavers disbanded in 1952, although they reunited for a triumphant Carnegie Hall concert in 1955. They signed a new recording deal with Vanguard Records, a company sympathetic to radical causes, and though they never had another hit record, they continued to do successful concerts in major cities for a loyal niche audience (even after Seeger left the group in 1959 and was replaced by Erik Darling).

Folk-Pop Crossover

Even before the heart of the folk song revival from 1959 to 1964, folk music had some impact on the pop scene. The West Coast group the

Easy Riders recorded six albums for Columbia Records between 1952 and 1959, with their major hit "Marianne" released in 1957. Two of the members of the group, Frank Miller and Rich Dehr, had been active in the West Coast People's Songs. Harry Belafonte had a moderately successful career as a jazz singer before turning to American folk music. Like the Weavers before him, he appeared at the Village Vanguard in 1952, and landed a contract with RCA Records. His success peaked with his calypso recordings, notably "The Banana Boat Song." The New York folk trio the Tarriers had also had a hit with a different version of the song a year earlier.

The Tarriers had no direct political associations, although original member Alan Arkin was the son of David Arkin, a member of the West Coast People's Songs. Belafonte, however, had performed for some radical groups, and he was an outspoken proponent of racial equality. In various interviews he has stated that he was on the blacklist during the McCarthy period, but possibly he was able to maintain his career for the same reasons that Josh White was able to survive professionally. Certainly the music that Belafonte recorded was relatively innocent from a political viewpoint.

Another folk-oriented hit of this period was Tennessee Ernie Ford's 1955 recording of Merle Travis' song "Sixteen Tons." "Sixteen Tons" described the life of the coal miner, and used the refrain "I owe my soul to the company store." The other major pop hit was Lonnie Donegan's version of Leadbelly's song "The Rock Island Line." Donegan was a British artist, and his record initiated the skiffle music fad in Britain. Skiffle was a sort of British version of a jug band, with a bass made out of an old tea chest. Although the song was a hit in America, skiffle did not catch on here.

The Kingston Trio

The Kingston Trio was the group that galvanized the folk revival. Formed in 1957, they scored their first hit record with the old Southern murder ballad "Tom Dooley." Peculiarly enough, the trio, who never made any claims of authenticity, performed in a folkier manner on their recordings than the Weavers had originally done. The

trio played banjos and guitars, and they didn't augment their recordings with many other musicians. The members of the trio had no political background, and they were so crew-cut, mom-and-apple-pie
appealing that it would have been unthinkable to identify them with
radical causes. In 1961 Dave Guard, the original leader of the group,
left and was replaced by John Stewart. The first recording of the new
group was Pete Seeger's song "Where Have All the Flowers Gone?"
This was an antiwar song, by a blacklisted writer. The Trio got away
with it because the image of the group was so clean and all-American
that to accuse them of being communists would have appeared ri-
diculous. It was also ten years after the original controversy about
the Weavers, and anticommunist fever was somewhat less prevalent.
Hot on the trail of the Kingston Trio's successes came a string of folk-
pop groups. Among them were the Brothers Four, the Limeliters, the
Highwaymen, and the Chad Mitchell Trio. Although Lou Gottlieb,
an avowed radical, was the leader of the Limeliters, their music was
not political. In fact, of these groups only the Chad Mitchell Trio
sang about political issues. They specialized in songs that mocked the
right wing John Birch Society, Senator Barry Goldwater, and Texas
entrepreneur Billie Sol Estes. The John Birch Society song included
the lyrics

> We've got the Red Cross, and we're after Pinky Lee,
> And the day we get Red Skelton,
> Won't that be a victory?

The two beloved American comedians referred to in the song were
about as far from being "reds" as one can imagine. The satire of the
Chad Mitchell Trio was popular in colleges, but the group did not
perform for radical causes.

This brings us to Peter, Paul & Mary. PP&M mixed up-front social concerns with entertaining pop-folk performances. Mary Travers
had sung in a small choral group that had recorded with Pete Seeger
during the days when he was blacklisted. They became identified

with the civil rights movement, partly through their recording of Bob Dylan's song "Blowin' in the Wind." The song referred to not only the civil rights movement but also the arms race. The format of the song was to raise a series of questions about social inequity and war, and answer them with the hook line "The answer, my friend, is blowin' in the wind."

In 1962 Peter, Paul & Mary scored a huge hit with the Pete Seeger–Lee Hays anthem "If I Had a Hammer." Although the lyrics to the song are somewhat vague, the lines about "love between my brothers and sisters" were generally taken to refer to racial equality. Latino rocker Trini Lopez also had a hit with the song a year later. Once again a Pete Seeger song had become a big hit at a time when he was still blacklisted, unable to appear on American radio and television. The folk-rock group the Byrds had a huge hit with Pete Seeger's antiwar song "Turn, Turn, Turn" in 1965. They also recorded his coauthored song "The Bells of Rhymney." Meanwhile, I remember vacationing in western Canada in 1966 and seeing Seeger on the long-running and popular Pierre Berton show—noting that Seeger could appear on network TV in Canada, but not in his own country!

A year later the Smothers Brothers had Seeger on their CBS-TV show, but the network would not allow him to sing his song "Waist Deep in the Big Muddy." The song was a parable that linked a stubborn sergeant with President Lyndon Johnson. In January 1968 the network finally relented and allowed Seeger to sing the song on a return visit to the show.

Music and the Civil Rights Movement

The coal mining and textile communities sang songs that were widely known, and the performers came from within the communities themselves. In the case of the civil rights movement, which included the same sort of musical consciousness, the music that was universally known to the participants was gospel music and blues.

Most of the music that was actually sung at sit-ins, in jails, on Freedom Rides, or at movement gatherings was gospel music. New lyrics were set to old tunes reflecting contemporary struggles. A number of African American singers were active in the movement, including James Collier, the Freedom Singers with Bernice and Cordell Reagan, Len Chandler, Bill McAdoo, the Reverend Frederick Douglass Kirkpatrick, and Julius Lester. The music used in the movement included not only gospel music, but also soul. Curtis Mayfield, the lead singer and composer for the Impressions, was a favorite artist of many people in the movement. In Guy Carawan's book *Sing for Freedom,* he prints three movement adaptations of Mayfield's songs. The Chicago movement added some lines to Mayfield's big hit "People Get Ready": "Don't want no Toms, or any sorry Negroes, / Comin' to me sayin' they won't go."

White Performers in the Civil Rights Movement

A number of white politically-oriented artists were involved to some extent in the struggle for civil rights. Pete Seeger, as usual, was on board. Guy and Candy Carawan ending up devoting the bulk of their adult lives to the movement, working at the Highlander Folk School in Tennessee. They have also documented the history of the struggle in several songbooks. Famous folk-oriented singers like Judy Collins and Phil Ochs sang for voter registration rallies in the South, as did numerous other performers.

The signature song of the civil rights movement was a blend of gospel music and adaptations by white folk song performers. An early version of it was used in a 1945 strike by black food and tobacco workers. The late Zelphia Horton, who was the original music director at Highlander, made some changes to the song and taught it to Pete Seeger. He in turn taught it to Guy Carawan. Guy made some further changes, together with his sometime musical associate the superb guitarist Frank Hamilton, and it is this version of "We Shall Overcome" that spread throughout the entire world.

The original song was called "I Will Overcome." The revised version stressed the coming of a new world where everyone can live in peace, and where all men are free. The song became so famous that when Lyndon Johnson became president of the United States he actually used the title of the song in a speech advocating civil rights.

Protest Singers of the Sixties

Bob Dylan, Phil Ochs, Len Chandler, and Tom Paxton were all New York-based singer-songwriters in the 1960s. Although all of them spent some time in Mississippi, Chandler was the only one who devoted a major part of his energies to the civil rights struggle. Not coincidentally, Chandler was the black artist in the group.

Since there are more than enough books about the quixotic Mr. Dylan, it doesn't seem necessary here to go into great detail about every aspect of his career. Dylan pursued two career tracks soon after his arrival in New York in 1961. On the one hand Dylan wrote topical songs and became the shining star of *Broadside Magazine*. *Broadside* was a radical magazine that published new topical songs. Between 1962 and 1964 it published twenty-three Dylan songs and poems. This was far more than those authored by anyone else, except for Phil Ochs.

On a different track, Dylan performed at a club called Folk City and played harmonica on a Columbia album recorded by Carolyn Hester and produced by John Hammond. Hammond became quite intrigued by Dylan and signed him to the label. Just after this, Dylan acquired a manager in the person of Al Grossman. It was Grossman who got Dylan's songs to Peter, Paul & Mary, which set the singer on the road to success.

Dylan's first album only had one original song, a relatively innocuous piece about Woody Guthrie. His second album, *The Freewheelin' Bob Dylan,* included the song "Blowin' in the Wind." By this time Dylan was recording and performing all original material, and he had become the darling not only of the radical movement but of such folksingers as Joan Baez and Judy Collins. *The Times They Are a-Changin'* followed. The title song was essentially Dylan's warning to the denizens of the Old Left to get out of the way, because a new sheriff had come to town. *Highway 61 Revisited,* released in 1965, featured the new rock-and-roll Dylan.

Dylan's original left wing supporters were now freaking out. It had appeared that Dylan was going to be the first artist to bring radical propaganda to the masses. The subject range of his early songs included nuclear war, racial injustice, and a large dose of anti-governmental radical sentiment. It comprised almost a litany of radical causes. The song "Only a Pawn in Their Game" pointed out that the murderer of Mississippi civil rights leader Medgar Evers was only a pawn in the racist game. Another of Dylan's songs discussed the accidental murder of a domestic servant named Hattie Carroll. Other songs warned that hard rain (radiation) would fall, and Dylan railed against the masters of war.

It turned out that Dylan's political stance was too good to be true. Dylan had gained the confidence of the inner circle of the radical movement. Pete Seeger endorsed his work, such respected younger artists as Joan Baez and Judy Collins loved and recorded his songs, and Broadside circulated them to other singers.

But even more significantly, he had gained access to a mass audience through recordings of his songs by many artists, and his own recordings. Few observers grasped that Dylan, shepherded by his manager Grossman, was headed in another direction.

At the summer 1965 Newport Folk Festival Dylan unveiled an electric rock band with guitarist Mike Bloomfield. The folk establishment railed in rage and frustration as the sound blasted through the audience. Supposedly Alan Lomax and Al Grossman were rolling on the ground and wrestling over the volume of the band's amplified sound. Pete Seeger even wanted to pull the plug on the electricity so that people could hear the lyrics over the electric instruments.

Dylan became the most controversial figure that the folk music revival had ever seen. Folk music buffs thought he had betrayed them. Some writers, like Paul Nelson, writing in *Sing Out,* saw Newport as the death of the old-line radical movement and the dawn of a new visionary art.

Bob Dylan

Phil Ochs   Evph

The old radicals were left with Phil Ochs as their safe political ora-
cle. While even Dylan's radical songs had bordered on the abstract
and surrealistic, as in "Hard Rain," Ochs's style was much more
direct. Various musicians and critics have reported that Ochs continually felt trumped by Dylan, who sometimes taunted him with
being a journalist rather than an artist. Ochs's songs were much
more explicit than Dylan's. Even the titles, like "I Ain't Marching
Anymore," or "Love Me, I'm a Liberal," clearly indicated where the
songs were going. Most young people were simply not galvanized by
lyrics like this one, from "I Ain't Marching Anymore": "For I stole
California from the Mexican land, / Fought in the bloody Civil
War." Listeners should compare this to Dylan's menacing "Ballad of
a Thin Man."

On the other hand, some of Ochs's songs were open to interpretation. I had the odd experience of playing in a pickup band accompanying Florida orange juice queen Anita Bryant at the 1975 Colorado
State Fair. Bryant did a medley of Ochs's song "The Power and the
Glory" and Woody Guthrie's "This Land Is Your Land." Ochs's song
was a tribute to a possible and more equitable America, with a stirring chorus. Bryant did not sing the Guthrie protest lyrics, and I
suspect she was unaware of their existence. It was truly a surrealistic
experience!

It turned out that Ochs was every bit as ambitious as Bob Dylan
had proved to be. He tried various musical experiments, included a
sort of pseudo-Elvis pose, before experiencing problems with drugs
and alcohol that reduced him to a shell of himself. The almost inevitable result was suicide.

Tom Paxton

Other protest singers of the sixties were less intent on competing
with Dylan, and found niches for themselves. Tom Paxton, whose
career continues to the present day, made a name for himself by writing two types of songs. One of Paxton's trademarks was his romantic,

idealistic songs like "Rambling Boy" and "The Last Thing on My Mind" that were somewhat reminiscent of some of Guthrie's songs, but with original melodies. The other aspect of his writing was humor and satire. A few of his subjects were disgraced Senator Gary Hart, drug testing ("We're Filling a Bottle for Ronnie"), yuppies, and the government's 1979 bail-out of Chrysler.

Bob Dylan's Voyage

Dylan has always made a habit of being quixotic and unpredictable. In a book edited by Craig McGregor, Dylan told two interviewers that "I became interested in folk music because I had to make it somehow." In the same interview, he later professed to like folk music. In another article, Dylan told interviewer Frances Taylor that he wrote antiwar material because "that was my chance. . . . In the Village there was a little publication called *Broadside*, and with a topical song you could get in there. I wasn't getting far with the things I was doing, songs like I'm writing now, but Broadside gave me a start."

Once Dylan renounced political songwriting his songs moved in a number of other directions. During the late 1970s he underwent a religious conversion, and did three albums of music that reflected his (temporary) born-again Christian ideology. A large number of his songs have been songs about romances, realized or failed. Dylan has also continually mined folk song territory, performing such American folk songs as the murder ballad "Little Sadie," and the mountain song "Little Maggie." In some other songs he has thrown in images from folk songs together with lyrics of his own.

Periodically Dylan, like a sleeping giant, has awakened and has written songs that reflect social concerns. Analysis of the songs in the 2001 publication *The Definitive Bob Dylan Songbook* indicates that, for whatever reason, Dylan's social consciousness seems to become much exercised when it comes to injustices against professional boxers and outlaws, literary or metaphorical. In 1971 he wrote a song about George Jackson, a black prisoner murdered by prison guards in New York.

In 1975 Dylan collaborated with poet Jacques Levy, writing a song about Rubin "Hurricane" Carter, a professional boxer who was unjustly accused of a murder and sentenced to prison. In 1981 it was comedian Lenny Bruce who captured Dylan's imagination. Dylan describes Bruce as a truth teller and an outlaw, but someone who never hurt anyone. As Dylan tells it, Lenny "fought a war on a battlefield where every victory counts."

In 1983 Dylan wrote two songs that expressed opinions about social issues. The song "Neighborhood Bully" appears to be about Israel, regarded by its immediate neighbors as a bully. Dylan recites the various injustices that the Arab nations feel about Israel in a sarcastic tone, affirming Israel's struggle.

Dylan's other political song from 1983 is "Union Sundown." The singer reels off a list of goods that Americans import, ranging from flashlights to dresses to belt buckles coming from various parts of the world. The song states that capitalism is "above the law," but then describes unions as big business in themselves, "goin' out like a dinosaur."

In 1989 Dylan continued on his cynical, apolitical track with the song "Political World." The song reflects considerable bitterness, with such phrases as "a stacked deck," "people are put up against the wall," and so forth.

Dylan himself has said that no one could continue to write such songs as "Hard Rain" into middle age. As his songwriting moved from social to personal issues, and later to religious ones, he switched from folk to rock, to country, to gospel music, with periodic revisitations of folk. Dylan continues to write and record music, and to tour more widely than in his more famous days of the 1960s. The identity that he has carved out, miles away from Woody Guthrie's persona, could be characterized with the title of an old country song, "You Don't Know Me."

However one criticizes Dylan's real intentions or his shifting politics, more than any other artist Dylan introduced the notion of writing songs about social issues to American popular music. He was the first popular singer to find (or create) an audience for these songs. This was more than the Weavers were able to do, and it went far beyond what any of the Almanac Singers or the stalwarts of People's Songs had even attempted to accomplish.

Suze Rotolo, Dylan's girlfriend during his initial New York successes, recently wrote a memoir of her life with Dylan. Two of her comments may represent the last word on the subject of Dylan's withdrawal from writing political music: "An artist can't be made to serve a theory," and "He [Dylan] wasn't ready to accept the torch they were trying to pass on to him."

Protest Music After Dylan

Dylan spawned a huge outpouring of folksingers who turned to songwriting. The early revival singers, starting with the original Kingston Trio, did not write songs. When Dave Guard left the group, however, he was replaced by John Stewart—one of the first people in the revival who viewed himself as a songwriter. Although he was not associated with radical folksingers, starting in the mid-sixties he began to write many songs that were a blend of social concern, American history and mythology, and the new frontier of the Kennedy brothers. Stewart left the group in 1967 and toured with Bobby Kennedy's presidential campaign. After Kennedy's death Stewart went on to write numerous songs and record many albums. Although his music definitely reached many people through his concerts and recordings, he has in effect been "written out" of the revival because of his earlier connections with commercial music.

A number of singer-songwriters emerged out of the New York scene. We have already mentioned some of them in the discussions of Broadside Magazine. Jean Ritchie was a traditional folksinger from Kentucky, who after some years of performing began to write songs about coal mining and the hard lives of the people in the mountains. Several of her songs, such as "Blue Diamond Mine" and "The L&N Don't Stop Here Anymore," have been recorded by a number of artists.

Although this book generally avoids discussions of non-American groups, it is impossible to deny that the Beatles had an enormous influence on all contemporary music of the sixties, and later music. John Lennon in particular was oriented toward social issues in his post-Beatles songs, like "Give Peace a Chance" and "Woman Is the Nigger of the World."

Rock music has its own chapter later in the book, but there were a number of artists who reduced social protest to a sort of lowest common denominator of concerns about such in-depth issues as hair length, or being denied admission to restaurants because of wearing odd clothes. During the height of the opposition to the war in Vietnam in the late sixties, it became fashionable and even commercial to express some level of opposition to the war. Earlier we mentioned Glen Campbell's recording of Buffy Sainte-Marie's song "The Universal Soldier." P. J. Sloan, a scruffy nineteen-year-old Los Angeles Dylan psuedo-clone at the time, cowrote a big hit for Barry McGuire in 1965 called "The Eve of Destruction." His cowriter was Steve Barri, a noted rock producer. The song listed many of the trouble spots of the world, and the impending doom that awaited the world. It used the repeated refrain, "Don't you know, we're on the eve of destruction."

Protest Music Today

By the mid-eighties music had witnessed disco, punk, rap, and heavy metal. A whole new crop of folk-oriented singer-songwriters emerged. Tracy Chapman, the Indigo Girls, and Suzanne Vega were examples. Judy Collins and Joan Baez had taken to writing their own songs as well.

Suzanne Vega's song "Luka" concerned an abused child. It was a career record for Vega, and certainly an unusual subject for a hit song. Vega's subsequent work is more personal and less involved with politics.

This brings up the subject of the narcissism and self-absorption that became such a large part of the singer-songwriter mystique. The songs of Baez, Collins, Carl Simon, James Taylor, and even for the most part Joni Mitchell focused on personal stories, usually their own. It was as if Dylan had given a license to singer-songwriters to break free from social commentary. For folksingers like Pete Seeger, social issues were an indelible part of their commitment to the music. For the younger writers, social issues represented a much milder commitment. Mitchell did touch on the failures of urban life, and some of her songs did break out of the confessional mode that nevertheless seemed to be at the core of her work.

Tracy Chapman captured the heartbeat of the country with her 1988 songs "Fast Car" and "Talkin' 'Bout a Revolution," which I have used as the title for this book. "Fast Car" is the wistful story of someone seeking to leave the constricting live of the ghetto, or any other urban slum. The heroine's father is an alcoholic, and she and her boy friend are living in a shelter. The song ends with the singer saying that she and her friend need to make a decision to leave or they may be stuck in the same place forever.

It is astonishing that "Talkin' 'Bout a Revolution," with its numerous references to the inequities of our society, received tremendous airplay and became a huge hit record. The song describes people standing in a welfare line, others drawing unemployment or waiting for a promotion. She concludes with the powerful and incendiary thought that the poor people are going to "rise up and take what's there."

To hear these songs all across American pop radio during the George H. W. Bush presidential years was truly astonishing. One can only wonder what radio music directors and disc jockeys thought about the revolution that the singers advocated. Of course some of these same people had played Bob Dylan twenty-five years earlier, but none of his hit singles had been so incendiary.

An odd sidelight is that Chapman, who is African American, received no airplay on "urban contemporary" radio stations. Her music was regarded as being unacceptable to these stations because it was folk-rock rather than R&B or rap.

Contemporary Protest Writers

Si Kahn is a civil rights, union, and community organizer who is also a singer and a songwriter. John McCutcheon, Charlie King, Anne Feeney, Rebel Voices, Tom Juravich, David Rovics, and the black female vocal group Sweet Honey in the Rock are all artists who devote a large segment of their repertoire to current social issues. Many of these artists, especially Anne Feeney, are quite literally as apt to be found on picket lines as in concert.

The late Joe Glaser had a unique role in that his "straight" job was working for the United Textile Workers education department. The rest of his time was spent composing and recording pro-labor music. Glaser's song "The Mill Was Made of Marble" became popular in the union movement. It is a sort of fantasy for the working man, laboring in a factory where no one ever gets tired or becomes old. Glaser was a non-communist liberal, and one of his recording projects was an album of songs satirizing the communist movement. His song "Our Line's Been Changed Again" includes the lyric

> The party says
> The time has come. . .
> Don't call a socialist a bum. . . .

Another verse asserts the strength of the communist party and how they will coalesce with the bourgeois groups. Glaser also established a record company that issued recordings by himself and other labor songsters, and he was active in organizing the Labor Heritage Foundation. This group of pro-labor songwriters and performers holds annual meetings where singers network and exchange songs and organizing techniques. More than any other group, these singers represent the heritage of the Almanac Singers.

The labor songsters of today sing about many of the same issues that the Almanacs raised in the 1940s. Wages, working conditions, and job security are among the subjects raised, along with such contemporary issues as automation, the two-job family, health care, and environmental and safety issues.

Anne Feeney's "Whatever Happened to the Eight Hour Day?" asserts: "We got to bring back the eight hour day, / Can't feed a family on one person's pay."

Charlie King specializes in humorous commentary, exemplified by his song "Buy, Buy the American Car." One of his lines is: "These robots deserve your support."

John O'Connor has written quite a few songs about specific struggles and issues. His song "Easy Street" discusses joblessness in Gary, Indiana, with such lines as "They shut down the big mills before we knew / What the hell they were trying to do."

John McCutcheon combines virtuoso instrumental ability on various instruments with songs of social protest. His song "Christmas in the Trenches" relates a remarkable incident during World War I. For one night at Christmas, the Germans and British ceased their warfare to sing Christmas carols, play soccer, and exchange reminiscences about their families. The last verse delivers the moral:

Joy - TE

> The ones who called the shots
> Won't be among the dead and lame,
> And at each end of the rifle we're the same.

Tom Juravich is a college professor and labor organizer who has written a number of songs for the United Mine Workers. Although most of the labor songsters operate out of the folk tradition, Juravich's *Out of Darkness* recording uses a rock and roll rhythm section.

Hazel Dickens's songs generally refer to her coal-mining heritage, or the position of women in our culture ("Don't Put Her Down, You Put Her There"). One of her songs, "Will Jesus Wash the Bloodstains from Your Hands?," concerns the Korean War. Her music has also been featured in several movies about miners, including *Harlan County, U.S.A.* and *Matewan*. Dickens has no formal connection with the union movement, but sings at folk festivals and concerts, and makes records.

Ani DiFranco is a unique artist whose music is known for its strong feministic themes. However, she also has a role in political music that extends beyond women's issues. She teamed up with the late Utah Phillips to do two albums of protest songs in 1996 and 1999. They also did some touring together. Because Ani was some thirty years younger than Utah, the effect of this tour was to create a brand new audience for him.

During the 1990s I wrote a number of songs for the Oil, Coke, Chemical & Atomic Union Workers. These songs dealt with contemporary and historical struggles that the union waged in the volatile oil and chemical industry, including such issues as the loss of jobs from companies to independent contractors, and poor safety procedures in the industry. The song "Out of Control" contained the lines

> Contract workers aren't trained,
> To see the danger signs;
> They're afraid they'll get in trouble,
> If they step out of line.

Several other songs were about Karen Silkwood, a member of the union whose car was forced off the road in Oklahoma as she was on the way to meet a reporter from the *New York Times*. Silkwood's briefcase documenting safety violations at the Kerr-McGee plant disappeared during the "accident." The company denied involvement in the accident, but agreed to a large cash settlement to her family

Vietnam Blues

An album called *In Country: Folk Songs of Americans in the Vietnam War* is a collection of song written by Vietnam veterans. Although the songs were all written in the sixties, the recording was not made until 1991. Captain Herschel Gober's "Six Clicks," written in 1966, asserts that "Every step you take, death is close at hand in Charlie's land."

Charlie was the name used for the North Vietnamese soldiers. According to the album's liner notes, "Tchepone" was the most popular song of the war. It was written in 1968 by Toby Hughes, who flew 208 combat missions. It contains the following sobering lines: "We felt a bit sorry for folks down below, / The thought passes quickly."

Ex-rocker vet Bill Ellis's song "Firelight" says:

> War is hell,
> Lead was flyin'
> Men were dyin'.

A 1993 album of songs about the war called *Soul of Vietnam* was issued on the Risky Business label, distributed by Sony. Delia Gartrell, singer and coauthor of "Can't You See What You Done," sings the tragic story of her son going to the war and returning as a heroin addict. She sings:

> Can't you see what you done, to my only son
> While he was fighting for your war.
> I didn't know you'd send him back to me a stone junkie
> I watched him one day take some money from my purse,
> That's when I knew his habit was getting worse.

On the same alum Swamp Dogg recorded a song by John Prine called "Sam Stone." Prine is a singer-songwriter who has recorded a number of songs about social issues. Like Gartrell's song, this one concerns a Nam vet who becomes addicted to heroin. The disturbing lyric states, "There's a hole in daddy's arm / Where the money goes."

The Homeless

There have been a half-dozen albums of songs by or about the homeless. Some are collaborations between professional musicians and homeless people, and others are songs written by homeless people who are also semiprofessional musicians.

The 1993 MCA release *Voice of the Homeless* is a collection of songs sung by artists who were homeless at the time of the recording. The song "Catman Jimmy" was written by Joe Wasyl, and is performed on the album by Leo Porter. The chorus states that

> Catman Jim lives alone
> A burned-out shack for a home,
> One more stray on his own.

Other songs on this album describe marshals evicting poverty-stricken renters. In the anthem called "Voice of the Homeless," by David Mitchel, the singer pleads: "Hear me now, / I'm the homeless of the world."

Environmental Issues

The L'il Green Songbook is a radical-ecological book of songs about environmental issues. "Johnny Sagebrush" compiled this collection of songs ranging from descriptions of guerrilla ecology tactics to complaints about the destruction of natural resources. As was the case with the old Wobbly songs, many of the songs are poems set to well-known melodies.

Other environmental songs appear of albums by the Indigo Girls, Joni Mitchell, and others. Over the last twenty-five years Pete Seeger has written many songs about preserving the environment, often based on his efforts to clean up the Hudson River with his boat the *Clearwater* and a volunteer crew.

Music That Advocates for the Status Quo

There are two types of right-wing songs that take opposing viewpoints to radical protest songs. The more extreme songs, which I will refer to as the music of hate, will be covered in a later chapter. The other category of songs defends the status quo from the attacks of radical song makers or politicians.

During the Korean War, many songs appeared defending American intervention in Korea. Many of these songs were country music hits. Such songs as "The Red That We Got Is the Old Red, White and Blue," "Advice to Joe (Stalin)," and "Thank God for Victory in Korea" represent similar attitudes toward the war.

On the subject of Vietnam, country artist Stonewall Jackson recorded "The Minute Men Are Turning in Their Graves" in 1966, objecting to antiwar protesters. Dave Dudley recorded the "Vietnam Blues," written by Kris Kristoffersen. (By the eighties, Kristoffersen had become radicalized and was writing songs celebrating Latin-American revolutionaries.)

In his 1967 song "Letter to My Teenaged Son," Victor Lundberg denounced draft dodgers and promised to disown his own son if he exhibited such behavior. Merle Haggard's "The Fighting Side of Me" and "Okie from Muskokee" in turn reflect patriotic and small-town values. In an unanticipated turnaround, "Okie" is sometimes sung by such "radical" types as Woody Guthrie's son Arlo as a sort of parody. In 1966 an ex-Green Beret soldier, Sergeant Barry Sadler, enjoyed sales of over seven million copies of his record *The Ballad of the Green Berets,* celebrating the elite corps of soldiers.

Over the years country music artists have sometimes run for public office, and conservative politicians have used country music or country musicians in their election campaigns. Jimmie Davis, author of "You Are My Sunshine," became governor of Louisiana. W. Lee (Pappy) O'Daniel was a governor and senator from Texas who had a Texas swing band before he had a political career. Roy Acuff, one of the leading performers on the Grand Ole Opry and co-owner of Acuff-Rose Music Publishing, unsuccessfully ran for governor of Tennessee. Senator Robert Byrd of West Virginia plays the fiddle, and occasionally has done so at election rallies. Country stars Brooks and Dunn made appearances for John McCain, the Republican candidate for president in 2008.

Popular Protest

Starting in the 1980s such popular artists as Peter Gabriel, U2, Sting, Bruce Springsteen, Don Henley, Jackson Brown, John Mellencamp, and Willie Nelson have been associated with such causes as Amnesty International, Earth Day, Farm-Aid, and ecological issues, such as Henley's attempt to save wildlife sanctuary Walden Pond. Henley and Bonnie Raitt usually avoid political statements but have supported anti-nuclear causes, and numerous artists were involved in Bob Geldof's relief efforts for Africa. Jackson Browne, author of pop hits like "Doctor My Eyes" and "Lawyers in Love," has also taken on hunger, wars, soldiers fighting on foreign soil, and the question of what constitutes true patriotism in "Soldiers of Plenty" and "Lives in the Balance." He has been active in anti-nuclear benefit concerts and has sung and spoken out against American involvement in wars in El Salvador and Nicaragua.

Of particular interest is Bruce Springsteen, who has moved in a direction exactly opposite to that of Bob Dylan. Springsteen's early work was mostly personal, focused on his experiences growing up as a troubled teenager on the New Jersey shore. These songs featured romances, fast cars, and teenage moves, to paraphrase Bob Seger. Springsteen's 1978 song "Badlands" begins to adopt more of the Woody Guthrie attitude, identifying the singer with working-class struggles and tribulations. The 1982 song "Atlantic City" continues in the same vein, describing a man who is broke, goes to the casinos, and concludes, "I guess everything dies."

Springsteen's 1984 "Born in the U.S.A." adopts the voice of a troubled returning veteran whose buddy fell in love with a woman in Saigon, but who is "all gone." Many, including presidential candidate President Reagan, missed the song's dark message because of its powerful "born in the U.S.A." rock chorus.

Subsequent Springsteen songs have described abandoned stores and disappearing jobs ("My Hometown"). Springsteen went further in his 1993 song "Streets of Philadelphia," where he took on the role of homosexual afflicted with AIDS.

Bruce Springsteen

We have seen how Dylan essentially chosen to abandon social commentary in his music. In contrast, Springsteen has directly identified with Woody Guthrie in his *Ghost of Tom Joad* album. Springsteen has occasionally toured as a solo acoustic, which places more emphasis on the songs and less on the "act." In 2007 he did an album that was essentially a tribute to the repertoire of Pete Seeger, called *The Seeger Sessions,* and toured with the Sessions band instead of his usual E Street rock band.

The Future of Protest Music

Whatever cause or political viewpoint a singer may initially favor, the amount of energy and commitment that he or she may be willing to make may be closely related to the direction of his or her career. In other words, once one achieves mass popularity, one may not remain loyal to the smaller core audience that helped establish one's career. Who can determine the level of an artist's sincerity? Was the radical movement simply a vehicle for Dylan's ambitions, or was it a belief that he modified, or in his mind outgrew?

Songs are about whatever their authors want to write about. Certainly artists will continue to write songs about social and political issues, and sometimes the songs reflect changes in the writer's ideas.

Many artists write songs about a specific issue that concerns them, rather than focusing their entire careers on such songs. From time to time Stevie Wonder, John Mellencamp, and many other artists produce such songs. An event like the war in Iraq, or the 9/11 attack, which we will discuss in more detail later, may inspire a particular artist to write a song about that event from his or her point of view. Toby Keith, the Dixie Chicks, and Allen Jackson have all done this. This doesn't magically transform them into protest singers.

We will leave the question of whether songs create social movements, or social movements inspire songs, for the conclusion of this book.

Why Folk Music? Then and Now

In the revival of the sixties, there were two groups of people that became involved with the music. The first were casual music fans who simply enjoyed the music, and found its rural simplicity an attractive alternative to rock and roll. By 1960 rock had temporarily run out of steam. Buddy Holly had died in an airplane crash, Jerry Lee Lewis was largely removed from the public eye due to his marriage with his thirteen-year-old cousin, and Elvis Presley was turning more and more toward movies and away from public performances. A good deal of the rock that was available was mindless and synthetic, and the Motown Records musical revolution hadn't yet begun. Consequently, folk was a pleasant albeit temporary alternative to rock for college students. Many of the folk groups consisted of people not much older than the students, and their dress, humor, and general style had a lot in common with their college audiences.

Another side of the revival was the community that became dedicated to the roots of the music. Many of the older traditional musicians, like Mississippi John Hurt and Dock Boggs, had just been rediscovered and were touring in the major cities and at folk festivals.

In many of the cities and on college campuses a fellowship of people developed who wanted to learn how these people played. Many of the participants were disgruntled by middle-class life styles and sought an identity in these older styles of music.

This second stream of the revival never really died, but it certainly had fewer adherents by the late 1970s and into the 1980s. The music got promoted by lesser-known record labels, like Rounder Records, through acoustic music stores, at folk festivals, and at summer instructional camps, many of which were located in the Southern mountains. By the year 2000 a group of younger fans started to take to the music. Their patron saints were the New Lost City Ramblers, a sort of anti-folk-pop group from the sixties. The Ramblers played mostly old-time music, mountain music that preceded bluegrass.

The old-time music movement was particularly popular in the West. Portland, Oregon has an annual Old Time Music Gathering that started in 1999. The participants tend to be under thirty-five or over fifty-five. It is as if an entire generation was skipped. This is a participatory music: people come to the event with their instruments and participate in jam sessions. It is not at all a political movement, but it is a search for a community outside the world of cell phones, video games, and consumerism that permeates American middle-class life. It is not a technophobe community; in fact the event is promoted almost entirely from a web site, called Bubba Guitar. There is an even larger annual festival in Berkeley, and other hotbeds of the music are Denver and Seattle.

Another community connected with folk music consists of people involved in song circles and house concerts. Song circles usually take place in people's houses. There is an emphasis on singing along, and usually people take turns singing songs. Sometimes song circles are also connected to acoustic music stores.

House concerts are concerts presented in the houses of music fans, or people who are themselves musicians. There is a nominal door charge, and performers play for anywhere from ten to a hundred people, depending on the size of the house. Some of the presenters have large e-mail lists and present regularly scheduled events, and others present music when it is available, or when it is convenient for them to do so.

The glue that binds all of the aspects of the current interest in folk music is that it generally is unconnected to commercial enterprises. Promoters of house concerts do not take fees, and most of the people in the old-time music community are not full-time professional musicians. The notion of sharing music rather than selling it may strike the reader as a quaint anachronism, but it is very much a part of the current face of the folk music revival.

When musicians in this community decide to become full-time professionals, they generally become involved with the North American Folk Music and Dance Alliance. For many of the artists the Alliance represents something of a contradiction in terms. It holds an annual national gathering in Memphis that mixes jam sessions with talent showcases. Presenters seek talent, and agents and managers and self-directed artists try to make deals for gigs, and with the folk record companies that attend the event. Numerous workshops are intended to assist musicians in advancing their careers. There are also a half dozen regional meetings that represent the same general format, but with a smaller number of attendees and exhibitors. Musicians and music fans disagree about the degree of community that these events represent. The community has also become somewhat splintered and factionalized by subgenres. There are bluegrass musicians, blues musicians, old-time music musicians, and, most of all, singer-songwriters. In a sense the Folk Alliance is caught up in the contradictions of the revival itself, and of the commercial world that most of us live in.

The blues and bluegrass communities have their own festivals, summer instructional camps, and annual meetings and award ceremonies. Many of the same observations apply to these communities, although the commonality of musical style tends to result in less musical separation of the adherents. Nevertheless, the adherents of electric or acoustic blues, and of old and new bluegrass styles, have their own tensions and disagreements.

What all of these groups have in common is the sense that they are operating outside of the commercial mainstream that is utilized to create and sell popular music in the United States. The radio play that these genres receive is usually limited to specialized radio shows or community or public radio stations. Once in a great while these artists break through to a wider audience, such as with the *Oh Brother, Where Art Thou?* movie soundtrack that sold over seven million copies, or the records of Allison Krauss.

By and large the music is associated with alternative lifestyles and an emphasis on community rather than monetary values.

6
SPANISH-SPEAKING GROUPS

The Southwest

In order to understand the Spanish-language music of the Southwest, it is important to understand the history of the area. Two of the Spanish settlements in the United States actually preceded the coming of the English settlers. St. Augustine, Florida was settled in 1519, and Santa Fe, New Mexico sometime between 1608 and 1610. The descendants of the original settlers in New Mexico and south-central Colorado regard themselves not as Mexicans (though these areas were part of Mexico until the mid-nineteenth century), but as Spanish Americans. Not only do they not look toward Mexico as their homeland, but they have a somewhat racist attitudes towards recent Mexican immigrants. From their point of view, their culture, language patterns, education, and lifestyle are superior to those of the "newcomers."

Folklorists and folk song collectors like Americo Paredes and J. Donald Robb have collected a considerable amount of lore and many songs that have their origins in Spain. The isolation and pride of the descendants of these original settlers parallels the situation found by folk song collectors in the early part of the twentieth century in the

Southern Appalachian Mountains, where people had retained the songs and language of Elizabethan England.

When the Spaniards came to the American continent, it was populated by a number of Indian tribes. As we have seen in the chapter about American Indians, attempts to utilize the Indians as slaves were not very successful. The population of the Caribbean countries in particular was decimated by a combination of disease, warfare, and cruelty. Debates in Spain between the Catholic Bishop Bartolome Las Casas, who chronicled the cruelty toward the Indians in books to inform the Spanish court, and the theologian Juan Gines de Sepulveda, who defended the colonists' domination of the native population, ultimately resulted in the Spanish government siding with Las Casas. According to author Earl Shorris, by the time the debate was resolved, the Spaniards had already killed fifteen million Indians. Of the million who had lived in Hispaniola, the second largest of the Antilles islands, only five hundred remained.

Shorris also points out the irony that the Spanish themselves were the mestizos of Europe, deriving from a mixture of Celtic tribes, Phoenician sailors, soldiers, and settlers from Carthage. The latter included Greeks, Hebrews, Romans, Visigoths, and Moors.

The importation of African slaves to work in the Spanish mines and farms created the mixed-blood population of the southwestern United States and Central America. The Spanish settlers, who had not brought families with them, soon had children with Indian and African women, creating the population that we now refer to as Hispanics or Latinos.

Mexico outlawed slavery, however, in 1830, more than thirty years before the United States did so. This was a source of tension between the neighboring countries. Another was the Anglo cattlemen, ranchers, and prospectors who established large settlements in California, New Mexico, Arizona, Texas, southern Colorado, and Utah, all part of Mexico. The Mexican government attempted to prohibit any further immigration from the United States to Texas, but this proved to be a futile exercise, and by 1835 there were twenty thousand

Americans in Texas, but only four thousand Mexicans. The Anglos declared the "Lone Star Republic" as an independent nation, and in 1836 they were defeated at the battle of the Alamo. Most of the rebels were killed in the battle, and Mexican General Santa Anna executed four hundred American prisoners. In turn the United States annexed Texas in 1845, which led to the Mexican War a year later.

The Spanish had colonized California in 1767 and established twenty-one missions up and down the coast to convert the Indians to Catholicism. Spain attempted to attract settlers from other parts of Mexico to settle in California by offering large land grants to new settlers, but by 1781 there were only six hundred Spanish settlers there. In 1821, when Mexico became independent from Spain, California was part of Mexico, but there were only three thousand Mexicans in the state, most of them descended from the original Spanish colonists. On June 6, 1846, thirty armed Americans awakened General Mariano Vallejo, occupied the area, and created the Bear Flag Republic, following the example of the Texans.

The Mexican War (also treated in chapter 1) that began that year was a result not only of the events in Texas and California. The American government had adopted the view that it was their "Manifest Destiny" to control a nation that would span the distance between the Atlantic and the Pacific Oceans, and to be bordered on the southwest by the Rio Grande River. The war was relatively quick and painless for the Americans. In 1848 the Mexicans signed the treaty of Guadalupe-Hidalgo, giving the United States over a million square millions of territory for a payment of fifteen million dollars. This included California, Texas, Utah, Nevada, and parts of Arizona, New Mexico, and Colorado. It represented a reduction of the land area of Mexico by half. Five years later the United States peacefully acquired the rest of Arizona and New Mexico for a payment of an additional ten million dollars.

The Mexican War was distinguished by numerous acts of cruelty and violence by American soldiers. Generals Grant and Meade were themselves horrified at the senseless murders and thefts perpetuated by

American soldiers. These crimes and the loss of face Mexico suffered with the drastic defeat of their troops created an antagonism between the two countries that persists in the music of Mexican Americans. Nonetheless, internal revolutions, repressive governments, and poor economic conditions in Mexico have led to the legal and illegal immigration that continues to this day. America's need for cheap labor, especially acute when wars have occurred or the American economy is booming, influences the extent of this immigration at any given point in time. According to the 2000 United States census, 66.1 percent of the U.S. Latino population is Mexican. The second-largest group, 14.5 percent, consists of Central and South American immigrants, excluding Cuba and Puerto Rico. Since this includes nations from Brazil to Haiti, it does not represent a single identity. Nine percent of the U.S. Latino population is Puerto Rican, and four percent is Cuban. Political and economic conflagrations in Nicaragua, San Salvador, Haiti, and Guatemala have resulted in American "colonies" of these groups in various American cities, just as Miami is the center of the influx from Cuba. "Latino music," it should be noted, is not a single style, but includes idioms that are peculiar to each national group. Even specific genres, like salsa, are a blend of musical styles and mannerisms from a variety of Latino cultures.

Immigration

Despite the efforts of the Immigration and Naturalization Service to restrict the flood of illegal immigrants, immigration from Mexico has generally continued unabated. Huge maquiladora factories have grown up on the Mexican side of the American border. Goods imported from the United States are assembled in these facilities and then returned to the U.S. In a 2008 study, professors Joseph Heinzeman and Gian Marco Valonitini of Hodges University reported that as of 2007 there were about 1,200,000 workers in the maquiladoras.

On the American side of the border, Mexicans work on a seasonal basis on American farms, often entering illegally, living in squalid huts and returning home at the end of the growing season.

Others work as laborers in large cities. In many American cities there are sections of the town that function as illegal hiring halls. Mexicans gather on the corner, and people drive by and hire them for day labor as gardeners or handymen.

Immigration and Politics

Immigration from Mexico has become an important issue in American politics, especially as economic opportunities in the United States are limited by our current recession. When many American workers are unemployed, they object to immigrants working in the United States. This is as much a psychological problem as a real one, in the sense that in many cases American workers don't want to do the jobs, such as farm work, that are often performed by migrant laborers. This is particularly true in states like California, Arizona, and Texas that are located right on the Mexican border. Conservative groups have demanded stronger policing of the border states, and a fence is currently under construction on the Texas and California borders (the New Mexico and Arizona segments are completed). The fences serve a dual purpose, restricting illegal immigration and also the importation of illegal drugs. Because there are 1951 miles of border between the two countries, this is a herculean undertaking.

Among the many issues surrounding immigration are the education of the children of immigrants, the issue of whether illegals should be able to obtain driver's licenses, and the questions surrounding the distribution of health, welfare, and social security benefits.

Bilingualism is a particularly controversial issue. Many Anglos and conservative Hispanics, such as Linda Chavez, feel that there is no reason to encourage a bilingual culture. Chavez points out that no other immigrant groups have insisted that their own languages be taught in the public schools. However, since many of the Mexican illegals do not intend to stay in the United States permanently, their motivation to join the existing American culture is minimal. Moreover, there is a strong concentration of Mexican Americans in the southwestern United States, and of Puerto Ricans in New York City, enough that these populations constitute a majority in some neighborhoods or even congressional districts. This has happened before during earlier waves of immigration to the United States, but never so dramatically as it has with Mexican Americans.

Political Militance

Mexican American political militance parallels the agitation by African American citizens during the 1960s. Some of the issues that have taken hold among Mexican Americans include the low wages of migratory farm workers, the attempt to establish political organizations such as La Raza Unida, and the assertion of land rights derived from charters issued by the Spanish government dating back long before the Mexican War. These issues were followed by the emergence of Mexican American political figures.

Denver mayor Federico Peña and San Antonio mayor Henry Cisneros were elected in the late seventies and eighties. The current mayor of Los Angeles is Antonio Villarigosa, and Ken Salazar was a Colorado senator until he was appointed by President Obama as Secretary of the Interior. Salazar's brother John serves as a Colorado congressman.

Mexican American Music

There is a rich and active Spanish musical tradition all over the southwestern United States. *Corridos* are a large part of that tradition. A *corrido* is a ballad that tells a story. The late Americo Paredes, a famous folklorist and folk song authority, believed that the *corrido* actually originated on the American side of the border. Others believe that Mexico was its birthplace.

Corridos functioned like newspapers, speaking about current events and celebrating historic ones as well. They had particular importance among non-literate people, for whom *corridos* in effect *were* their newspapers. Paredes collected many songs about conflicts between Anglos and Mexicans on or near the border. In his book *A Texas-Mexican Cancionero,* he printed six songs from colonial days, thirty-five about border conflicts, eight for special occasions, eleven romantic and comic songs, and seven songs about "pochos," the Mexican name for over-Americanized Mexican Americans.

Many of the songs about border conflicts were recorded in the 1920s and 1930s, often on small, regional record labels. Chris Strachwitz has issued them as CD compilations on his Arhoolie record label. Possibly the most famous of these songs is the "Ballad of Gregorio Cortez." The ballad is based on a true story that occurred in 1901. Cortez's brother was shot by a Texas sheriff who accused him of being a horse thief. Cortez in turn killed the sheriff, then fled, evading pursuit by walking seventy miles in forty hours. He survived a gunfight and led the deputies on a three-day pursuit on horseback. Hundreds of men were chasing Cortez, and special trains transported horses and dogs.

Ultimately Cortez was captured because another Mexican betrayed him, allegedly for a thousand-dollar reward. A series of trials took place. Some ended in Cortez's acquittal, but eventually he received a life sentence. The sentence was commuted after eight years. Here are some of the many verses of the song:

Said Gregorio Cortez
With his pistol in his hand
"I'm not sorry for having killed him.
It's for my brother that I feel sorry."
Came the hound dogs
They came on his trail
But to reach Cortez
Was to reach a star.
The Americans said
"If we see him, what shall we do to him;
If we face him head on,
Very few will return."
Gregorio Cortez said,
With his pistol in his hand,

"Don't run, you cowardly Rangers,
From one lone Mexican."
Now with this I take my leave
In the shade of a cypress,
Here we finish singing
The tragedy of Cortez.

There are a number of interesting aspects of this *corrido*. It paints Cortez as a heroic sort of Lone Ranger, pitted against the entire American police apparatus. The Americans are quoted as being afraid of this one man, and he in turn begs them not to run, but to face him.

To a population still smarting from the loss of half of their homeland fifty-three years earlier, the notion of this single hero successfully aligning himself against superior American might had to be inspiring and reaffirming. These verses are only a handful of the dozens that have been recorded or collected. In 1983 the ballad was made into a movie starring Edward James Olmos.

There are numerous other *corridos* that tell of lone Mexicans heroically taking on cowardly Americans, often the hated Texas Rangers. The Rangers were notorious for their brutality against Mexicans in the border areas, which were pervaded by lawlessness and violence. Raids across the border by Mexican bandit-revolutionaries took place from time to time, and sometimes these resulted in armed encounters with the Texas Rangers or American vigilantes.

Many of the Mexican bandits were depicted as Robin Hoods, who had the interests of the poor at heart. One of the most famous of these *corridos* concerns the outlaw Joaquin Murrieta. Unlike Cortez, Murrieta was a professional outlaw who was not driven by any injustice done to him. Nevertheless, to the poor immigrant he represented something of a heroic figure. Below are some of the lyrics of the song.

Joaquin Murrieta
I am not an American

But I understand English.
I learned it from my mother
Forwards and backwards
And any American I make tremble at my feet.
From the greedy rich,
I took away their money.
With the humble and the poor
I took off my hat.
Oh, what laws so unjust
To call me a highwayman.
Through bars I went
Punishing Americans.
"You must be the captain
who killed my brother,
You grabbed him defenseless,
You stuck-up American."
My career began
Because of a terrible scene.
When I got to seven hundred killed,
Then my name was feared.
When I got to twelve hundred
Then my name was (really) feared.

If Cortez was a brave man avenging a great injustice, Murrietta was by contrast a sort of thug Superman. The notion of one Mexican man killing twelve hundred Americans represents a far-fetched fantasy, but increasing the numbers against Murrietta may make the character seem more heroic, and less like an outlaw. There is a certain cognitive dissonance involved in conflating a Robin Hood character and a mass murderer. Of course America has its own "superhuman outlaw" ballads about such comparable "heroes" as Billy the Kid and Jesse James.

In general, *corridos* tell stories about illegal border crossings, ordinary workers, separation from a lover or the acquisition of a new one, hostile attitudes towards gringos and the injustices committed by them, politics or heroes, and the drug trade (*narcocorridos*). As we will see later in the chapter, there has been an explosion of *narcocorridos* that has paralleled the drug wars currently taking place in Mexico.

Corrido Structure

Maria Herrera-Sobek, a professor of Spanish and Portuguese at the University of California, Irvine, and the author of several books on the music of northern Mexico and southern Texas, points out that *corridos* are constructed according to a general formula. The opening verse is an initial call from the singer to the public. of the singer then sets the place and date of the tale, and names the protagonist. An exposition then precedes the arguments of the protagonist. This is followed by a message, the protagonist's farewell, and the farewell of the singer. Herrera-Sobek describes this sequence as follows:

> Reiterated phrases admonishing the audience to remember the event that is being related
> An exclamation or reflection that the singer makes about the story
> A brief biography of the protagonist
> A summary and synthesis of the main theme
> An invitation to buy a broadside containing the *corrido*
> An invitation to stay for the second part of the song
> The name of the song's author and the beginning of the second part of an analogous *corrido*

Corridos and Women

Very few *corrido* singers are women. Herrera-Sobek describes the main images of women in *corridos* as being the domineering mother, the mother goddess, the lover, and the soldier. The mother is regarded as a key figure in the Mexican family, powerful and good, yet expected to be subservient. Occasional *corridos* show women murdering husbands or lovers, or acting as traitors and betraying men. Some of these roles are historically determined, and others derive from literary traditions.

Corridos and Immigration

There are a number of *corridos* that detail specific situations involving illegal immigrants (braceros) or the working conditions that Mexican American immigrants had to endure. The *corrido* "The Kansas Contractors" reveal some of the labor conflicts between immigrants and American workers.

> One day the third of September,
> Oh what an unusual day
> When we left Laredo
> Signed up for Kansas.
> When we left Laredo
> I committed myself to the strong saint
> Because I was traveling illegally
> On that side of the bridge.
> The Americans said
> With a great deal of bravery:
> "Round up the Mexicans
> So as to put them in the union."
> We replied to them:
> "We will not join this thing called union
> This is not our flag, because we are Mexicans."

Some of the immigrant *corridos* contain a sort of gallows humor: a bitter if amused view of the place of Mexicans in American life. The song "About the Railroad Worker (The Dishwasher)" is a good example:

> I dreamed in my youth of being a movie star,
> And one fine day I came to visit Hollywood.

One day, desperate from all the revolutions,
I crossed to the USA without paying the immigration.
The gringuitos would ask me, "Do you like what you see?
It used to belong to the Mexicans, now it is all ours."
Goodbye American men, goodbye American girls,
I take my leave; goodbye, I am going to see my Mexican girls.

In 1944 Private Felix Longoria, a Chicano soldier from Three Rivers, Texas, was killed in action in the Philippines. He was buried there, and when his body was shipped back to Texas, it was refused entry at the local funeral home. A *corrido* called "Discrimination" was written, calling on (then) Senator Lyndon Johnson to intervene. Johnson did so, and the body was buried with full military honors at Arlington National Cemetery.

Chris Strachwitz, owner of Arhoolie records, says that today's *corridos* are usually fictional, because radio stations and record companies fear lawsuits from the people mentioned in these sometimes outspoken songs. He claims that true *corridos* can only be found in private gatherings and cantinas, which are relatively safe from possible legal action from offended parties. However, there are exceptions to Strachwitz's rule. A number of *corridos* concerned Cesar Chavez and his attempts to organize Mexican American farm workers. John Storm Roberts cites "El Corrido de Cesar Chavez": "We don't ask for charity, only a better way. / That's Cesar Chavez's demand to help the people."

Another pro-union *corrido* is "Los Rinches de Texas," written by melon workers in south Texas in 1968. The song concerns an unsuccessful strike that was broken largely through the efforts of the Texas Rangers. This *corrido* was used in a subsequent election against the county attorney, who was the one who had called in the Rangers. The attorney was swept out of office. The lyric to the song is printed in Manuel Peña's book *Musica Tejano*. It refers to the beating of the strikers, and describes the Texas governor, John Connolly, as "the evil governor." The song ends with the verse

I take my leave, my brothers,
with an aching heart.
Like good Mexicans
join the union.

The United Farm Workers Union often presented touring plays for the farm workers, and the plays included music.

Strachwitz does acknowledge the rash of *corridos* composed after the assassination of John F. Kennedy. Dan William Dickey, author of the monograph *The Kennedy Corridos,* collected several dozen *corridos* about Kennedy, who was a much-admired figure among Mexican Americans. Some are simply tributes to him; others describe the assassination or the grieving of his wife, Jackie.

Dickey, writing in 1978, also cites Cesar Chavez and Reies Lopez Tijerina as being the current subjects of *corridos.* Tijerina was involved in the 1967 occupation of a New Mexico courthouse over the issue of land ownership where the United States had overridden Spanish land grants given before the Mexican War.

Evolution of Musical Style in Mexican American Music

In northern Mexico and southern Texas a musical genre called conjunto evolved during the 1920s and 1930s. The original instrumentation for the style included the accordion and the *bajo sexto,* an instrument similar to the twelve-string guitar. During the 1940s and '50s bass and drums were added to the mix. At the same time a musical idiom called *orquesta* developed, which introduced brass instruments and more complex musical arrangements. Today Southwestern Tex-Mex music is grouped under the general label "tejano." It usually includes brass, electric guitars, a rhythm section, and an accordion, and covers the entire musical spectrum, including country music, pop, rock, and *corridos.* Every year there is a giant festival of conjunto music in San Antonio, and a few of the musicians, such as accordion player Flaco Jiminez, have become world-famous.

Orquesta has been replaced by banda, which uses larger orchestral ensembles, and also reflects jazz influences. Banda is popular on the West Coast. Ranchero music is often juxtaposed against banda as a sort of Southwestern, cowboy-oriented music. The performers wear cowboy hats, and the music features guitar and a handful of other instruments. Banda appeals to a more middle-class group who are somewhat snobbish about ranchero, regarding it as sort of the equivalent of hillbilly music. Mariachi music, featuring trumpets, guitars, and acoustic bass guitars called *guitarrons,* is another style of Mexican music that had its adherents. There are also regional styles, such as the music of Vera Cruz, which features a harp as the lead instrument.

Just as there are few female corrido artists, there are not many female conjunto artists. What women do enter the field are generally linked to men who are conjunto musicians. When women are involved in the music, men may serve as managers or band leaders. Essentially, they become buffers to the general public. This enables women to retain their traditional cultural place as secondary to the men in the band, and draws attention away from their suspicious social status as conjunto musicians. That role is often identified with

Tipica orchestra

recklessness, the abuse of drugs or alcohol, and a sexually promiscuous lifestyle; and in the context of Mexican American culture, these are not acceptable activities for women.

Tish Hinojosa is a self-contained artist, a singer-songwriter who is an exception to the women's roles described above. She has recorded for one major and one independent record company and tours widely. Some of her songs are in English, and some in Spanish. The songbook she has compiled from two of her albums contains fourteen love songs, one song about migrants, five songs with lyrics printed only in Spanish, and one song by another songwriter about a rambler. The selection "Something About the Rain," about the use of pesticides and the resulting diseases suffered by farm workers, includes the verse

> Cause there's something in the rain
> But there's more here in our hands.
> Buelita (grandma)'s right about the things of man
> Whose profits rape the land.
> And the rains are falling down
> From the growers to the towns.
> And until we break the killing chains
> There's something in the rain.

Hinojosa's album *Homeland* includes a song about immigrants called "Joaquin." One verse states that

> Joaquin loves his homeland
> But it can't give him enough
> He wants a god life, a job and a wife
> And some children with dreams that come true.

Hinojosa is herself the youngest of thirteen children, and her song "The Far Side of Town" describes her family and her poor but generally happy childhood.

Mexicans in Anglo Music

Anglo ballads about Mexican women generally play up the stereotypical Latin sexpot aspect. The song "Border Affair," also known as "Spanish Is the Loving Tongue," portrays the woman as "inferior but desirable," as Herrera-Sobek puts it. Another song, "The Texas Cowboy," is about a heroic Texas fellow who can make any senorita love him.

Some of these songs also include an underlying theme that Latino women can be dangerous to cowboys. In the song "Juanita," when the Anglo says that he must leave his love, she stabs him in the heart. In the huge country music hit "El Paso," it is not the woman who kills the cowboy, but his Mexican rival. By playing the femme fatale role, she has destroyed him.

The treatment of Mexicans in American pop music also tends to reinforce cliches. Peggy Lee's 1945 song "Mañana" is a description of a lazy Latino who always puts things off until tomorrow. An uglier stereotype was offered by a disc jockey named Randy Miller in San Diego in 1986. Using the tune of the old folk song "She'll Be Coming Round the Mountain," Miller wrote that,

> They'll be carrying drugs and handguns
> So they can have some real fun
> They will not have a green card,
> But they sure know how to run hard
> Now all they know is Spanish, and if you don't they will vanish.

Miller also mentioned Frito Lay, tortillas, and Taco Bell in his song. Eventually it was removed from the station because of listener complaints.

Ian Tyson and Neil Young have written a number of songs about Mexican Americans and their Indian heritage. Young in particular has written a trilogy about the extermination of Indians by the Spaniards. The late Texas singer Doug Sahm, who was an Anglo, formed a country-Mexican group called the Texas Tornadoes with Augie Meyer, the late Freddy Fender, and Flaco Jiminez. Fender also made a number of recordings where he sang verses alternately in Spanish and English.

Puerto Rican Life and Music

The United States acquired Puerto Rico in 1898 as a result of the Spanish-American War. Puerto Rico is a United States Commonwealth, so Puerto Ricans may enter and leave the mainland at will. There are 3,913,055 Puerto Ricans living in Puerto Rico, and roughly the same number in the continental United States. In a 1993 vote, 47 percent of the people favored the continuation of the current commonwealth status, 46 percent preferred statehood, and 4 percent opted for independence from the United States. Commonwealth status provides tax exemptions unavailable stateside. On the other hand, statehood would grant seats in the U.S. Congress, as opposed to the current nonvoting status that Puerto Ricans representatives are granted.

According to musicologist Ruth Glasser, the early songs of Puerto Ricans in New York were laments of homesick migrants that recalled their homeland as a tropical paradise. During the 1920s and 1930s, trios and quartets formed in Puerto Rico, featuring guitars or guitar-like instruments, re-formed when the members arrived in New York. Each wave of settlers assisted the new immigrants who followed them. There were Latino ethnic clubs and regular dances. Barber shops and pharmacies sold recordings that were not available at record stores at that time. Julio Roque had the first sponsored radio show of Puerto Rican music in New York, and the Apollo Theater in Harlem presented bufos. Bufos resembled North American minstrel shows, with performers wearing blackface.

By the 1940s most of the night clubs were owned by whites, but managed by Latinos. Puerto Rican musicians played to the prevailing Anglo stereotypes of Latinos, but at the same time they made fun of these cliches. The song "El Buen Borincano" ("The Good Puerto Rican"), recorded in 1939, exhibited a sort of sardonic humor. Glasser reprints the lyrics:

If I had not been born
In the land in which I was born,
I would regret
Not having been born there.

Some other songs of the period decried the fact that Puerto Rico was not independent, as seen in the lyric "Nothing remains to them but a cry that drowns in the heart." Another political song, "Estan Tirando Bomboas," written in 1935, even criticized the governor of Puerto Rico for his role in a police massacre of four people who were demonstrating for Puerto Rican independence. Other songs took as their subject farm relief during the Depression and hurricanes.

Puerto Ricans expressed ambivalence towards America's appropriation of their island. The song "Pobre Borinquen" ("Poor Puerto Rico") is expressive of these contradictory feelings:

With flowers we welcomed them
With music and flags
With guitars and violins
We stared at the colors
Of their starry banner
And the enthusiastic island
Never for once imagined
It would find itself so helpless
When the Yankees took us over.

Glasser points out that several of the best-loved and most nationalistic songs, including "Lamento Borincano" and "Pedro Flores," were composed by Puerto Ricans living in New York. Ethnomusicologist Peter Manuel cites a number of songs that give voice to familiar themes from the immigrant songs discussed in the first chapter of this book. These songs cite such issues as the cold weather, the lack of good Puerto Rican food, and the difficulty of making a living as an immigrant in New York. On the other hand, Manuel mentions that some songs offer support for the decision to come to New York. He also points out that after the late 1960s few songs even discuss migration.

Ultimately, traditional Puerto Rican music was overwhelmed by the popularity of Cuban dance music, which was more modern, exciting, and flashy. Today's salsa music blends elements of Cuban and Puerto Rican music into one somewhat heterogeneous stew. In turn salsa has been influenced by merengue and other South and Central American music styles, and has become ubiquitous throughout Latin America and in many of the Spanish-speaking cities and radio stations in the United States.

A recent innovation in Puerto Rican music is a dance music style called reggaeton, which represents a fusion of Panamanian reggae with Puerto Rican hip hop music. While Daddy Yankee, whose music is basically intended for partying, is the one artist in this idiom who has achieved a good amount of success in the U.S. music market, another reggaeton artist, Tego Calderon, has addressed the issue of racism in some of his songs.

Reggaeton had its biggest successes in the United States in 2005–6, when some Spanish music radio stations converted their formats to feature the style. At the present time, it appears that the fad has subsided, and the idiom will take its place alongside numerous other Latin dance music forms.

Cuba and the Exodus

The first significant immigration from Cuba to the United States occurred in the 1830s, when middle- and upper-class Cubans came to Key West. In the 1880s a largely blue-collar population moved to Jacksonville and Tampa, where they worked in the cigar industry. As late as 1959 there were only 30,000 Cubans in the United States. In 1959, after Castro assumed power in Cuba, an exodus to the United States began. In that year alone 26,527 Cubans came to the United States. Within the next ten years an additional 230,000 Cubans came to the United States.

Most of the early anti-Castro immigrants were members of the upper economic class. Over the years Castro began to deport undesirables and enemies of the regime. He emptied jails and mental hospitals not only of political prisoners, but of many others whom he chose to export in order to avoid paying for their support. During the 1980s, many more black Cubans, and Cubans of lower economic status, entered the United States.

Many Cuban immigrants settled along the Miami-Fort Lauderdale corridor. This transformed the lifestyle and image of the area of what had been primarily a tourist and retirement destination to a center for South American trade. According to a 2004 U.S. Census Survey, there were 1,448,684 Cubans living in the United States at that time. Nine hundred ninety thousand lived in Florida, with the next highest number, eighty-one thousand, living in New Jersey. Clearly Florida is the core community of Cuban Americans.

The U.S. government regarded Cuban immigrants as supporters of the United States against a communist country and provided them with special aid programs, jobs, college loans, free certification for professionals, food stamps, cash allotments, and citizenship exemptions. This created a considerable amount of resentment in the Miami African American community, who had no such status.

Spanish-language culture quickly became a powerful force in the life of Miami. MTV Latino headquarters in Miami, and there are two daily and various weekly

Latina singing folk songs, circa 1940s

Spanish-language newspapers. Several of these cater to Argentines, Venezuelans, Nicaraguans, and Colombians, reflecting the fact that Miami has become a center for Central and South American trade and culture.

Like most Latin Americans Cubans trace their history to original Indian settlers, Spanish conquest, and the importation of slaves, creating a blend of Spanish, Indian, and African culture and ethnicity. Black Cubans deal with racism from "white" Cubans, as well as from the Anglo population. Despite Latin Americans' insistence that this prejudice is an American phenomenon, it is prevalent in most of Central and South America and reflected in terms of job opportunities, even among musicians. Miami's black Cubans are virtually invisible, and live apart from other Cubans. Because of their strong anti-communism Cubans are generally more conservative than other Latinos, and tend to vote Republican.

The Miami Sound

Miami has become a major recording center for the production of Spanish-language music that circulates not only in the United States, but throughout Central and South America. The major record companies all have offices there. In addition to recordings of Latin artists, Miami is a center for recordings in Spanish by Anglo artists who are attempting to enter the South American market.

Miami is also the home of the "Miami sound," the slick and popular music of Gloria and Emilio Estefan and the Miami Sound Machine. The Estefans, both refugees from Cuba, met and married in the United States in 1978. Emilio is a record producer, and the Miami Sound Machine he formed as a vehicle for Gloria has been a major influence on America's pop scene. The band recorded only in English for ten years, beginning in 1984, but in 1993 Gloria began singing in Spanish. The music, a sort of Latin-tinged crossover soft rock, has been enormously popular, selling 26.5 million records in the United States, and 90 million worldwide. In addition, Emilio has produced recordings by a number of successful Latino artists, including Ricky Martin and Marc Anthony. There is little political sentiment in the music of the Miami Sound Machine, other than nostalgia for the Cuban homeland.

Salsa

Over the years America has had a lengthy love affair with the rhythmic and brass band music styles that have originated or developed in Cuba. These include the guajira, the mambo, the bolero, and the boogaloo. Several Cuban musicians, notably percussionist Chano Pozo, played an important role in the development of bebop. Pozo played briefly with Dizzy Gillespie, and has received much credit during his brief career for pointing Gillespie in the direction of understanding and playing sophisticated Latin rhythms.

In the early 1970s a New York record company called Fania capitalized on the development of salsa. Musicians like Willie Colon, Ray Barretto, and Eddie Palmieri achieved considerable popularity not only in the New York Latino community, but throughout the nation. Rock and roll adopted the boogaloo, which according to author Hernando Calvo Ospino, was an adaptation of the Cuban guajira rhythm by Puerto Ricans in New York. The same author regards salsa as a creation of hybrid Latin musicians in New York based on the harmonic and rhythmic patterns of the Cuban music. Latin music scholars attribute salsa to varying degrees of Cuban or Puerto Rican influences.

The breakthrough album of salsa was *Siembra*, by bandleader Willie Colon and singer Ruben Blades. Blades is a Yale-educated lawyer, actor, and musician from Panama. In the song "Plastico" he shows his left-wing orientation with such lines as "He is always thinking money, she of fashion in Paris. / Telling their little five-year-old not to play with colored kids."

Blades recorded another song about the death of a guerrilla in an army ambush. Colon also wrote some socially conscious songs, including one against drugs.

Cuban immigrant Celia Cruz became the vocal superstar of salsa. Cruz was a strongly anti-Castro refugee whose song "Camino para Volver" reflects her desire to go back home, and asks for the blessing of her native country, because "I am your daughter, and have never failed you." In another song, "En Estados Unidos," Cruz calls for unity and exhorts her listeners, "Don't let anyone persuade you / To abandon your Spanish language."

Although the songs of early anti-Castro refugees expressed a longing for the homeland, and these nostalgic sentiments still occasionally appear in Cuban American music, author Gustavo Firmat Lopez comments that "I am struck by how apolitical, by how rootless the sound of Miami often seems. . . . If New York salsa unfolds in the barrio, Miami salsa happens in the malls."

According to Ospina, salsa today is more dance-oriented and less socially relevant than it once was, and much of the production has shifted to Puerto Rico. There is even a Japanese salsa band, Orchestre de la Luz, which tours internationally and has made a number of recordings despite the fact that the band members do not speak Spanish but sing it phonetically. The orchestra is entirely non-political, but their very existence indicates the importance of salsa as a worldwide musical phenomenon. It is interesting to observe the evolution of a music that can be used to represent anti-Castro sentiment, pro-revolutionary left wing agendas, or no political viewpoint at all.

What's Going On: Chicano Consciousness and Music

During World War II, many Mexican Americans served in the armed forces. They came home to a country scarred by a series of riots in which other American soldiers had chased and beaten Latino barrio gang members. Like returning African American soldiers, these veterans were keenly aware of the inequities of American society.

After the war some small independent record labels like Imperial recorded Mexican American artists, but the overwhelming popularity of rhythm and blues and later rock and roll made these companies

Los Lobos

concentrate on Anglo music. Long before Jimi Hendrix surfaced, a San Antonio guitarist named Lorenzo Caballero was setting his guitar on fire and playing guitar solos with his tongue. Eventually, in the 1970 and '80s, South American rhythms began to exert an undeniable influence on North American rock. A common identity developed between black and Latino musicians as Latin musicians played in jazz groups, and jazz musicians worked in some of the Latin big bands. The black band War was heavily influenced by Latino rhythms, and in 1972 the band El Chicano had a #1 national hit record.

By 1984 there were 2,100 Latino bands in Los Angeles. Such bands as Thee Midnighters and Tierra recorded a number of albums with some success, but Los Lobos was the first Chicano rock band that broke out in a big way. Their breakthrough record was the song "La Bamba" from the 1987 film of the same name. Los Lobos was a unique band, because they deliberately set out to integrate traditional

Mexican music into their performances. They even learned Spanish in order to do so. In concert they played rock instruments, but they also mastered instruments and instrumental styles used in traditional Mexican music. For years they performed locally at fiestas and schools, building up support in the mass music market while maintaining their roots in the community where they lived. Their allegorical song "Will the Wolf Survive" was a hit record by country "outlaw" Waylon Jennings. Los Lobos achieved national distribution through a deal with independent Slash Records, which was distributed by conglomerate Warner Brothers Records.

One of the oddest success stories in Chicano rock annals is the odyssey of the band Redbone. The core of the band was two brothers named Vasquez, who recorded under the name Vegas.

Initially they wanted to play surf music, but, according to cultural theorist George Lipsitz, their agent told them that the world was not ready for a Mexican band that played surfing music. They changed their identity, creating a band called Redbone, a slang expression describing a light-skinned black person.

In the late 1960s they met an American Indian drummer named Peter de Poe who informed them that their band sounded Indian, and that they needed to hire him because he was an Indian. The band began to wear stage clothes that resembled the apparel of Plains Indians, and to sing songs about Native American history. In a conversation with their grandmother they found out that in fact they had Indian blood in their heritage.

To confuse matters further, the Indian drummer left, and was replaced by a Filipino-Chicano drummer. The band had one major national hit, "Come and Get Your Love," but on the same album they also recorded "We Were All Wounded at Wounded Knee." That song was also released as a single, and was a #1 record in some European countries. In the United States it was banned by some radio stations for its "inflammatory" political lyrics, and did not chart. In its persona and its very existence, Redbone still represents a fascinating hodgepodge of ethnic and racial identities.

Chicano Rap

Groups and artists emerged in Los Angeles who are essentially barrio rappers. The group Chicano Soul Power uses a rap format and is heavily political, if vaguely sexist. Most of their songs are in English, with occasional Spanish phrases. They offer a celebration of Chicano pride, as in this lyric in their song "Latin Lover": "I ain't no hispanic, a proud chicano / There's no need to panic."

Another song, "Jimmy," is about a junkie who cleans up his act after going to jail.

Crudos is a young punk rock group that sings political lyrics in Spanish, in a style somewhat similar to the rock band Rage Against the Machine. Their song "Fight to Be Heard" warns:

> Peasants, slaves, starving families
> There are no alternatives
> They are desperate to survive.
> Armed they'll take you seriously
> Defend yourself and you'll survive
> If not they'll kill you.

Dr. Loco's Rockin' Jalapeno Band is a modern horn band that sings about such matters as Immigration and Naturalization Service (INS) agents shooting illegals. They also sing about picketing and Chicano pride.

In 1990 Kid Frost, another barrio rapper, sang: "You say we are assassins, train ourselves to kill / It's in our blood to be Aztec warriors."

In a 2008 book, Pancho McFarland claims that Chicano rap emerged in the years 1989 to 1996. He describes the Los Angeles environment as one where Latino income levels lagged way behind those of both whites and blacks, and as part of a state where Latino prisoners outnumbered any other ethnic group behind bars (35.27 percent of prisoners in 2002, compared to 30 percent for blacks and 29.2 percent for whites).

McFarland traces the attraction of misogynist rap as being culturally rooted in the attitude toward women exhibited in corridos and conjunto music. Women in these genres are rarely mentioned independently of their relationship to men, as though they lack an autonomous existence.

McFarland cites a number of socially conscious Latino rappers, beginning with Frost, formerly known as Kid Frost, and including more recent artists Street Platoon, the Movement, and Krazy Race (Mark "Markie" Ramirez). The multicultural group Cypress Hill includes an Italian, a Cuban, and a Chicano/Cuban. In 1999 they made their first all-Spanish recording. They continued their musical explorations with the 2000 *Skull and Bones* album, which had one CD in hip-hop style, while the second album utilized rock-punk fusion. A 2004 album had some reggae tracks. The band Psycho Realm's album *War Story Book I* took on police violence, drugs, and the Rodney King case, and its 2003 successor, Book 2 continued these political themes.

McFarland analyzed a sample of 470 Chicano rap lyrics. He reveals the following characteristics:

336 concern themselves with violence
170 refer to women as sluts, whores or freaks
141 concern violence between police and Chicano youths
98 have women as their subject
98 reference sexual intercourse
37 present competition between men over women
Only 19 involve misogynistic violence (4.5 percent of the total, as opposed to studies that indicate a figure of 22 percent for African American rappers)
11 deal with "good women"—loyal wives or daughters

McFarland also mentions several Chicana rappers. Ms. Sancha is a sort of Chicana Li'l Kim, whose sexually explicit lyrics are written by her male producer.

Cypress Hill

Chicana rapper JV writes songs about self-empowerment and controlling her own destiny. They represent resistance against the patriarchal control of women that is a common part of Latino culture. McFarland says that JV too sometimes slips into sexist language to express her power over others.

Narcocorridos

If not for the *narcocorrido*, it is quite possible that the *corrido* form would be on the way out, or even dead, by now. *Narcocorridos* are ballads about drug smuggling and smugglers. As is the case with rap, certain slang expressions represent different aspects of the trade, such as specific drugs.

The group Los Tigres del Norte, the superstars of music that spans the Texas-Mexico border, have made the *narcocorrido* their trademark. According to Cathy Ragland's fascinating book *Música Norteña: Mexican Migrants Creating a Nation Between Nations,* they have sold over 35 million records since recording their first *narcocorrido* in 1973. Unlike American rock stars, the group does not write its own music, but searches for music on both sides of the border that will appeal to Mexican American laborers and to the Mexican working class.

Elijah Wald's book *Narcocorrido: A Journey into the Music of Drugs, Guns and Guerrillas* traces the history of the idiom. Wald traveled to various places in Mexico, Phoenix, Los Angeles, and San Antonio in search of *narcocorrido* artists and composers. He believes that the first example of this genre dates back to 1934, and a recording in San Antonio by Jean Gaytan. The song was called "El Contrabandista," and describes the arrest of a smuggler in Texas.

Rosalino "Chalin" Sanchez was a legendary artist who, as a composer of *narcocorridos*, also assumed the violent stance associated with the subject matter. Like later gangster rappers, he ended up being murdered. And, as in the world of gangster rap, his death seemed to result in increased interest in the genre and fascination with the trade.

Of all Wald's colorful stories and interviews, the oddest was his Los Angeles encounter with the Rivera family. Pedro Rivera was Chalino's record producer, and owns the Cintas Acuario record label. Two of the artists on the label are his son Lupillo and his daughter, Jenni. Unlike Chalino, these artists are not thugs or drug-involved, but simply artists who have seized an opportunity to establish musical careers. One might say that the Rivera family is to *narcocorrido* as the Beastie Boys are to rap! Pedro records all sorts of *corridos*, ranging from songs about Mexican presidential candidates to songs about the L.A. riots and the Gulf War. Initially disc jockeys thought the *corridos* were old-fashioned, but sales on the street and listener requests brought Pedro Rivera's songs to the radio.

As a woman singing *corridos*, Jenni is an oddity. Although Wald points out that some women have sung *rancheras*, Jenni Rivera is the only one who has enjoyed radio hits with *narcocorridos*. To go with the image she has created with her music, she also has cultivated her own style of dress that presents her as tough but attractive. For the Rivera family *narcocorridos* are not really a way of life; they are a financial opportunity that only someone with roots in the Mexican American community could have grasped.

Since the 2001 publication of Wald's book, the drug wars have greatly escalated, not only in Mexico itself, but in American border towns, or cities located in fairly close proximity to the border. There have been thousands of people killed in the drug wars in the last five years. A dozen of them were musicians involved in the *narcocorrido* world, according to a story published in the *Christian Science Monitor* on April 8, 2008. Some of the border towns, notably Tijuana and Juarez, have literally been experiencing wars between competing drug cartels. Policemen, judges, and government officials have been murdered, as have innocent bystanders caught up in the gunfire. The fatal adoption of the drug runner profile by singers eerily parallels the deaths of various gangster rappers in New York and Los Angeles.

Several of Wald's informants told him that they are careful not to mention too many names in their corridos, for fear that the person being written about, or his competitor, will be angered by the song; the story in the Monitor also cited one singer who has given up singing *narcocorridos* because he is afraid for the safety of his family. Many of the Mexican radio stations refuse to play songs celebrating drug trafficking, and as the situation has become increasingly violent, some American Spanish-language stations have followed suit. Meanwhile, according to Ragland, the lyrics of several California groups have become increasingly violent since the mid-nineties, and some drug cartels even commission songs to be recorded.

Narcocorridos remain popular on both sides of the border, especially—like gangster rap—with young people. Aside from the attractiveness of the themes Wald describes—"beautiful women, powerful friends, the hottest guns, the finest cocaine, drug shipments sneaked across the border past stupid gringos, brave men shot and friends avenged"—censorship leads to creating a taste for forbidden fruit. Ragland points out that the narcocorridos are recorded on independent record labels that are not affiliated with the four multinational record labels (EMI, Sony-BMG, Universal, and Warner Music).

These smaller labels, including the relatively large Fonovisa (a division of the Spanish-language TV network Fonovision) in San Jose, Haciendas and Freddy Records in Corpus Christi, Texas, and Joey International in San Antonio, are less subject to censorship and more flexible in their operations than the major labels.

Besides the artists already mentioned, Pedro Rivera, Jan Rivera, Grupo Exterminador, Los Huracanes del Norte, and Originales de San Juan are among a dozen or so artists who specialize in the genre. Some of these groups focus on *narcocorridos* as their bread and butter, while others perform music in other genres. Los Tigres del Norte, for example, also record songs about illegal immigrants, or *mojados*. *Narcocorridos* contain elements of protest, in the sense that they are about illegal drugs and sometimes border crossings, and they sometimes make fun of the border guards. The songs about *mojados*, however, are much more direct, and some of the ones that Ragland has translated include discussions of border guard brutality, the difficulties of pursuing a stable family life when the entire family has not emigrated, and the difficulties of working in the fields for low pay.

Rock En Espanol

Cultural theorist Josh Kun writes about this genre in his book *Audiotopia: Music, Race and America*. A number of groups have become popular on both sides of the border singing rock in Spanish, or in Spanglish, a hybrid of the two languages. Initially the Mexican rock bands all sang in English. By the mid-1980s and early 1990s, as Kun tells it, the major record labels began to see the commercial possibilities of rock sung in Spanish. Café Tacuba was a successful act in Mexico, and several Argentine acts emerged as well. The Grammy Awards added a Latin rock category in 1998, and MTV Latin America spread the gospel.

Sometimes this means embracing a very clear message. The Tijuana No band, based in both Tijuana and San Diego, wrote and performed some songs denouncing California's anti-immigrant legislation. One of their songs was titled "Gringo Ku Klux Klanes."

Mexican rock band Vecindad y Los Hijos del Quinto Patio wrote the song "Mojado" in 1989 about an illegal who suffocates while riding in a truck attempting to cross the border. Other songs aim for a broader appeal; some of the Mexican rock bands have rewritten the lyrics to such classic rock songs as "Hang On Sloopy" or "Fever," putting a fresh spin on the notion of cultural appropriation. The band Café Tacuba combines techno and punk music with traditional Mexican instrumentation. They sing original songs, and also covers of other material from various parts of South America. As Kun puts it, their music is "simultaneously local and global."

As the Mexican American population, the fastest growing ethnic group in the United States, becomes larger and larger, it is inevitable that America will become more of a bilingual society. Who knows what strange musical hybrids await us in the years to come?

Ry Cooder

It was difficult to decide where to place Ry Cooder in this book. On the one hand Ry is more of a musical revolutionary than a protest singer as such. In his early work his particular vision was integrating musical styles that had not previously been joined. He worked with musicians like San Antonio conjunto accordion player Flaco Jiminez and Hawaiian guitarist Gabby Pahinui, and joined them on slide guitar. He also served up an incredible mixture of Hawaiian music, blues, country music, and rhythm and blues, quarterbacking the whole experience with his own special vision.

During the 1980s Cooder successfully integrated his encyclopedic knowledge of musical styles into various film scores, notably *Paris, Texas*. In the nineties Cooder played with Indian and African musicians, inspiring a whole series of music experiments and combinations attempted by such musicians as David Lindley, Henry Kaiser, Bob Brozman, and Taj Mahal.

In 1997 Cooder went to Cuba and put together a group of eighteen older musicians whose music captured the ambiance of pre-Castro Cuba. The album was called *The Buena Vista Social Club,* and it sold over eight million copies around the world. The music was entirely nonpolitical, except in the sense that the U.S. government would not allow Cooder to return to do a sequel, because of its restrictions on Cuban travel and trade.

But it is Cooder's work from 2005 that places him in this section of the book. In 2005 he recorded a magnificent album called *Chavez Ravine.* The album commemorates the destruction of a Mexican American neighborhood that was bulldozed in the 1950s. The original intent was to build an experimental public housing facility, but in an ugly land grab the area was turned into the home of the Los Angeles Dodgers baseball team.

The album comes with a booklet that contains photos of the area and lyrics to the songs. Among them is a song about Frank Wilkinson, a man who had the vision to create a revolutionary home for the poor, to be designed by famous architect Richard Neutra. Instead Wilkinson was jailed after refusing to testify before the House Un-American Activities Committee. The song, which references J. Edgar Hoover, the head of the FBI, and also the Los Angeles Chief of Police, contains the lyric "Don't call me red."

Cooder's band on this album includes various Anglo and Mexican American musicians and songwriters, and all of the lyrics are printed in English and Spanish. There is a song cowritten by David Hidalgo of Los Lobos, several songs written and performed by Lalo Guerrero, and a vocal by Don Tosti. University of California, San Diego professor George Lipsitz sums up the value of this record with the comment that it may be "American studies'" greatest (and so far, only) hit.

Since the *Chavez Ravine* project, Cooder has written and recorded two other albums, *My Name Is Buddy,* and *I Flathead,* that comment on the history and "development" of California with a definite social conscience.

7

ROCK AND ROLL

Why Rock and Roll?

All of the other sections of this book are based on music with a political agenda. As a musical form, rock and roll does not have a specific socially conscious origin or agenda. However, I have placed it in is own chapter because the music itself presented many ingredients of a social revolution. Because I've tried to keep the focus on music that offers cultural commentary, the chapter excludes styles like house music, electronica, industrial music, goth music, and emo.

Post–World War II prosperity introduced a middle-class lifestyle to millions of Americans. Women were freed from some of their onerous household tasks by the widespread purchase of dishwashers, washing machines, and dryers. Many families acquired an additional car, so that the two-car family became a common feature of American family life. With the help of federal loans, many soldiers returning from the war were able to attend college and/or buy homes, often in the suburbs. Even without a college education, many blue-collar workers settled into the suburban lifestyle that was a product of this era, supported by high-paying jobs in such industries as steel or auto manufacturing.

The counterpoint to this era of peace and plenty was the fear generated by the Cold War. Russia became the enemy, and soon China joined it. Many people anticipated that another war would occur, and when Russia developed the capability of producing atomic and hydrogen bombs, these fears were further aggravated.

In 1949 communist North Korea invaded South Korea, and the United States sent troops to assist South Korea. When American soldiers crossed the Yalu River in North Korea, China entered the war on the North Korean side. The war ended in a stalemate, and the boundaries of the two countries were restored. Thirty-three thousand Americans died in the war, and many considered it the predecessor of a forthcoming epic struggle between communism and capitalism.

Teenagers

In earlier days teenagers had little or no discretionary income. Before World War II we had experienced a long-term depression, and young people had to scramble for nickels and dimes. It now became customary for teenagers to get allowances, and to work part-time. Some even earned enough money to drive old cars. With this increase in purchasing power, a new teenage culture developed, and it was only natural that this culture had its own definite musical preferences.

Rock and Roll History

Rock and roll represented a social revolution in its own right. It wasn't a revolution in a directly political way, but it was a sea change in the way that American popular music was created, how it was promoted, and, to some extent, even who bought it. Though there isn't general agreement on when rock and roll started, by the mid-1950s it had clearly become the engine that drove American popular music.

Just about everyone concurs that rhythm and blues was the most immediate source of rock and roll. Critics differ on the extent to which country music was an influence. Others cite gospel music vocal styles and a sense of abandon, and still others mention Latin rhythms, such as the famous Bo Diddley guitar riff.

In my opinion, too much is made of this sort of musical segregation. In the same way historians seem to have assumed that after the age of ten, there was no social contact between whites and blacks in the American South. It has become increasingly obvious that this is not an accurate assessment. Many white musicians were taken with the blues. Dock Boggs, Frank Hutchison, and the Allen Brothers were among the white musicians who sang and recorded blues during the 1920s and 1930s. Although we have tended to see the pre-bluegrass string band tradition as being white, in fact there were black fiddle and banjo players from slavery days. The Library of Congress recorded some of these musicians in the 1940s and 1950s, and their repertoire and playing styles were quite similar to what white bands were playing. Interviews with such country musicians as Bill Monroe, Merle Travis, and Hank Williams Sr. all cite specific black musicians as major influences. A number of country artists liked and to some extent listened to Blind Lemon Jefferson's blues recordings. The fingerpicking guitar styles of Etta Baker and Mississippi John Hurt are quite similar to the guitar techniques used by Merle Travis and Sam Magee. By the same token, quite a few black artists, like Muddy Waters, have revealed that they listened to country music on the radio while they were growing up. These interviews generally express a commonality between the two styles, reasoning that both country and blues songs "told a story."

The most obvious major difference between the white and black musicians is in their vocal stylings. Listen to Frank Hutchison's guitar work, and he might easily be a black blues player; his slide playing, bending of notes and picking styles are clearly influenced by various black blues artists. When you hear him sing, however, you know he is white. We could say the same thing in reverse about Mississippi John Hurt, Elizabeth Cotton, or John Jackson.

Alan Lomax created an entire theory, called *cantometrics,* based on the difference between white and black singing styles. Without going into all of the trappings of the theory, the fundamental difference is between singing with an open throat and singing with a closed throat. Aretha Franklin is an open-throat singer. Her sound is free, unconstrained, and capable of great volume. Many country singers, like Hank Williams Sr., sing or sang with a closed throat. The sound is parched, tense, and constricted.

Before rock and roll, a rhythm and blues hit, by definition, was one that was played on black radio stations and sold to black consumers who lived in black neighborhoods. In the early 1950s, however, artists like Ruth Brown and Big Joe Turner were singing songs that began to cross over to white audiences. In 1954 Turner recorded a song called "Shake, Rattle and Roll." It became a major rhythm and blues hit, but is also generally considered the first real rock record.

The first all-market rock and roll hit was recorded by a Michigan native, Bill Haley, whose own musical preference was for Western swing, the cowboy-music-with-horns style popularized by Bob Wills. The guitars represented the country-and-western element of the sound. After hitting pay dirt with the tune "Crazy Man Crazy," Haley signed with Decca, one of the three major U.S. record labels, in 1953. Haley's record producer was jazz buff Milt Gabler, who tried to model the sound of the Comets after the sound of Louis Jordan's Tympany Five. Jordan's band had had a number of big R&B hits that crossed over to the mainstream, and Gabler had produced some of Jordan's records in the 1940s.

Inadvertently starting a trend that continued for some years, Haley's version of the Turner song cleaned up the mildly bawdy lyrics to make them more radio-friendly. The original lyric referred to dresses that the sun comes shining through, worn by the heroine who "ain't no child no more." The lyric about the sexy dress got transformed into a more innocuous line about wearing dresses and having nicely styled hair, though the singer still ventured to say, "you look so warm, but your heart is cold as ice." The end line about not being a child becomes "I can look at you, but you don't love me no more."

"Rock Around the Clock"

"Shake, Rattle, and Roll" was a major hit, but it did not usher in any sort of musical revolution. Haley's follow-up record, "Rock Around the Clock," released in 1954, was a different story. The song initially didn't go anywhere, but it was included in the film *Blackboard Jungle*. This hit movie portrayed juvenile delinquency and teenaged thugs in a high school. The record went on to become a rock and roll classic, and sold over a million and a half copies. More importantly, it established an identity for rock and roll. That identity was focused on opposition to parents, and (relatively) innocent gang-like behavior. There is an unforgettable scene in the movie where the kids destroy the record collection of a jazz-loving teacher, who has brought in his rare 78 rpm records to play for the class. It was almost like a message to parents that their old swing records were now passé, because there was a new musical kid in town.

It was an anomaly that Haley's band, a group of club musicians, all thirty-ish, would be involved with that image. Haley himself was 29 and was losing his hair. Within a short time Haley himself had become an oldies relic. His mantle, however, was about to be taken over by one Elvis Aaron Presley and the Sun Records hit-making machinery in Memphis, Tennessee.

Elvis and Sun Records

Sam Phillips was a Memphis entrepreneur who opened a recording studio called the Memphis Recording Service in 1950. There were two aspects to the business. On the one hand Phillips rented it out to anyone who wanted to make a demo recording of a song. On the other, he recorded a number of black blues artists, including B. B. King and Howlin' Wolf. He produced the records and then leased them to various labels, including the Chess label in Chicago. Phillips produced some R&B hits, including Little Walter's "Juke" and Jackie Brenston's "Rocket 88." (Some people describe the Brenston record as the first real rock and roll record.)

In 1952 Phillips decided to form his own label, Sun Records. He had some success, again in the world of R&B, but in the back of his mind was another plan. Philips believed that R&B would always be a limited market, but that if he could find a "white boy that could sing the blues," the opportunities would be boundless.

In 1953 that white boy walked in to make a record for his mother's birthday. His name was Elvis Presley. In 1954 Phillips recorded Presley singing a blues song by Arthur "Big Boy" Crudup called "That's All Right Mama," backed by Bill Monroe's Blue Moon of Kentucky.

The story of Elvis Presley's successes has been told many times in many other places. Suffice it to say that rock and roll was now on its way to dominating the American popular music scene, and Sun quit recording black artists and instead focused on "rockabilly," the

Elvis Presley

fusion of rock and hillbilly music. Among its successful artists were Johnny Cash (who was not then considered a country singer), Jerry Lee Lewis, Carl Perkins, and Charlie Rich.

More than this, Elvis brought a social revolution in his wake. His hairstyle, his dance movements, and his love for African American music added up to a package that made American suburban parents uncomfortable. When "Elvis the pelvis" appeared on the Ed Sullivan show, his dancing was considered so provocative that the camera only showed him from the waist up. Eventually, after a string of hit records (RCA Records had bought his contract from Sun), Elvis became increasingly involved in the movie world, and in performances in Las Vegas. Still, he was the trailblazer, the great representative of crossover, who had absorbed black music and translated it to white audiences.

Rock and White Supremacy

The idea of "race mixing" was an anathema to the white supremacists who held sway in many areas of the South. Asa Earl (Ace) Carter, the head of the Alabama White Citizens Council, denounced rock and roll as "sensuous Negro music." He claimed that it was endangering the moral structure of Christianity.

Since the great racist fear was that white women would be attracted to rapacious black studs, the idea of mixed-race dancing, or even of teenagers bowing at the feet of black artists, was frightening. To cite just one instance from personal experience, in 1963 I was playing in a pop-folk band called the Journeymen. We attended a fraternity party after performing at Hampton-Sydney College in Virginia. A black pop R&B group was performing, and the singer–piano player was singing Smoky Robinson's song "You Really Got a Hold on Me." A young blonde coed was leaning over the piano staring at the musician, displaying considerable flesh for all to see. The tension in the room was palpable. I literally began to get sick, because I was afraid for the singer's life and safety. I left the room, not wanting to see how the situation would unfold.

Little Richard

Little Richard, as wild a performer as he was, consciously presented himself as androgynous or gay so as to avoid such difficulties. But
what was a white supremacist to make of Chuck Berry, flagellating
his guitar and doing his famous dance, the duck walk? To complicate
matters, disc jockeys didn't always know which artists were black and
which were white. When Elvis was first played on Memphis radio,
the disc jockey had to make a point of telling his listeners that Elvis
had graduated from the all-white Humes High School. In another
odd turnaround, when Buddy Holly and the Crickets were hired

at the Apollo Theater in the neighborhood of Harlem in New York City, the theater managers were astounded to find that the whole band was white, not black.

Cover Records

One of the major controversies in rock and roll was the re-recording of R&B records by white artists. Pat Boone is generally cast as the villain in this particular scenario for his covers of songs by such artists as Little Richard. One of the most outrageous figures in early rock and roll, Richard was a dynamic performer, screaming and jumping around on stage while singing songs like "Tutti Frutti" and "Long Tall Sally." David Somerville was the leader of the Diamonds, a white doo-wop group. He told my friend John Phillips that they had appeared at the Paramount Theater on a show with Little Richard, and one day they'd walked in after taking a break to find Richard singing "Tutti Frutti." Instead of his usual nonsense lyrics, Richard improvised the words "ram-a-lam-a-ding-dong fuck Pat Boone." The Diamonds were rolling on the floor laughing at this concise analysis of Pat Boone's cover record of his song.

The ingredients of these cover records generally involved several revisions of the original versions:

The new versions were usually faster than the originals.

The lyrics sung by some of the R&B artists, like Little Richard, were difficult to understand. The cover records were sung "white," with the words clearly audible.

The original R&B arrangements usually had a strong accent on the second and fourth beats of the measure. This accent was reduced or eliminated in the white cover versions.

The lyrics were rewritten to avoid any bawdy sentiments, and to correspond better to what record companies believed white teenagers wanted to hear.

The original recordings were often on minor labels, while the cover records were on more established major labels or strong independent ones. Because the majors had better distribution, the cover records were available in many more markets than the originals were.

Among the people who recorded cover records were Bill Haley, Elvis Presley, Theresa Brewer, Georgia Gibbs, the Diamonds, the Crew Cuts, and, of course, the leading "offender," Pat Boone.

Many of the R&B songs that were covered by white artists had been hits on the R&B charts, but had not crossed over into pop to any great degree. The white cover records often did become major pop hits, as was the case with Pat Boone's cover of Ivory Joe Hunter's "I Almost Lost My Mind." Naturally the original artists resented not getting national attention, but in the case of those who had written their own songs, like Little Richard, at least they enjoyed significant royalties as songwriters. Those who did not write their own songs were out of luck.

Syd Nathan established King Records in 1945. His notion of cover records was different from the one described above. Nathan liked to buy songs outright, so that he owned not only the publishing rights but also the songwriter's share. He would make two recordings of the same song, one a country version, the other an R&B version. For some reason King was more successful making R&B versions of country hits. Nathan also was unique in hiring music arranger Henry Glover as a record producer. Glover had both country and R&B hits, which was revolutionary in its day and would even be unusual in today's record marketplace.

Not all cover records crossed racial lines. Mitch Miller, who was the head of Artist & Repertoire at Columbia Records for many years, recorded Tony Bennett singing the Hank Williams song "Cold, Cold Heart" in 1951. Still, Ray Charles's hit crossover album of country and western songs, released eleven years later, was inevitably more surprising in addition to being more successful (three hit singles).

"The Sound of Young America"

The sixties saw the emergence of Motown Records in Detroit. Whereas Atlantic Records had focused on recording black musicians with relatively few musical compromises, Motown consciously wanted to use black artists to make records for teenagers of all colors. Motown used a production system that made the producers and songwriters the stars. Instrumental tracks were recorded, and then various artists competed until the producers decided that a particular artist was best suited for a specific song. Motown's records carried the slogan "The Sound of Young America."

A number of television dance parties for teenagers emerged in the late fifties and early sixties. The artists would come in and either lip-synch or perform the songs to teenagers who would dance to the music. Dick Clark's *American Bandstand* show had very few black teenagers in attendance, and white and black couples did not cross the color line in their choice of dance partners. In Los Angeles, disc jockey Dick "Huggy Boy" Hugg presided over radio and television shows where he did not observe the color line with teenage dancers. Of course, Huggy Boy didn't have a network show.

Politics of the Sixties

John F. Kennedy was elected president in the midst of the folk revival. Along with him he brought an atmosphere of hope and possibility. The civil rights movement was in flower, and seemed to be poised to make some real changes in the United States. Kennedy heavily promoted the Peace Corps, an idealistic attempt to send young Americans abroad to help Third World countries. The elephant in the room was still the Cold War. France had surrendered to the North Vietnamese, but under Kennedy America started to send military advisers to assist the government of South Vietnam.

After Kennedy was assassinated June 1963, new president Lyndon Johnson helped to get strong civil rights legislation through

John F. Kennedy and Jaqueline Kennedy

Congress. He promoted the "Great Society," an attempt to bring economic and political equity to all. However Johnson heavily supported the war in Vietnam, and America soon found itself fighting a major war against a minor power. All of the good will that Kennedy had created and that Johnson had capitalized upon went up in smoke. At first most Americans supported the war, but as soldiers began dying in large numbers and little progress was made, tremendous resistance developed against the war.

Peace, Love, Flowers, Drugs, and Music

After the end of the folk revival in and the invasion of English rock groups in the mid-sixties, a number of American folk-rock groups emerged, especially in California. The Byrds, the Mamas and the Papas, and the Buffalo Springfield were among the Los Angeles bands of the mid to late sixties. San Francisco contributed a number of psychedelic rockers, including the Jefferson Airplane, Janis Joplin & Big Brother & the Holding Company, and the Grateful Dead.

Most of the bands of the day were involved in various kinds of drugs. LSD had become the drug of choice, and the so-called hippie movement created large numbers of "long-haired freaks" who spread out from San Francisco to many American cities. A literally communal culture developed, and large numbers of long-haired freaks and earth mothers lived on communes where they shared food, drugs, and just about everything else. There was a real and serious rift in American culture between the hippies and the straights.

The folk-rock musicians were either hippies or aligned with the hippie culture. Their music and their politics were radical by American pop standards. The Grateful Dead did extremely long shows and thought nothing of playing a tune for twenty minutes or more. The Airplane used drug references openly in their songs. Janis Joplin gloried in her reputation as being a "wild chick" who loved alcohol, drugs and sex, and it seemed as though all of the bands were indulging not only in marijuana but in other drugs as well. The most socially activist band was Country Joe (McDonald) and the Fish, who developed a chant as part of their "Fixin' to Die Rag," that had the audience joining in to spell the infamous F word. "For What It's Worth," written by Stephen Stills for the Buffalo Springfield in 1967, became known as an anti-Vietnam protest song, and has been used in various movies. A close examination of the lyrics, however (which are actually about a fairly meaningless teenage riot on Hollywood's Sunset Strip), reveals that Stills is not taking sides in the song. For example, he describes the teenagers as carrying signs that say "hooray for our side." Even so, it's not hard to sense defiance in the song, as when the singer tells the listener that if you step out of line the man (i.e., the police) will come and take you away.

Crosby, Stills and Nash, later joined periodically by Neil Young, were involved with political and social issues. Graham Nash wrote the song titled "Chicago" about police brutality during a Vietnam War protest at the Democratic Party convention of 1968. The song also protested the subsequent trial of eight of the demonstrators, including Bobby Seale and Abbie Hoffman. It asks the listener to come to Chicago to protest the trial, and includes such lyrics as "Let a man live his own life / Rules and regulations, who needs them?" Neil Young wrote the song "Ohio" about a tragic event at Kent State University in Ohio when four students who were protesting the war were gunned down by National Guards. Unlike Nash's song, "Ohio" is specific in assigning blame, with such lyrics as "Tin soldiers and Nixon's coming," and "This summer I hear the drumming, Four dead in Ohio."

Although both songs got some airplay, neither joined the group's major hits, such as their rendition of Joni Mitchell's song "Woodstock." Young's song was used in peace rallies. He revived it in 1989 after the Chinese student massacre at Tiananmen Square.

Many books have been devoted to the music of the sixties. For our purposes we can simply say that the mid to late sixties was the most political time for rock music. The mood in the country was negative and defiant. The assassinations of Malcolm X, John F. Kennedy, Martin Luther King, and Robert Kennedy also led to a climate of violence, especially in the urban ghettos. After King's assassination, there were race riots in a number of American cities, and a strong impetus developed to remove whites from any position of authority in civil rights organizations.

The defining musical events of the era were easily the Woodstock festival in upstate New York and the December 1969 Rolling Stones concert in Altamont, California. Though they took place only months apart at the end of the decade, they exemplified, respectively, the hopefulness of the sixties and the dark new mood of the seventies.

The Woodstock festival took place on August 15, 1969. It was somewhat modeled after the Monterey Pop festival, held two years earlier in Monterey, California. Hundreds of thousands of people gathered on a farm near Woodstock, New York, and listened to the music of numerous rock and folk-rock favorites for three days. The atmosphere was generally peaceful, if the living conditions were uncomfortable, with a shortage of food and water and an excess of mud.

On December 6, 1969 the Rolling Stones headlined a concert in Altamont, California that featured another set of rock idols. The Stones made the unfortunate decision to use the Hells Angels motorcycle gang as their security, and violence on and off stage erupted, including the murder of a young black student named Meredith Hunter. "Bad" drugs were prevalent, and the general atmosphere was exactly opposite to what had taken place at Woodstock. The era of peace, love, flowers, and psychedelic drugs had come to an end.

Peace, Love, and Disillusionment

In August of 1972 Republican operatives authorized by President Nixon's staff broke into Democratic National Headquarters in Washington, D.C. This became known as the Watergate scandal, named after the commercial and housing complex where the Democrats had their offices.

Initially President Nixon denied any responsibility for this occurrence, but over a two-year period investigations by the U.S. Congress and a special prosecutor proved that the break-ins had been at Nixon's instigation. Impeachment proceedings began, and Nixon resigned on August 9, 1974.

Shortly after the Watergate break-in occurred, Defense Secretary Henry Kissinger signed a treaty with the North Vietnamese, and the United States withdrew all of its troops from Vietnam.

After the President had been revealed to be involved in what was basically a criminal action, a strong climate of cynicism prevailed in the United States. With the president totally discredited, and the war over, liberals and radicals withdrew from politics. To many it seemed that there was no longer anything left to agitate for, or to fight against.

Disco

Folk-rock had worn itself out, and although groups like the Grateful Dead and the Jefferson Airplane retained some popularity, the San Francisco sound was no longer the music that was selling. Instead, competing genres fought for the attention of the rock audience.

Disco was a dance-oriented style that became popular in gay clubs on Fire Island and in San Francisco. In disco the producer was king, and electronic drum machines, synthesizers and samplers could be manipulated by producers without the presence of session musicians. Artists like Donna Summer, the Silver Convention, and the Village People were pawns, and in the latter case even creations, of their producers. The Village People were an all-gay integrated group whose songs made fun of their own gay identity. A song like YMCA traded on the well-known "underground" notion that the Y could function as a pickup place for homosexuals.

Not all of the disco groups were electronic. K.C. and the Sunshine Band and Chic were live bands who were involved in writing their own songs and producing their own records.

Disco songs had no social message beyond "shake your booty." In a sense disco represented a revolt against message songs. In songs like "Rock the Boat Baby" the lyrics simply served to extend the length of what were essentially opportunities for dancing.

The social importance of disco was that it was the first open recognition in rock and roll that there was a gay community, and that music could be tailored for it in the same way that it could be crafted for long-haired teenagers.

The height of the disco craze occurred with the 1977 release of the movie *Saturday Night Fever*. The film featured a soundtrack by the falsetto-loving Australian group the Bee Gees. Songs like "Staying Alive" seem almost comical today, but they were great dance tracks. Another foreign group, Abba, achieved worldwide popularity, but less notoriety in the United States. Their lyrics were similarly innocuous.

On June 12, 1979 a Chicago disc jockey led a "disco sucks" rally as part of a baseball game at Comiskey Park. Fans stormed the field as records were destroyed, and there was such a furore that the baseball game had to be canceled. Many observers regard this as the moment disco began to phase out.

Punk

If disco was slick and techno-oriented, punk was the ultimate in raw and simple music. Punk's patron saints were the New York band the Ramones and England's Sex Pistols. The whole idea was that anyone could play or sing, because the music was so simple. What made it "punk" was *attitude*.

The dancing that accompanied punk music was as far as possible from slick disco dancing. People jumped up and down and flailed

The Ramones

their arms in a style known as pogoing (because they looked like pogo sticks). Disco musicians dressed up and looked professional in a glittery sort of way, but punk rockers wore cast-off old clothes and banged their instruments around. Mohawk hair styles appeared, with hair often dyed in multicolored hues.

Rock has always had a component of existing to infuriate both parents and middle-class people, and punk accomplished both of those ends. The musicians represented a new generation of rockers and audiences who were beginning to regard the Who and the Rolling Stones as middle-aged and stodgy.

The Politics of Punk

The lyrics of disco songs had no message at all. The lyrics of punk were another story. The ideology that went with the music was nihilism. Nothing mattered, the world was terrible, and the establishment and the middle class were the enemy. So were organized musical forms. Some of the bands, like the B52s, frankly acknowledged that they were playing professionally without knowing how to play. As crazy as this sounds, there was something refreshing about their attitude, which contrasted with the slickness (and stiffness) of such bands as Crosby, Stills and Nash (less so when Neil Young was involved), or Emerson, Lake and Palmer.

Inevitably, punk's lack of vision led to modifications of the idiom's lyrics in bands that believe in political activism, rather than nihilism. In 1979, two members of the new group the Dead Kennedys started their own label, Alternative Tentacles, and the band recorded songs criticizing United States imperialism and the moral majority. As an extension of his ideology, band leader Jello Biafra ran for mayor of San Francisco in 1979, finishing fourth out of ten candidates, and received 4 percent of the vote.

In 1986 the band was charged with distributing material harmful to minors, because one of their albums had a cover painting by Swiss surrealistic artist H. R. Giger that the police regarded as being obscene. The case ultimately ended with a hung jury.

Considering the band's supposedly high-minded convictions, the circumstances of their eventual breakup in 1998 were bizarre. The other band members claimed that Biafra's record label hadn't paid them appropriate royalties, while Biafra contended that the reason for the dispute was that he had refused to license the bands' songs for a Levi-Strauss commercial.

Hard Core

Punk wasn't musically powerful enough to meet the requirements of some American bands, so they revved up the tempo and the volumes in a style that became known as "hard core." Bands like Black Flag, Husker Du, and Sonic Youth positioned themselves outside the mainstream of middle-class American values. Part of the culture of hard core was slam dancing, a violent form of dancing where the dancers actually slammed into each other's bodies. This bizarre custom sometimes resulted in physical injuries. It was representative of the macho, torn-T-shirt-and-big-biceps attitude that was part of hard core.

Greg Ginn, who started Black Flag, also founded a record label called SST to promote hard core. When the label started it had a sort of communal mystique, but according to Michael Azzerad's book *Our Band Could Be Your Life,* bands complained that the label didn't pay proper royalties, including their most popular band, Sonic Youth, who left SST in 1988 after a three-year tenure.

Straight Edge vs. Punk's Underbelly

Many books have been written that provide encyclopedic detail on punk and hard core music. From the standpoint of this book, the most socially conscious music and ideology grew out of the straight edge movement, centering around Ian McKaye. MacKaye had established his reputation with the band Minor Threat, but when he formed Fugazi in 1987 he had more in mind than writing and recording music. He established that all shows would be open to people of any age group, because he felt that many rock shows discriminated against teenagers. He also instituted a uniform $5 fee for tickets in order to make the shows as affordable as possible. MacKaye also formed his own record label, Dischord. He sold records at concerts and by mail, but consciously avoided the normal channels of record distribution and promotion. The band also actively promoted the avoidance of drugs and alcohol.

In the song "Merchandise" Fugazi sings, "Merchandise keeps us in line / Common sense says it's by design." In "Suggestion," MacKaye takes on the role of a sexually harassed woman, asking, "Why can't I walk down the street free of suggestion? / Is my body the only trait in the eyes of men? The song "Cashout" concerns a family that is evicted from their home. One of the lyric lines is "Development wants this neighborhood."

In a sense MacKaye was the first, and virtually the only rock artist whose politics and music entirely matched one another. Although other artists have created their own record labels, they have not limited their ticket prices or entirely controlled their own distribution apparatus as a conscious choice.

Because of Fugazi's insistence on minimal ticket prices, very few promoters are interested in presenting their shows. The band seeks out alternative spaces, like basements or community centers, and they often stay with the people who are presenting the shows.

There are other people in the world of rock and roll who have taken radical political stances, but I am hard-pressed to name anyone who has walked the talk to the extent that MacKaye and Fugazi have done.

On the other hand, though the prevailing image of punk identifies it with the political left wing, Reebee Garafalo's book *Rockin' Out: Popular Music in the U.S.A.* points out that there was a sort of underbelly of the idiom. A number of punk groups used Nazi memorabilia in their stage attire, and the band the Eels used lyrics in their song Spin Age Blasters that were taken from a Nazi Party display. Garafalo further adds that some punk uses of fascist symbols may have been intended as irony, but that the audience may not have received these messages in that spirit.

Heavy Metal and Eighties Rock

During the early seventies, British groups like Led Zeppelin and Deep Purple turned up the volume and created the style that became known as heavy metal. In the late seventies, a group of British bands like Iron Maiden and Def Leppard, and an Australian band called AC/DC, toured the United States, and American hard rock bands like Aerosmith, KISS, and Ted Nugent all had chart-making albums. In the eighties, American band Van Halen became a major hit-maker, and other bands like Motley Crue entered the fray. Even more extreme metal bands like Metallica and Megadeth escalated the volume and tempo to create offshoots of the style, known as speed metal, thrash, and death metal.

Metal Themes

Like hard core, metal was a musical form that was ultra-masculine and violent, and it consciously excluded all but the most determined women from the idiom. The same nihilism that had characterized punk was in play, but the lyrics had become even darker than before.

Some of the bands did exhibit environmental concerns, but presented them in the context of a civilization that is doomed. Metallica's song "Blackened" describes the death of Mother Earth and ends with the lyric "Earth dies." Similarly, their song "And Justice for All" paints a hopeless picture, with such lyrics as "Hammer of Justice crushes you" and "Nothing can save you."

Virtually all of the songs by the thrash metal band Testament reflect an apocalyptic vision of the future, with the destruction of civilization coming about through man's despoiling the environment. The band started in 1983, writing political songs like "Over the Wall," "So Many Lies," "Reign of Terror," "Raging Waters," "Greenhouse Effect," "First Strike Is Deadly," and "Nuclear Assault," and is still active today. The band Nuclear Assault's song "Inherited Hell" takes a similar view, describing the end of the world "not far away."

Some metal musicians, such as guitars Randy Rhoades and Yngwie Malmsteen, were classically trained, and would unleash long classical guitar solos amidst the loud, heavy metal assaults. Certain bands, like Queensryche, veered into art music, while others, like Bon Jovi, quieted down and achieved mass popularity with three-minute pop songs.

One of the most successful bands was Guns N' Roses. Its leader, Axl Rose, was notoriously difficult to deal with. He recently released an album with a new band that he had been working on for fourteen years! Some of Rose's work crosses over into what I call the music of hate, which will be discussed in the next chapter.

Professor Harris M. Berger did extensive research on heavy metal music in Akron, Ohio, described in his book *Metal, Rock, and Jazz: Perception and the Phenomenology of Musical Experience,* published in 1999. According to Berger, hardcore music has both left- and right-wing political factions, while death metal music expresses little interest in politics. Death metal has some Satanic adherents as well. Berger's primary informant on metal, Dann Saladin, was

Kurt Cobain

essentially apolitical but open-minded, and pointed out to Berger that some members of the metal audience also attended punk shows.

Grunge

Grunge music is the term that has been used to describe the exploding Seattle rock scene of the late eighties and early nineties. A string of bands, including Soundgarden, Nirvana, Alice in Chains, and Pearl Jam all achieved national popularity at about the same time. Nirvana was the poster child for "grunge." The band wore flannel shirts (connoting the Northwest working class) and played punk-flavored music with an antiestablishment attitude. Although Kurt Cobain wrote most of the songs and was the lead singer, it was bass player Krist Novoselic who was the most political voice in the group, appearing at rallies and even considering a run for political office.

Pearl Jam was the most openly political of the Seattle bands. Lead singer and lyricist Eddie Vedder cavorted around stage destroying a George Bush mask prior to the 2008 election. The song "Army Reserve" evokes the anxieties of a wife and mother whose husband is fighting in a war. "Cropduster" speaks to environmental concerns. One part of the lyric says, "Daddy's gone up in flames," and another lyric warns, "This ain't no book you can close / When the big lie hits your eye." The song "Education" is a philosophical statement, "questioning my education."

There's a bit of Fugazi in Pearl Jam. In 1994 they sued Ticketmaster, attempting to limit the price of tickets to their shows to $20, with a $1.80 service charge for Ticketmaster. Pearl Jam lost this antimonopoly suit, and for four years attempted to avoid using Ticketmaster's services. At the end of that time the band capitulated, and resumed using the ticketing organization.

A Pearl Jam concert tour that took place in the nineties illustrates an important factor in any discussion of music and politics; the sheer power of fame. I no longer remember where I read this story, but I believe that it was in some sort of promotional piece for Native American artist Bill Miller, who opened for Pearl Jam on the tour.

At the first show that Miller played with the band, he was greeted with total indifference by the audience. He had looked forward to doing the shows, because obviously Pearl Jam played to much larger audiences than Miller usually did, and came off the stage extremely depressed, wondering how he'd be able to stomach night after night of this over the course of the tour.

Because he wasn't especially familiar with Pearl Jam, he didn't recognize the person who came up to him as he left the stage: the band's lead singer, Eddie Vedder. Vedder told Miller how much he had enjoyed the show, and how important he felt it was for the audience to understand Miller's message.

The next night Vedder came out on stage and introduced Bill Miller. He told the audience that he wanted them to listen carefully to Miller, because he had some important things to tell them. The audience listened with rapt attention and gave Miller a tremendous ovation when he finished his show.

Obviously, what Miller had to say was not more important on the second night than it had been the night before. But at the second show he had received an endorsement from the person the audience most wanted to see. To influence an audience's ideas, a musician must get their attention. Pearl Jam had that ability thanks to their successes and popular image. For Miller to reach that status, he had to borrow from Pearl Jam's credibility. The importance and even the accuracy of his message were beside the point.

Jokers in the Deck

Alice Cooper and Marilyn Manson represent the glam aspect of rock and roll. Cooper is actually a golf-playing Republican, but for years he drove middle-class parents crazy with his overwrought makeup and over-the-top stage act featuring guillotines, electric chairs, and cutting off the heads of baby dolls. At one point journalist Bob Greene joined the band on tour, dressed as Santa Claus, and each night the band would "kill" him on stage.

What some feared and denounced as being un-American and evil was essentially just another night in show business for the act. The lyrics of Alice's songs are innocuous, with such sentiments as "Give the kid a break." Even the famous song "School's Out" simply states that a school has been blown up. Since this was some thirty years before the Columbine High School tragedy, it is difficult to believe that anyone took this lyric seriously.

Marilyn Manson is another story. His very name is a fusion of movie star Marilyn Monroe and psychotic murderer Charles Manson. If Cooper's lyrics are innocuous, Manson's tend to be vitriolic. The song "White Trash" mentions porn, oral sex, and date rape, and contains the line "Why are all the 'niggers' in the unemployment line?" In "Rock 'n' Roll Nigger" Manson refers to himself as the antichrist, and claims that outside of society is the place that he wants to be. The song "Mutilation Is the Most Sincere Form of Flattery" features liberal use of the F-word. Manson's songs periodically wax pseudo-philosophical, as in the lines from Mutilation: "The young get less bolder / The legends get older."

In 1999 two teenage high school students attacked Columbine High School in suburban Denver, killing twelve students and a teacher, and wounding twenty-three other students. Initially it was believed that Marilyn Manson was one of the two killers' favorite artists, but it turned out that a German metal band called Rammstein was their favorite. Manson had to cancel three concerts after the killings.

The issue of how music influences teenage behavior often comes up with rap and various forms of heavy metal. There have been several unsuccessful lawsuits filed as a result of suicides which parents tried to connect with recordings of various rock artists. None have been successful.

Mainstream Artists

There are a number of popular rock artists who periodically have written songs that raise social issues. Singer-songwriter-pianist Billy Joel wrote the song "Allentown" in 1981. The song has a simple and straightforward theme: the decline of the American industrial plant, and the loss of economic opportunities that Americans anticipated.

In 1981 Joel wrote "Goodnight Saigon." This is a powerful antiwar song that does not lay blame, but simply describes the hopelessness of the Vietnam War. The lyrics are touching, with such lines as "Remember Charlie, remember Baker, / They left their childhood on every acre." Joel's 1989 song "The Downeaster 'Alexa'" is to the fishing trade as Allentown was to factory life. One of the lyrics proclaims, "There ain't no island left for islanders like me."

In the same year Joe wrote "We Didn't Start the Fire." This song is a recitation of world leaders and pop heroes, with the hook line "We didn't start the fire, / No we didn't light it, / But we tried to fight it." Yet another 1989 song, "Leningrad I," is sung from the standpoint of Joel meeting a clown in Leningrad, with both of them understanding the futility and senselessness of the Cold War.

John Mellencamp made his original reputation as a chronicler of teenage romances, notably his song "Jack and Diane." By the mid-eighties he was bemoaning the decline of the American farmer. His song "Rain on the Scarecrow" describes a man losing his farm, and expresses his regrets that he won't be passing his legacy on to his children. In the song "Small Town" Mellencamp pays tribute to the closeness of friends and family that is part of living in a small town.

Randy Newman uses satire and sarcasm to make his political points. The song "Rednecks" satirizes not only the good old boys, with lines like "We're too dumb to make it in no Northern town / And we're keepin' the niggers down," but Northern liberals, pointing out at the end that the Northern black man is free, "Yes he's free to be put in a cage." Newman's song "Sail Away" is like a commercial intended for prospective African slaves, describing how they will get to sing about Jesus and drink all day, eat watermelon and buckwheat cakes, and: "You'll be as happy as a monkey in a monkey tree."

Of course, the problem with satire is that the listener has to have a reasonably sophisticated sociopolitical background in order to grasp the joke. This is another way of saying that for the most part, Newman is preaching to the choir.

Rage Against the Machine

This band merits its own section for its unique fusion style, combining Zach de la Rocha's raps with aggressive hard rock music, and for its committed focus on political issues.

The roots of Rage Against the Machine go back to the sixties and the MC5 in Detroit. The MC5, which performed together from 1964 to 1972, became associated with radical agitator John Sinclair, who founded the White Panther Party as a sort of tribute to the Black Panthers. The band played at many radical rallies.

In addition to endorsing radical causes, Sinclair was a strong proponent of legalizing marijuana, and served several prison terms for possession of that drug. The band's Elektra album received notoriety and some success, partly based on the controversy whirling around their song "Kick Out the Jams." (The song used the word "motherfucker," and was therefore censored by radio and some record stores.) Eventually the band fell out with Sinclair, who was managing them, and the musicians gradually drifted apart from one another.

Like the MC5, Rage Against the Machine is almost entirely devoted to social protest. Songs like "Know Your Enemy" or "Freedom" protest against the police, the American political establishment, and public apathy. De la Rocha and guitarist Tom Morello are strong political activists, and have been involved in numerous protest demonstrations. Morello was jailed during a protest against clothing manufacturer Guess, and the band has demonstrated for Philadelphia prisoner Mumia Abu-Jamal and done benefit concerts for him. They also demonstrated at the 2008 Republican convention and the 2000 Democratic convention.

Rock and Roll and Race

Rock and roll was born from black music, but black musicians were not widely accepted in the idiom. In the early years of rock and roll Little Richard and Chuck Berry were the most visible musicians whose popularity crossed over into the white marketplace. In the sixties, Jimi Hendrix was another such exception, although he did not achieve broad popularity until he moved to England and played with a white bass player and drummer.

Arthur Lee had a psychedelic rock band in the sixties called Love that was signed by Elektra. Unfortunately for Lee, Elektra signed the

Doors at about the same time. Although Elektra president Jac Holz-man liked Lee's music, he was unwilling to do much to promote it, and the success of the Doors quickly eclipsed Love.

Sly and the Family Stone was an integrated band, with a black leader and producer and black female performers, that was quite popular in the late sixties and early seventies. The song "Family Af-fair" is a fascinating portrayal of ghetto life. The song concerns two sons, and a mother's love for each of them. One of them is "Some-body that just loves to learn," while the other is "Somebody we just love to burn." Sly's song "Don't Call Me Nigger, Whitey," is a sort of abridged version of Curtis Mayfield's "Choice of Colors." Both of them were written in 1969. Sly's song has a very brief lyric, in which two angry people confront one another and "neither could change a thing." Mayfield's lyric is a more complex one, not just depicting the conflict between the races but calling on people to get together. Although Mayfield's records did cross over, he was not specifically a crossover artist, as Sly and his group were.

In the mid-eighties, Prince took after Sly's example with a racially and gender-integrated band. His songs were oriented toward chal-lenging sexual mores rather than the political process, however.

Living Colour was a metal rock group of black musicians that fea-tured guitar player Vernon Reid. Reid was a cofounder of the Black Rock Coalition, a group of New York musicians. Mick Jagger himself produced their demo and helped them to get a deal at Epic Records in 1988. Before the band was able to get Jagger's help, major labels did not see a market for black rock and roll. A further example of this attitude occurred when moviemaker Spike Lee wanted to sign the black rock band Faith to his 40 Acres and a Mule label in 1992. The label was a subsidiary of Columbia Records, which refused to sign the band, despite Lee's interest.

The other notable black rock star is Lenny Kravitz, who has been making records since 1989. His music includes elements of funk, hard rock, folk, soul, and reggae, showing a versatility that has helped en-sure and sustain his popularity with a wide audience.

Women and Rock

Unfortunately, a good deal of rock and roll is macho nonsense that is based on the subordination of women in general. It has always been difficult for women in rock music to garner respect. In gender-integrated bands, women in rock were relegated to the "chick singer" role, even when they played an important role in songwriting and arranging, as was the case with Grace Slick of the Jefferson Airplane. And all-women bands like the Go-Go's and Fanny did not generally receive the publicity or credit, or enjoy the record sales of their male colleagues.

Madonna has been a major star for twenty-five years now. She has sustained her career through artfully manipulating the media, and through reinventing herself from album to album, using different producers to capitalize on different musical styles. She has also received an amazing amount of publicity, based on her "outrageous" styles of dress and behavior, and her role as the CEO of her own record Maverick Records. She has continually directed media attention to her career by working as an actress, writing children's books, and studying an obscure Jewish sect. Adopting African children has also kept her in the news. As such she has generated enormous interest among cultural studies students and professors, who provide a sort of intellectual ballast to a career that seemingly would be of little interest to academicians. For purposes of comparison, pop singer Barbra Streisand has always been regarded as a very strong woman, who has had a long musical career and a far more successful acting career than Madonna. She also has sold many records over the years. The difference, however, is that Streisand, who is sixty-seven, has made no efforts to appeal to the hip young-adult population, while Madonna, at the age of fifty-one, remains a subject of interest among people young enough to be her adult children. I am not aware of any college classes or cultural studies books that discuss Streisand.

Because rock and roll is an "in your face" kind of music, featuring loud volume and instrumental athleticism, there has been a tendency to exclude the majority of female players from its inner sanctum.

Lita Ford, the Wilson sisters of Heart, and Bonnie Raitt are among the few rock instrumentalists that are widely respected, as is guitarist Jennifer Batten, who played in Michael Jackson's band. Portland (Oregon) has a rock and roll camp for teenage girls, and the Daisy Rock Company is currently manufacturing guitars that are appropriately shaped for women. As Bob Dylan put it, in an entirely different context, "the times they are a changin'."

There have been a few notably successful indie-rock bands fronted by women, such as Sleater Kinney and Sonic Youth. Suzi Quatro, Pat Benatar, and Patti Smith are among significant female rock singers, and in the world of heavy metal Vixen and Lita Ford have achieved credibility. However, the majority of female singers, like Linda Ronstadt, Carole King, or Melissa Manchester, lean toward soft rock, or even pop rock. Although athletic and powerful pop singers like Aretha Franklin, Whitney Houston, and Mariah Carey are at the top of anyone's list of vocal stars, fewer female rock musicians can claim this distinction.

Rock and Roll Today

The problem in dealing with politics and rock and roll is that even the most nihilistic artists tend to be corrupted by commercials, TV placements, and the opportunity to make hit records and do stadium concerts. Many of the artists become involved with rather safe charity causes, like feeding the hungry. Possibly Willie Nelson's Farm Aid is the one cause where American artists can see direct results from their generosity, in terms of saving some small farms from extinction. The other charity events, like the Live Aid shows, are media events as much as they are political statements. But the essence of rock and roll, from its inception, is rebellious energy. Though rock and roll is saturated with genres and subgenres by now, each generation produces new artists that fit under this umbrella, who embody this timeless rebellion and reflect the issues of their specific period in time.

8

THE MUSIC OF HATE

Throughout this book we have seen songs that expressed various levels of prejudice against different ethnic or gender groups. I define the music of hate as being an expression of right-wing politics that would correspond to left-wing protest music. In other words, the music of hate wishes to exclude or even eliminate various groups. It expresses itself by making fun of the habits of other groups, and by criticizing their work ethic or intelligence. The most extreme version of this genre of music advocates violence against specific groups, notably, but not limited to, African Americans.

Most cultural studies scholars have a liberal or radical world view, and they have practiced avoidance behavior in ignoring the music of hate. The reader should be warned that the lyrics discussed in this chapter may be obnoxious, hateful or even intolerable to them. Ignorance of their existence is not a solution to the sentiments that govern them.

Anti-African American Music

Scholarly studies of openly racist music are rare. The outstanding study available is Henry Glassie's "Take That Night Train to Selma," a long portion of a book called *Folk Songs and Their Makers*. Glassie discovered a singer in upstate New York who regularly wrote songs that insulted African Americans. One of these songs, written about Martin Luther King, included the lyric

> The wops had Mussolini,
> And then they lost the war.
> And then they joined the niggers
> And they joined up with CORE.

CORE was the Congress of Racial Equality, a relatively radical civil rights group. Other songs by the same author refer to old stereotypes of blacks with razors, and jungle-style rapes. It is important to mention that Glassie's informant was not a professional singer. His music was confined to picnics and family gatherings. The only recordings of it were made by Glassie himself.

George Wallace, Lester Maddox, and Orville Faubus were all racist Southern governors who utilized country bands at their election rallies. A company called Rebel Records in Crowley, Louisiana used a "well-known country star," whatever that meant, to record songs that glorified the Ku Klux Klan and other racist groups. This singer, named Johnny Rebel, was featured on an album called *For Segregationists Only*. One of Johnny's lyrics urged:

> Move them niggers north
> If they don't like our Southern ways. . . .
> They're trying to start trouble by mixing up the races
> They'd be a whole lot better off by staying in their places.

Some of Johnny's other song titles include *Some Niggers Never Die* (*They Just Smell That Way*), and "Kajun Ku Klux Klan." In the latter song Klansmen torture a black man named "Levi Coon" after he demands service in a restaurant. According to an article in *X Magazine* in 2001 by Thilo Pieper, Johnny Rebel was a little-known Cajun musician named Clifford "Pee Wee" Trahan.

Klu Klux Klan

The most bizarre aspect of these recordings is that they were produced by Jay Miller, who had produced a number of black blues artists, including Lightnin' Slim and Slim Harpo. Macho country singer
David Allan Coe recorded a ditty called "Nigger-Lovin' Whore." It
contains the lyric "To think I'd ate the pussy where that big black
dick had been."

On the Arlington, Virginia Hatenanny label, Odis Cochran &
the Three Bigots recorded "Ship Those Niggers Back." This country
song portrays African Americans being shipped back to Africa. The
name Hatennany is obviously a play on the word hootenanny, which
was used by left-wing folk singers for their group concerts.

It is difficult to know how popular any of these records were, or
where they were sold. I also wonder how many folklorists encountered
material like the songs that Glassie collected, and chose to ignore them.

Neo-Nazi Music

Neo-Nazi music is semi-invisible until one goes to the Web. There
is also a 1999 publication called *Soundtracks to the White Revolution*

that outlines the various sub-genres of the music. Much of the music sic centers around a company called Resistance Records, currently based in West Virginia. The label, founded in Windsor, Ontario by George Burdi in 1993, became involved in various disputes with the U.S. and Canadian governments—with the former over tax issues, and with the latter over distributing materials that promote hatred. In 1999 Dr. William Pierce, the head of an American Nazi organization called the National Alliance, bought the company and moved it to West Virginia, apparently bringing an end to its legal troubles.

Pierce's goal was to use music popular with young people to draw them into the Nazi movement. The so-called skinhead movement started in England, and involved two competing factions, one a racist group, the other one favoring racial equality. The former movement was taken up in the United States, and Resistance was the leading record label for the music. The songs are variously anti-Semitic, homophobic, anti-African American, and anti-Latino.

According to the Soundtracks book, neo-Nazi music has also infiltrated death metal music, some electronic music, and even folk music. The book reprints a song by the band Mudoven that includes the lyric "Our job is done, the war is won / When all of you are killed." The band Intimidation One checks in with a song that begins with the lyric "Die, Jew. I hate you." It goes on to threaten violence and includes various obscene words as well. The focus on anti-Semitism is certainly part of the association with the neo-Nazi movement.

Resistance sells over a thousand CDs, as well as computer games, clothing, books, and other items. The games allow the player to choose an identity as a Nazi skinhead or a Klansman running through a ghetto and killing blacks and Latinos. After that is accomplished, the player goes into the subway system and murders Jews. *Soundtracks to the White Revolution* contains a list of twenty-five additional labels and record distributors, spread out across many American cities and states.

One scholar who did pay attention to neo-Nazi music was ethno-musicologist Henrietta Yurchenko, who died in 2007. In an undated article posted online, called "Skinhead Serena: The Songs of Neo-Nazis," Yurchenko quotes the band No Remorse: "We gotta get rid of the niggers and the Asians." Their song "Niggers Came Over" threatens, "Your wife and kids are going to the camps, / With all of the queers and the nigger-loving white slags." Christianity is also a target, Yurchenko notes, in the song "Let's Start a War," by Attack: "Or your whore Christianity / They will pay for your insanity." Another song by the same band, titled "Dirty Bitch (Feminist)," jeers, "You'll just keep fighting for equality / All you really want is a lesbian society."

As a result of the events that occurred before and during World War II, advocating Nazism or hate crimes is not an acceptable point of view in contemporary Germany. Neo-Nazi bands have been prosecuted for inciting hate crimes in many European countries, and particularly in Germany. Because the United States protects many aspects of freedom of speech under the First Amendment to the United States Constitution, the government does not prosecute speech as such.

The difference between neo-Nazi music and music that promotes stereotypes, or even promotes racism, is that neo-Nazi music is specifically designed to recruit young people into the Nazi movement. As such it encourages violence and racism as socially acceptable and even desirable.

In 1989 Axl Rose, of Guns N' Roses, wrote and recorded the song "One in a Million," which railed against "niggers" and "faggots." Axl responded to criticism of the song by saying that the viewpoint of the song's protagonist was not his own, and by pointing out that his guitarist, Slash, was half black. Axl's defense is remarkably similar to the way that gangster rap artists defend their lyrics that encourage violence and demean women.

Although the most virulent gangster rap is misogynist, and at times encourages violence against the police, one can only imagine what would happen if rap records called for the extermination of white people. This is exactly what neo-Nazi music does in its depiction of minority groups.

Currently we are living in a severely depressed economy. If unemployment increases, and economic opportunities diminish, it is certainly possible that disaffected young people could be drawn into the Nazi vortex through music.

9

THE TWO GULF WARS, 9/11/2001, AND AFGHANISTAN

The Gulf War of 1991

The first Gulf War came about as a result of Iraq occupying Kuwait in August of 1990. The United States immediately worked through the United Nations in an attempt to persuade Iraq to withdraw their troops from Kuwait. Efforts by the UN to bring about a peaceful solution failed, and ultimately a coalition army that consisted primarily of American and British troops, with additional troops from thirty-four nations, bombed and then invaded Iraq. The actual land invasion lasted less than two weeks, and on February 22, 1991 Iraq accepted a cease fire and both sides withdrew their troops.

Because of the swiftness of the war, and the small number of American casualties (148 died in combat, 453 were wounded), the war was generally popular in the United States. It also had the effect of restoring America's pride in its armed forces, a pride that had been deeply wounded in the Vietnam conflict.

Songs Supporting the First Gulf War

Because the war was so successful and was supported by a large number of troops from other countries, comparatively little

Hank Williams Jr.

music about the first Gulf War immediately emerged. Country music immediately registered their support of the war, notably in the revival of Lee Greenwood's 1983 song "God Bless the USA." The song, with the hook line "I'm proud to be an American," pays tribute to soldiers who have died defending America, and proclaims the singer's love for the country. The same song surfaced again after the terrorist attacks of September 11, 2001 and the subsequent second Gulf War, even though the song itself makes no reference to these wars.

Hank Williams Jr.'s contribution in support of the war was the song "Don't Give Us a Reason." Williams informs Iraq's then president Saddam Hussein that Americans are not afraid of him, and advises him not to give Americans a reason to "come gunning for you."

Songs Protesting the First Gulf War

Again, the war's short duration meant that most of the songs opposing the war didn't surface until after the fighting had ended. Such songs also faced an uphill battle for the ear of American listeners, since the war had been a popular one.

American Indian activist John Trudell's song "Bombs over Baghdad" was released in 1992. He refers to George H. Bush as "Queen George," and to business tycoons with government ties as "vampires": "Their violence works, it hardly ever fails." The song ends as it began, with the lines "Bombs over Baghdad, Dancers of Death."

Of course Trudell received very little airplay for this song, or, for that matter, for most of his political songs.

Erik and Rakim have long been regarded as among the most creative of all rap artists. In 1991 they released the song "Casualties of War." The song takes the position that America's enemy in the Gulf War was not clearly defined, and it compares the Gulf War to the conflict in Vietnam. It is a powerful lyric, with such lines as "Addicted to murder, send more body bags," and "Go to the Army, be all you can be. Another dead soldier?" Declaring, "The war is over, for now at least," they say they would go AWOL rather than serve again.

The Seattle band Pearl Jam recorded the song "Yellow Ledbetter," with lyrics by Eddie Vedder, their lead singer. Though Vedder has referred to it as an "antipatriotic song," it is less direct than the last two songs discussed. Vedder has referred to it as an "anti-patriotic song." During an August 7, 2008 performance, Vedder said that the song stemmed from a friend's experience. The friend had a brother who died in the Gulf War. When he received the letter, Vedder's friend went for a walk, and passed a house displaying an American flag. He gestured toward the flag, preparing to salute it, but the people on the porch glared at him, probably because of his unconventional appearance and dress. The song refers to the incident, but does not explain it. Because of Pearl Jam's popularity, and perhaps also because of the song's vagueness, it made it to #21 on the *Billboard* magazine Rock Tracks chart in 1994.

Folk and topical singer-songwriter Utah Phillips was so outraged by the first Gulf War that he released an entire album of antiwar songs, *Poems and Reminiscences* in 1991. The album was called *I've Got to Know*. In addition to adapting the Woody Guthrie song "I've Got to Know," he included poems by Sara Teasdale, Robert W. Service, and others. Phillips was himself a Korean War veteran who had become opposed to war. In the song "Yellow Ribbon," Phillips writes that he cannot be an accomplice to things that he knows are wrong. The song "Killing Ground" starts with "another young boy going on to the killing ground" and ends with the young soldier coming back in a coffin on a railroad car. In "The Violence Within," Phillips tells us that "no one is immune or safe from the slaughter."

In 1991 John Lennon's son Sean, together with John's widow, Yoko Ono, and Lenny Kravitz, re-wrote John's song "Give Peace a Chance." The new lyric invokes environmental issues as well as the Middle East conflict. It was recorded with a large choir that included numerous rock and rap stars. It was an amazing assembly, including Felix Cavaliere, Bruce Hornsby, Lenny Kravitz, Cyndi Lauper, M.C. Hammer, Michael McDonald, and Tom Petty. Nevertheless, the song doesn't seem to have received much airplay, or made much of an impact.

9/11

On September 11, 2001, Americans in the Midwest and the South awoke to see their television sets showing the twin towers of the World Trade Center in flames. New Yorkers experienced the event live, so to speak. Another attack took place on the Pentagon in Washington, D.C., and a fourth was thwarted by passengers on a hijacked airplane that crashed in rural Pennsylvania.

Almost three thousand people died in the attacks, which were executed by nineteen Islamist terrorists affiliated with the Al-Qaeda movement. Many emergency workers also died or were disabled by lung diseases acquired during the rescue operations. With the support of the United Nations, America sent a military force to Afghanistan to pursue Al Qaeda and the self-acknowledged mastermind of the attacks, Osama bin Laden. A number of other nations participated, as they had done in the first Gulf War.

Music and 9/11

The reaction to 9/11 in the United States, and for that matter in most of the world, was absolute shock and horror. Many of the songs that reacted to the attacks registered a more subdued and thoughtful nationalism than the jingoistic response that wars often create. Country artist Charlie Daniels' "This Ain't No Rag, It's a Flag," does revert to the former ideology, with its insistence on revenge. So does comedic songwriter Ray Stevens' "Osama Yo' Mama," which not only threatens destruction in kind but imagines Osama's mother saying, "I can't do a thing wit'cha, told ya dubyah's gonna git'cha." ("Dubyah" refers to then President George W. Bush, who was widely known by his middle initial.) On a more exalted level, Bruce Springsteen's song "The Rising" refers to "wheels of fire" and "bells ringing." He invokes religion with the lines "May their precious blood forever bind me / Lord as I stand before your fiery light." The song ends with a plea for all of us to get together and "come on up for the rising"—to get together and rise, united, to meet the challenges of this barbarous act.

Folksinger John McCutcheon wrote the song "Not in My Name," which points out that "It's the innocent who die for the crime." He reminds listeners of the pacifist trope that "An eye for an eye and a tooth for a tooth / Leaves the whole world toothless and blind."

Ground zero: Rudolph Giuliani and President George W. Bush

Country superstar Alan Jackson wrote and performed the song "Where Were You," invoking the notion that people would remember where they had been at the time of the explosion, in the same way that Americans over the age of fifty or so almost invariably can tell you where they were on the day that John F. Kennedy was assassinated. The singer asks not only where we were but how we responded, and humbly suggests that faith and love can be a force for good in the world. Somehow Jackson succeeded in capturing the confusion and despair of a whole nation in a three-minute song. In that sense, despite the lyric's profession of unworldliness and political ignorance, the song made a powerful social statement.

Rapper Wyclef Jean, one of the Fugees, wrote "War No More" in 2002. He commented that "The street pack more heat / Than the Middle East" and maintained that "We don't want the war no more / Let me hear the streets. Peace, oh peace."

The Second Gulf War

In the aftermath of 9/11, America was a confused and disturbed nation. Osama bin Laden had claimed credit for the 9/11 attacks, but the American military were not sure where he could be found. Intelligence indicated that he was somewhere in the border region between Afghanistan and Pakistan. Afghanistan was controlled by a religious sect called the Taliban, who were willing to help hide bin Laden. Pakistan was (and more or less remains) an ally of the United States, but the government has little control of the mountainous regions near Afghanistan.

The United States, with military assistance from a number of other countries, bombed Afghanistan, and also sent troops there. The Taliban was overthrown, and a new government under Hamid Karzai took over.

Meanwhile, the United States began to institute heavy security measures at home, especially at airports. Congress passed the Patriot Act, which gave the government the ability to gather all sorts of intelligence in the United States, to deport immigrants suspected of terrorist acts, and to regulate financial transactions by foreigners. A number of Americans objected to the act, because of its restrictions on civil liberties, but nevertheless it was passed and signed by the president.

Iraq came under considerable pressure from the United States and the United Nations to reveal any weapons of mass destruction, in response to the U.S. government's claim that such weapons were being developed, posing a threat to the security of the entire world. A series of inspections by United Nations representatives failed to reveal the presence of any such weapons, but Saddam Hussein obstructed the searches. This led to the conjecture that there were indeed such weapons, but that they were hidden.

In March 2003, the United States elected to bypass the United Nations and invade Iraq without their support. With assistance from British forces, and to a lesser degree from Australia, Spain, Poland, and Denmark, the invasion went forward.

Initially, the Iraq war had widespread support in America. Over time, however, that support dropped off. Many of the U.S. soldiers were members of the National Guard, who had never dreamed that they would be asked to fight a war. Since the military had trouble recruiting new members, many of the troops were compelled to stay for extended periods of time. And the weapons of mass destruction they had undertaken to discover and destroy never materialized.

Like the first Gulf War, this one ended quickly. Baghdad was occupied in April 2003, Saddam's regime was overthrown, and he was captured, tried, and executed. Unlike the first war, however, the United States lacked widespread international support and military participation. The other major difference was that in the first war, President George Herbert Walker Bush had quickly withdrawn American soldiers, and we had not attempted to occupy Iraq. In the second war we became committed to staying in Iraq, rebuilding the country, and making it into a "democracy."

In planning this long-term occupation, George W. Bush had not taken into account the internal feuds in Iraq between the various religious sects and ethnic groups. As American soldiers continued to die, and many more were wounded, the American people turned against both Bush and the war. In addition, the billions of dollars being spent on the war resulted in deficits for the U.S. Treasury, and limitations on domestic programs to promote the general welfare and to maintain the somewhat crumbling infrastructure of the country.

It is now six years since the war started, and under President Obama, American troops are just now beginning to withdraw from Iraq. Meanwhile, the war in Afghanistan is not going well, and some American troops are being transferred there. Osama bin Laden has not been located or captured, the Taliban are in a resurgence, and the Karzai government is unable to restrain the drug trade, or the feudal tribesmen that control much of the country.

Music of the Gulf War

Because the second war has been going on for six years now, there is a considerable body of music about it. Since World War II, country musicians have typically supported America's wars, while rock has tended to question them. (This is a generalization that is not 100 percent accurate, but it usually has held true.) It is also traditional for country music stars to be Republicans, while rock stars have inclined more toward the Democratic Party.

The second Gulf War has challenged this image. While Lee Greenwood's "I'm Proud to Be an American" surfaced yet again, there have also been some surprises. One of the biggest of all country groups is the Dixie Chicks. In the late nineties and first years of the 2000s their albums out-sold virtually everyone's, coming in at over ten million copies. In March 2003, just before the invasion of Iraq, the Chicks were appearing in London. On stage during the concert, lead singer Natalie Maines told the crowd that they, a group of native Texans, were ashamed that the president of the United States (George W. Bush) came from Texas.

This statement created a firestorm of debate. Some stations stopped playing records by the group, some observers criticized the band for making such a statement on foreign soil, and some disc jockeys sponsored events where Dixie Chicks CDs were smashed. (This is oddly reminiscent of the Chicago disco-bashing event.)

Several major country artists registered their opposition to Maines's remarks. A feud subsequently developed between Maines and country star Toby Keith, author of the song "Courtesy of the Red, White, and Blue (The Angry American)." The song cites Keith's father's service in the Army, where he lost an eye, and refers to 9/11 as a "sucker punch" that America will avenge. Maines described the song as "ignorant" in a newspaper interview, and rejected its claims of association with country music. This led to more back-and-forth, including Maines wearing a T-shirt at a country music awards show that said "F.Y.T.K."

But the Dixie Chicks weren't the only country act questioning the war. Willie Nelson wrote "What Ever Happened to Peace on Earth?"

Willie Nelson

in 2004. While it does not specifically reference Iraq, it clearly concerns the war, and the closing lines "But how much is a liar's word worth? / Whatever happened to peace on earth?" are indeed strong medicine. Nashville rebel Steve Earle wrote a song, "John Walker," about an American who voluntarily joined the Taliban army and was captured by American soldiers in Afghanistan. The song is a long ballad in a sort of early-Dylanesque style that refers to televangelists and aging politicians who will not have to fight in the war.

In 2004 Earle recorded an angry album, *Revolution,* featuring the song "The Revolution Starts Now" ("The revolution starts now. Just follow your heart"). Another song pokes fun at Condoleezza Rice, then Secretary of State, and another, called "Rich Man's War," uses the line "Just another poor boy off to fight a rich man's war."

At the time of the Maines-Keith battle, the Dixie Chicks had a #1 single with the song "Travelin' Soldier," written by Bruce Robison, who is the brother-in-law of the Chicks' Emily Robison. The song, written in 1996 and revised in 1999, concerns a lonely soldier who meets a girl just before going to Vietnam. He falls in love with her, and when he dies in the war, the only person who misses him is the girl he left behind. Although the song is not about the Gulf War, it is ironic that it became a hit just when the controversy over the Dixie Chicks' political ideas was raging.

Kris Kristofferson wrote and recorded the antiwar song "When the President Talks to God," which includes the line "I want nothing but the end of the war." Kristofferson was pro-war during the Korean and Vietnam conflicts, but his political views turned left in the 1980s, when he supported the Sandinistas in Nicaragua. Merle Haggard, whose politics incline more toward libertarianism than toward either of the major political parties, did express antiwar sentiments in the 2003 song "That's the News," with the line "Suddenly the war is over, that's the news." The song takes the position that no one wins in a war, relates the death of an American soldier, and concludes by proclaiming that "Politicians do all the talkin', soldiers pay the dues."

In a chapter in the book *Country Music Goes to War,* writer Randy Rudder describes Darryl Worley as the most misunderstood artist in country music. Worley's hit song, "Have You Forgotten," was written about 9/11 and the American invasion of Afghanistan, but many listeners thought that it concerned the war in Iraq. The song refers to bin Laden, the people who died in the twin towers and the Pentagon, and the heroes who fought back and brought the fourth plane down in Pennsylvania. Worley wrote the song after coming back from entertaining American troops in Afghanistan, but by the time the record was released, we were at war with Iraq. Consequently listeners assumed that the song, like the U.S. government, was using the 9/11 attacks to justify the invasion of Iraq.

There are far too many antiwar rock songs available to analyze here. Neil Young has placed dozens of these songs, including some of his own compositions, on his web site. The punk band Green Day recorded a best-selling album, *American Idiot,* in 2004. The title song disavows any support that anyone could suspect them of harboring, as Americans, for the invasion, saying,

> I'm not a part of a redneck agenda
> And don't want to be an American idiot
> One nation controlled by the media.

Michael Franti is a singer-songwriter-band leader whose song "Bomb the World" was written after 9/11, just before the start of the second Gulf War. The theme of the song is that we can "Bomb the world to pieces / But we can't bomb the world to peace."

Veteran Portland, Oregon folksingers Steve Einhorn and Kate Power won a songwriting contest in Kerrville, Texas in 2006 with their song "Travis John (The Return)." The song is about a young soldier named Travis John Bradach-Nall, who was killed in Iraq while clearing land mines. The song's recurring lyric, "All the joy is dead and done / I am gone," encapsulates the sentiment of the song. The

Billy Joe Armstrong from Green Day

artists who recorded the song have a son who went to high school with Travis.

Other people who have written songs against the war include Billy Joel, whose song "Christmas in Fallujah" was recorded by Cass Dillon. The rappers Faithless' song "Mass Destruction" maintains that

"Terrorized, civilized / People livin' evil lives" and "Duct tape all your windows / But the smell is still inside."

A 2006 project, Voices from the Front Line, is a series of raps and personal messages and reminiscences from soldiers serving in Iraq. It is a nonpolitical document, simply describing the war rather than taking a political position in favor of it or against it. Two of the nine artist-writers are women.

A current book called *Sound Targets: American Soldiers and Music in the Iraq War* discusses music that the soldiers listened to during the war. Author Jonathan Pieslak, a professor of music at the City College of New York, found that soldiers used rap and heavy metal music in their tanks or before battles to rev themselves up for military action. He also discovered that the army blasted this music to irritate the enemy, and to discombobulate or torment enemy soldiers during interrogation.

Some rock artists, including Pearl Jam, have protested that they do not wish to have their music used in such interrogations. Although European record deals include the notion of moral rights, these clauses are not found in American record company contracts. Just as people download music illegally because they can, I suspect that interrogators will continue to play whatever music they think will work to achieve their goals.

Iraq and Vietnam

The music about the wars in Iraq seems to have developed in a similar way that protest music developed during the war in Vietnam. In both wars, patriotic sentiment initially was mostly in favor of the war. In each case, as the war continued, the American people became weary of the constant casualties. The difference between the conflicts is that America never won the war in Vietnam, nor did it conquer the enemy nation. In Iraq , we established military superiority quickly, and overthrew the regime of Saddam Hussein. The actual subjugation of the country, and an end to the serious ethnic and religious conflicts, has yet to come. As with Vietnam, as the war ground on, sentiment against it, both political and musical, increased in volume and intensity.

The September 11 attacks horrified virtually everyone. Although American feeling in favor of fighting the war in Afghanistan and bringing bin Laden to justice is less controversial than the Gulf War was, the outcome of this struggle is very much in doubt. We can certainly expect the focus of any antiwar music to increasingly shift from Iraq to Afghanistan.

10

MUSIC AND SOCIAL CHANGE

Omissions

This book represents a lifetime of playing, listening to, and reading about American music.

I need to frankly acknowledge some areas that this book does not even attempt to cover. This is a book *about* music, not a book with music. Consequently there is very little discussion here of the music itself. I wish to acknowledge that this is a shortcoming, because clearly musical style is part of the influence that a song exerts. This can be in the form of a stirring vocal performance, or the rhythm or melody of a song.

I haven't covered Canadians, unless they have moved (at least for the most part) to the United States. Therefore Neil Young and Joni Mitchell are very much a part of this book, but Bruce Cockburn, who is a very socially involved singer-songwriter, is not covered here.

I have not covered British artists to any extent. John Lennon lived here from 1971 until he was murdered in 1980. I felt that any detailed coverage of Lennon would force the book to cover other British artists who have lived here from time to time.

I have also not dealt with gay music, which is certainly a medium of its own. In addition, the last twenty years have seen a proliferation of gay choruses, both male and female. The audiences and even the members of the groups are not all gay, but the groups do perform repertoire that expresses solidarity with the gay community.

I have also not discussed the Christian music movement. Many people who are ignorant of this music are unaware that there is considerable disagreement within the Christian community about whether the message of contemporary Christian music reflects the depth and complexity of the Christian message. The late Larry Norman and Charlie Peacock are among the Christian musicians who have agitated for the music to be more expressive of these aspects.

It is also difficult to establish authenticity or motivations in the writing and performance of music. Are we to believe in the younger Dylan's songs, or should we accept his own contention that they only represented his attempts to establish a career in music? Is it also possible that the music represented his beliefs at one point in time, and that as his beliefs changed, so did his music?

Finally, no one could possibly be equally expert on all of the varieties of music covered in this book, and no one can have listened to all of the music performed or recorded that touches on social issues.

Now that you've received these warnings, I want to go ahead and discuss some of what I have concluded while researching and writing this book.

Music, Celebrity, and the Political Process

John Lennon once said that the Beatles had a bigger audience than Jesus, but had to backtrack when that statement threatened the career of his band. Peter Yarrow of Peter, Paul and Mary said that at their height they exercised so much power over young people that they might be able to elect a president. No one reacted much to this statement, because it seemed to reflect an exaggerated opinion of the group's clout.

Various musical figures have run for public office, with mixed results. Kinky Friedman ran for governor of Texas and lost. Roy Acuff, one of the stars of the Grand Ole Opry, ran for governor of Tennessee and was defeated. Jimmie Davis served as governor of Louisiana. Martha Reeves of Martha and the Vandellas is a member of the Detroit city council; John Hall, of the group Orleans, is currently

John Lennon

serving his second term in the U.S. Congress; and Sonny Bono also
served in Congress until accidental death put an end to his first term.

Other political figures use music as a sort of humanizing sideline.
Robert Byrd, the long-term senator from West Virginia, has played
his fiddle at political rallies, and Senator Orrin Hatch of Utah is a
songwriter who has had some of his songs recorded. By and large,
any direct connection between music and politics is thin. Like major
sports figures, musicians who are "stars" are in the public eye, and

have name recognition. This may or may not provide assistance in pursuing a career in politics.

Situations Where Music Had Influence

We have traced the use of music in American life in the political process, and in support of specific issues. Music seems to be most effective in the sphere of social change when the musical participants are involved in the political process itself. We have discussed how this happened in the mining and textile industries, in the civil rights movement, and to some extent in the antiwar movement of the sixties.

In each group that we have discussed, certain key figures are associated with demands for change. In the American Indian movement Peter La Farge and Buffy Sainte-Marie were the pioneers, and John Trudell is the most obvious current example.

In African American music Curtis Mayfield was a pioneer. Mayfield started out as a member of the Impressions. Their early records featured Jerry Butler and were oriented towards romance. When Butler left and Mayfield became the lead singer, he began to write songs that reflected social and political concerns. Initially, the messages were not very specific. His classic "People Get Ready," written in 1964, talks about a train that will soon be coming. Using the traditional language of the spirituals, Mayfield talks about the helpless sinner who will hurt mankind just to save his own.

In the same year, "Keep On Pushing" developed the message in a more explicit way. The song describes pushing obstacles ("a great big stone") out of the way. By 1967 Mayfield in "We're a Winner" told his audience to "keep on pushin', like your leaders tell you to."

In 1968 Mayfield wrote a sort of new black national anthem, "This Is My Country." The song refers to slavery and to the struggle to achieve equality, posing the question, "Shall we perish unjust or live equal as a nation?" In 1969 Mayfield wrote "Choice of Colors," in which he espouses education, asking his audience how long they have hated their white teacher, or loved their black preacher.

His songs were also used in the civil rights movement, often with slight rewrites and with Mayfield's permission. In the 1970s Mayfield had a successful career writing songs for films, notably *Superfly*. The songs for that movie concerned heroin and dope dealing in the black community. Unlike the movies they were written for, Mayfield's songs did not glamorize drug dealers and junkies, but rather presented them with insight and compassion. Of all the popular black songwriters, Mayfield exhibited the most consistent concern about social and political issues.

Jazz musicians Max Roach and John Coltrane, in different ways, supported not only social change but musical progressivism as well. John Coltrane, one of the most famous jazz musicians of all time, never considered himself a political figure, but he still used wordless compositions to make a statement and his protégés carried out this tradition as well. This type of musical expression was labeled "free jazz" and was heavily improvisational, with a sound that was often deliberately harsh and abrasive, intended to express the situation of the black musician in the United States. Musicians Cecil Taylor, Albert Ayler, and Pharaoh Sanders were among the leaders of this movement. Saxophonist-composer-playwright Archie Shepp, who like Sanders was a protégé of John Coltrane, included some of his poetry in his musical compositions, such as his poem "Malcolm, Malcolm, Semper Malcolm." Free jazz stretched the bounds of instruments and musical form; the effect made many of the older jazz fans uncomfortable, which if anything stimulated the musicians to expand their explorations.

In rap, N.W.A. and Public Enemy, particularly Chuck D., have been leading rap musician agitators. Pete Seeger and Woody Guthrie were the most prominent figures in protest music, and although there are many artists pursuing these ends today, no single artist stands out in this way. The whole notion of women's music has changed from the days when Holly Near and Chris Williamson were the major figures.

Today Ani DiFranco is the most obvious proponent of women's music, modified through her own particular punk-folk political sensibilities. Like Near, Ani elected to start her own record company, turning down numerous offers along the way. The company is called Righteous Babe, and it headquarters in the low-rent town of Buffalo, New York, where Ani grew up.

Ani achieved much of her original popularity with a gay audience, but along the way she revealed that she was bisexual, and then got married. Many of her songs are either directly political or have political overtones. They make fun of corporations and assert women's rights; her 1992 song "Fixing Her Hair" is about a woman who settles for a man whom the singer, her friend, considers an unworthy choice. Part of the lyric says:

I have met him before
And I think what is this
Beautiful woman settling for.

As the owner of her own record company, DiFranco can release albums whenever she wishes to. If she were recording for a major label, they would want her to tour nationally to promote each album for at least a year, and perhaps tour abroad after that to build up the international market, creating a gap of one to two years between albums. Because she controls her own career, she has been able to record thirty-nine albums. In 2006 alone she released four.

Very few Mexican American artists speak to the broad population, because many of them sing in Spanish, although Tish Hinjosa is one who sings in both Spanish and English. Many of the bands who perform in he Spanish language, like Los Tigres del Norte, bounce back and forth from *narcocorridos* to songs about immigration and social justice.

In rock and roll, Bob Dylan has passed the baton of his early folk and folk-rock agitation to Bruce Springsteen, while many other musicians, like Jackson Browne, Neil Young, or Don Henley, have specific causes that they are particularly active in. Many musicians confine their politics to benefit performances for certain causes or political candidates. There hasn't been a single cause like the civil rights movement that has galvanized a critical mass of artists to risk their own safety in solidarity with a specific issue. Some of the rap entrepreneurs, like Diddy (Sean Combs) and Russell Simmons, have been active in attempting to register young people to vote.

Can Music Cause Social Change?

Most songs are about three minutes long. It is possible, but difficult, to capture a major issue in such a short time capsule. The song "We Shall Overcome" comes to mind. Anyone who ever participated in the civil rights movement knows that this song beautifully represents that struggle. There are a number of problems in attempting to define social change, or even a specific issue, in such a brief format.

One problem is that many issues are too complex to be treated in this way, at least for a mass audience. Dylan's song "Only a Pawn in Their Game" is one of his more profound political songs. The basic concept of the song is that the murderer of Mississippi civil rights leader Medgar Evers was simply a representative of a hopelessly unjust system that convinces poor white people that they are superior to African Americans. Dylan cites the sheriffs, the police, politicians, and the educational system as all part of this machinery. In the final verse Dylan pays tribute to Evers, saying "they lowered him down as a king," a sort of loose play on the name Martin Luther King, as well as an eerie predictor of the tragic fate that awaited Martin Luther King five years later, in 1968.

This is truly a profound song, but it couldn't possibly have gained mass acceptance for several reasons. For one thing, the message is far too complex. For another, in deemphasizing blame for an individual and ascribing it to a system, the song removes the listener's ability to avenge the wrongful death. Compare this song to Dylan's "Blowin' in the Wind." That song has a great sing-along chorus, and it specifically refers to the oppression of African Americans. The hook line, "The answer is blowin' in the wind," inspired the pop-gospel singer Sam Cooke to write his own political song, "A Change Is Gonna Come." When all is said and done, the "Pawn" song is a teaching tool, offered to people who do not necessarily want the lesson. "Blowin' in the Wind" is a song that appears to raise issues, but in fact raises only questions, and offers no answers.

Even though a song cannot create social change, it can certainly be the inspiration that ultimately leads to such changes. "Solidarity Forever" tells the union member that by uniting with other workers it is possible to counteract the power of management. "Which Side Are You On?" told coal miners that their only chance was to join together in a union. These songs did not create change, but they certainly helped to pave the highway that could lead to change.

In the 1960s, the impetus for change captured the public imagination as never before. Some of the changes accomplished since then have clearly been for the better; others have been disheartening. Not only can black citizens vote, we have a black president. On the other hand we are still trying to extricate ourselves from a war, this time not in Vietnam, but in Iraq. We are not involved in a critical cold war with the U.S.S.R., but now our uncertainties concern the fanatical part of the Arab world, and another war in Afghanistan is unresolved.

Historically, such radical social scientists as Theodor Adorno saw popular music as being entirely the creature of the marketplace, and viewed it as musical drivel. Today's radical social theorists, like George Lipsitz and Josh Kun, have a more idealistic vision of what popular music can do. They marvel at capitalism's inability to control its content, and they laud the musical hybrids that involve different ethnic and racial strands.

Personally, I lean more toward the latter group, but I am disturbed that in today's popular music there is little difference between songs and commercials. Neil Young may be the last holdout of the artists who don't see commercials as a valid platform for their music. Dylan has licensed his revolutionary call to arms "The Times They Are a-Changin'" for five different commercials, and he himself appeared in a Victoria's Secret commercial.

I also find it daunting that a few small corporations own so many radio stations that the idea of a real protest song being widely played on the air is virtually unthinkable. The internet has its possibilities, but it is so fragmented that it may never provide the opportunity for a song to enjoy mass exposure, unless it is sung by an artist that is already well-known. Who knows what new platforms will arise, or how artists will utilize them?

Bibliography and Discography

1: Songs of the Immigrants and Songs in American History and Politics

Books

Abel, E. Lawrence. *Singing the New Nation: How Music Shaped the Confederacy, 1861–1865.* Mechanicsburg, PA: Stackpole Books, 2000.

Adler, Kurt, editor and arranger. *Songs of Many Wars: From the Sixteenth to the Twentieth Century.* New York: Howell, Soskin Publishers, 1943.

Begen, Theodore, and Martin Band. *Norwegian Emigrant Songs and Ballads.* Minneapolis: University of Minnesota Press, 1937.

Bergman, Marion. *Russian-American Song and Dance Book.* New York: A. S. Barnes, 1947.

Brand, Oscar. *Songs of '76: A Folksingers' History of the Revolution.* New York: M. Evans and Company, Inc., 1972.

Ewing, George W. *The Well-Tempered Lyre: Songs and Verse of the Temperance Movement.* Dallas: Southern Methodist University Press, 1977.

Finson, Jon. *The Voices That Are Gone: Themes in Nineteenth-Century American Popular Song.* New York: Oxford University Press, 1994.

Foner, Philip S. *American Labor Songs of the Nineteenth Century.* Urbana: University of Illinois Press, 1975.

Greene, Victor. R. *A Singing Ambivalence: American Immigrants Between Old World and New, 1830–1930.* Kent, OH: Kent State University Press, 2004.

Halker, Clark D. *For Democracy, Workers and God: Labor Song-Poems and Labor Protest, 1865–1895.* Urbana: University of Illinois Press, 1991.

Hausman, Ruth. *Sing and Dance with the Pennsylvania Dutch.* New York: Edward Marks, 1953.

Heaps, Willard A. and Porter W. *The Singing Sixties: The Spirit of Civil War Days Drawn from the Music of the Times.* Norman: University of Oklahoma Press, 1960.

Jackson, George Stuyvesant. *Early Songs of Uncle Sam.* Boston: Bruce Humphries Publishers, 1933.

Jacobs, Gertrude. *The Chinese-American Song and Game Book.* New York: A.S. Barnes, 1966.

Kornbluth, Joyce L., editor. *Rebel Voices: An I.W.W. Anthology.* Ann Arbor: University of Michigan Press, 1965.

Lawrence, Vera Brodsky. *Music for Patriots, Politicians and Presidents.* New York: Macmillan Publishing Co., 1975.

Levy, Lester S. *Grace Notes in American History: Popular Sheet Music from 1820 to 1900.* Norman: University of Oklahoma Press, 1967.

McNeil, Keith and Rusty. *California Songbook with Historical Commentary.* Riverside, CA: Wem Records, 2001.

Reyes, Adelaida. *Songs of the Caged, Songs of the Free: Music and the Vietnamese Refugee Experience.* Philadelphia: Temple University Press, 1999.

Rubin, Ruth. *A Treasury of Jewish Folk Song.* New York: Schocken Books, 1950.

Scott, John Anthony. *The Ballad of America: The History of the United States in Song and Story.* New York: Bantam Books, 1966.

Silverman, Jerry. *Jerry Silverman's Folk Song Encyclopedia, Volume 1.* New York: Chappell Music Company, 1975.

Tawa, Nicholas E. *A Sound of Strangers: Musical Culture, Acculturation and the Post Civil War Ethnic America*. Metuchen, NJ: Scarecrow Press, 1982.

———. *High-Minded and Low-Down: Music in the Lives of Americans, 1800–1861*. Boston: Northeastern University Press, 2000.

Wright, Robert. *Swedish Emigrant Ballads*. Lincoln: University of Nebraska Press, 1965.

Recordings

Brand, Oscar. *Presidential Campaign Songs: 1789–1996*. Smithsonian Folkways SFW CD 45051, 1999.

Chestnut Brass Company and Friends. *Hail to the Chief! American Political Marches, Songs and Dirges of the 1800s*. Sony SFK82485, 1996.

Cincinnati's University Singers. *The Hand That Holds the Bread*. New World Records 80267-2, 1997.

Seeger, Pete. *American Industrial Ballads*. Smithsonian Folkways, 1991.

2: Native American Music and Social Issues

Books

Allen, Linda. *Washington Songs and Lore*. Spokane, WA: Melior Publications, 1988.

Allen, Paula Gunn. *The Sacred Hoop: Recovering the Feminine in American Indian Traditions*. Boston: Beacon Press, 1986.

Barreiro, Jose, and Tim Johnson, editors. *America Is Indian Country: Opinions and Perspectives from Indian Country*. Golden, CO: Fulcrum Publishing, 2004.

Brown, Dee. *Bury My Heart at Wounded Knee: An Indian History of the American West*. New York: Henry Holt & Co., 2000 edition.

Burton, Frederick R. *American Primitive Music*. 1909. Reprint, Port Washington, NY: Kennikat Press, 1969.

Curtis, Natalie. *The Indians' Book*. 1922. Reprint, New York: Dover Publications, 1968.

D'Ambrosio, Antonino. *A Heartbeat and a Guitar*. New York: Nation Books, 2009.

Deloria, Vine. *God Is Red: A Native View of Religion*. Golden, CO: Fulcrum Publishing, 1994.

Densmore, Frances. *The American Indians and Their Music*. New York: The Women's Press, 1926.

Graeme, Theodor C. *America's Ethnic Music*. Tarpon Springs, FL: Cultural Maintenance Association, 1976.

Igliori, Paola. *Stickman: John Trudell*. New York: Inanout Press, 1994.

James, M. Antoinette, editor. *The State of Native America: Genocide, Colonization and Resistance*. Boston: South End Press, 1992.

Limerick, Patricia. *The Legacy of Conquest*. New York: W.W. Norton, 1987.

Matthiessen, Peter. *In the Spirit of Crazy Horse*. New York: Penguin Books, 1992.

McAllester, David P. *Indian Music in the Southwest*. Colorado Springs: Taylor Museum of the Colorado Springs Fine Art Center, 1961.

McAllester, David P. *Peyote Music*. New York: Viking Fund, 1949.

Pisani, Michael V. "I'm an *Indian Too: Creating Native American Identities in* Nineteenth- and Early Twentieth-Century Music." In *The Exotic in Western Music,* edited by Jonathan Bellman. Boston: Northeastern University Press, 1998, 218–237.

Scott, Derek B. *From the Erotic to the Demonic: On Critical Musicology*. New York: Oxford University Press, 2003.

Troutman, John W. *Indian Blues: American Indians and the Politics of Music, 1879–1934*. Norman: University of Oklahoma Press, 2009.

Wilkinson, Charles. *Blood Struggle: The Rise of Modern Indian Nations*. New York: W. W. Norton, 2005.

Wright-McLeod, Bryan. *The Encyclopedia of Native Music: More than a Century of Recordings from Wax Cylinder to the Internet.* Tucson: University of Arizona Press, 2005.

Recordings

Bobby Bee and the Boys from the Rez. *Reservation of Education.* Warrior CD-6, 1993.

Cash, Johnny. *Bitter Tears.* Sony B000002AN0, 1994 reissue of 1964 LP.

Haggard, Merle. *Greatest Hits.* Curb D4-77647, 1976.

In the Spirit of Crazy Horse. Four Winds Trading Co., 1992.

LaFarge, Peter. *Iron Mountain and Other Songs.* Folkways FN 2531, 1962.

McGraw, Tim. *Indian Outlaw.* Recording and video. Curb D3-77708, 1994.

Means, Russell. *Electric Warrior.* Warrior 603, 1993.

Miller, Bill. *The Red Road.* Warner Western 9 45324-2, 1993.

Ortega, Paul A., and Joanne Shenandoah. *Loving Ways.* Canyon, 1991.

Red Bow, Buddy. *Black Hills Dreamer.* Tatanka Records TRCD 41022, 1991.

Robbie Robertson and the Red Road Ensemble. *Music for the Native Americans.* Capitol CD B000002TCC, 1994.

Sainte-Marie, Buffy. *Best of the Vanguard Years.* Vanguard B0000AZKNV, 2003.

Secola, Keith. *Circle.* Akina, 1992.

Shenandoah, Joanne. *Peacemaker.* Silver Wave B00044R8PY, 2000.

Stuart, Marty. *Badlands: Ballads of the Lakota.* Universal South B000DB189C, 2005.

Till the Bars Break. Cargo Records, 1992.

Trudell, John. *A.K.A. Graffiti Man.* Rykodisc VR0223, 1992.

———. *Johnny Damas and Me.* Rykodisc RCD 10286, 1994.

———. *Blue Indians.* Ulftone B00000JORI, 2000.

Westerman, Floyd. *Custer Died for Your Sins.* Red Crow 4160.

Williamson, Chris. *The Best of Chris Williamson.* Olivia ORCD 959, 1990.

Without Reservation. *Are You Ready for W.O.R.?* Canyon CR 7035, 1994.

XIT. *Plight of the Red Man.* Soar 101, 1989.

————. *Relocation.* Soar 131, 1992.

Young, Neil. *Retrospective: The Best of Buffalo Springfield.* Atco 38-205-2, reissue of 1969 recordings.

3: African Americans

Books

Allen, William Francis, Charles Pickard Ware, and Lucy Garrison McKim. *Slave Songs of the United States.* 1867. Reprint, New York: Peter Smith, 1951.

Bastin, Bruce. *Red River Blues: The Blues Tradition in the Southeast.* Urbana: University of Illinois Press, 1986.

Bean, Anne Marie, James V. Hatch, and Brooks McNamara, editors. *Inside the Minstrel Mask: Readings in Nineteenth-Century Blackface Minstrelsy.* Hanover, NH: Wesleyan University Press, 1996.

The Big Book of Motown. Milwaukee: Hal Leonard, 2004.

Bozza, Anthony. *Whatever You Say I Am: The Life and Times of Eminem.* New York: Three Rivers Press, 2003.

Bradley, Adam. *Book of Rhymes: The Poetics of Hip Hop.* New York: Basic Books, 2009.

Brooks, Tim. *Lost Sounds: Blacks and the Birth of the Recording Industry, 1890–1919.* Urbana: University of Illinois Press, 2005.

Bryant, Jerry H. *"Born in a Mighty Bad Land": The Violent Man in African American Folklore and Fiction.* Bloomington: Indiana University Press, 2003.

Burns, Peter. *Curtis Mayfield: People Never Give Up.* London: Sanctuary, 2003.

Bynoe, Yvonne. *Stand and Deliver: Political Activism, Leadership, and Hip Hop Culture.* Brooklyn: Soft Skull Press, 2004.

Carawan, Guy and Candie, editors and compilers. *Sing for Freedom: The Story of the Civil Rights Movement Through Its Songs*. Bethlehem, PA: Sing Out Publications, 1992.

Carpenter, Bill. *Uncloudy Days: The Gospel Music Encyclopedia*. San Francisco: Backbeat Books, 2005.

Chang, Jeff. *Can't Stop, Won't Stop: A History of the Hip-Hop Generation*. New York: Macmillan, 2005.

Cheney, Cherise L. *Brothers Gonna Work It Out: Sexual Politics in the Golden Age of Rap Nationalism*. New York: New York University Press, 2007.

Cobb, William Jelani. *To the Break of Dawn: A Freestyle on the Hip-Hop Aesthetic*. New York: New York University Press, 2007.

Cohn, Lawrence, et al. *Nothing but the Blues: The Music and the Musicians*. New York: Abbeville Press, 1995.

Cohn, Nik. *Tricksta: Life and Death and New Orleans Rap*. New York: Vintage Books, 2007.

Cunard, Nancy, editor and collector. *Negro: An Anthology*. 1970. Reprint, New York: Continuum, 2002.

Darden, Robert. *People Get Ready: A New History of Black Gospel Music*. New York: Continuum, 2004.

The Definitive Blues Collection: Ninety-six Songs. Milwaukee: Hal Leonard, 1992.

Emerson, Ken. *Doo-Dah! Stephen Foster and the Rise of American Popular Culture*. New York: Da Capo Press, 1998.

Epstein, Dena J. *Sinful Tunes and Spirituals: Black Folk Music to the Civil War*. Urbana: University of Illinois Press, 1977.

Evans, David, editor. *Ramblin' on My Mind: New Perspectives on the Blues*. Urbana: University of Illinois Press, 2008.

Fisher, Miles Mark. *Negro Slave Songs in the United States*. Ithaca, NY: Cornell University Press, 1953.

Forman, Murray. *The 'Hood Comes First: Race, Space and Place in Rap and Hip-Hop*. Middletown, CT: Wesleyan University Press, 2002.

Franklin, John Hope, and Alfred A. Moss Jr. *From Slavery to Freedom: A History of Negro Americans.* 6th edition. New York: McGraw Hill, 1988.

Frazier, E. Franklin. *The Negro in the United States.* Revised edition. New York Macmillan, 1957.

Garon, Paul, and Gene Tomko. *What's the Use of Walking If There's a Freight Train Going Your Way? Black Hoboes and Their Songs.* Chicago: Charles H. Kerr Publishing Co., 2006.

Gellert, Lawrence. *Negro Songs of Protest.* New York: American Music League, 1936.

———. *Me and My Captain: Chain Gang Negro Songs of Protest.* New York: Hours Press, 1939.

Green, Jared, editor. *Rap and Hip Hop: Examining Pop Culture.* Farmington Hills, MI: Greenhaven Press, 2003.

Harris, Michael W. *The Rise of Gospel Blues: The Music of Thomas Andrew Dorsey in the Urban Church.* New York: Oxford University Press, 1992.

Heilbut, Anthony. *The Gospel Sound: Good News and Bad Times.* Updated and revised edition. New York: Limelight Books, 1985.

Jackson, Bruce. *Wake Up Dead Man: Afro-American Worksongs from Texas Prisons.* Cambridge, MA: Harvard University Press, 1972.

Jackson, George Pullen. *White and Negro Spirituals: Their Life Span and Kinship.* 1943. Reprint, New York: Da Capo Press, 1975.

Jah, Yusuf, editor. *Chuck D: Lyrics of a Rap Revolutionary.* Beverly Hills: Off Da Books, 2006.

Jasper, Kenji, and Natasha Womack, editors. *Beats, Rhymes and Life: What We Love and Hate About Hip-Hop.* New York: Routledge, 2007.

Jemie, Onwuchekwa, editor. *Yo' Mama! New Raps, Toasts, Dozens, Jokes, and Children's Rhymes from Urban Black America.* Philadelphia: Temple University Press, 2003.

Kelley, Norman, editor. *R&B Rhythm and Business: The Political Economy of Black Music.* New York: Akashic Books, 2002.

Kimball, Robert, and William Bolcom. *Reminiscing with Noble Sissle and Eubie Blake.* 1973. Reprint New York: Cooper Square Press, 2000.

Kitwana, Bakari. *Why White Kids Love Hip Hop: Wankstas, Wiggers, Wannabes, and the New Reality of Race in America.* New York: Basic Books, 2005.

Komara, Edward. *The Road to Robert Johnson: The Genesis and Evolution of Blues in the Delta from the 1800s Through 1938.* Milwaukee: Hal Leonard, 2007.

Krehbiel, Henry Edward. *Afro-American Folk-Songs: A Study in Racial and National Music.* 1913. Reprint, New York: Frederick Ungar Publishing, 1962.

Krims, Adam. *Rap Music and the Poetics of Identity.* Cambridge, England: Cambridge University Press, 2000.

Lee, Vera. *The Black and White of American Popular Music from Slavery to World War II.* Rochester, VT: Schenkman Books, 2007.

Lomax, Alan. *The Land Where the Blues Began.* New York: Pantheon Books, 1993.

Lomax, John A. and Alan. *Negro Folk Songs as Sung by Lead Belly.* New York: Macmillan Company, 1936.

Lovell, John Jr. *Black Song: The Forge and the Flame.* New York: Macmillan Company, 1972.

Mayfield, Curtis. *Poetic License: In Poem and Song.* Beverly Hills: Dove Books, 1996.

Neal, Mark Anthony. *What the Music Said: Black Popular Music and Black Popular Culture.* New York: Routledge, 1999.

Neate, Patrick. *Where You're At: Notes from the Frontline of a Hip-Hop Planet.* New York: Riverhead Books, 2004.

Odum, Howard W., and Guy Johnson. *Negro Workaday Songs.* Chapel Hill: University of North Carolina Press, 1917.

———. *The Negro and His Songs.* Chapel Hill: University of North Carolina Press, 1925.

Ogg, Alex, with David Upshal. *The Hip Hop Years: A History of Rap.* London: Channel 4 Books, 1999.

Oliver, Paul. *The Blues Tradition.* 3rd edition. New York: Oak Publications, 1970.

Perkins, William Eric, editor. *Droppin' Science: Critical Essays on Rap Music and Hip Hop Culture.* Philadelphia: Temple University Press, 1996.

Phinney, Kevin. *Souled American: How Black Music Transformed White Culture.* New York: Billboard Books, 2005.

Pomerance, Alan. *Repeal of the Blues: How Black Entertainers Influenced Civil Rights.* New York; Citadel Press, 1988.

Pough, Gwendolyn D. *Check It While You Wreck It: Black Womanhood, Hip Hop Culture and the Public Sphere.* Boston: Northeastern University Press, 2004.

Radano, Ronald. *Lying up a Nation: Race and Black Music.* Chicago: University of Chicago Press, 2003.

Ratiff, Ben. *Coltrane: The Story of a Sound.* New York: Farrar, Straus and Giroux, 2007.

Reeves, Marcus. *Somebody Scream: Rap Music's Rise to Prominence in the Aftershock of Black Power.* New York: Faber & Faber, 2008.

Rose, Tricia. *Black Noise: Rap Music and Black Culture in Contemporary America.* Hanover, NH: Wesleyan University Press, 1994.

———. *The Hip-Hop Wars: What We Talk About When We Talk About Hip Hop and Why It Matters.* New York: Basic Books, 2008.

Sackheim, Eric, compiler. *The Blues Line: A Collection of Blues Lyrics.* New York: Grossman Publishers, 1969.

Sarig, Roni. *Third Coast: Outkast, Timbaland, and How Hip-Hop Became a Southern Thing.* New York: Da Capo Press, 2007.

Saul, Scott. *Freedom Is, Freedom Ain't: Jazz and the Making of the Sixties.* Cambridge, MA: Harvard University Press, 2003.

Sharpley-Whiting, T. Denean. *Pimps Up, Ho's Down: Hip Hop's Hold on Young Black Women.* New York: New York University Press, 2007.

Smith, Bessie. *Bessie Smith Songbook: Empress of the Blues.* Milwaukee: Frank Music Corporation, distributed by Hal Leonard, 1994.

Southern, Eileen. *The Music of Black Americans.* 3rd edition. New York: W. W. Norton, 1997.

Spence, D., Preface. *Hip-Hop and Rap: Complete Lyrics for 175 Songs.* Milwaukee: Hal Leonard, 2003.

Stanley, Lawrence A., editor. *Rap: The Lyrics—The Words to Rap's Greatest Hits.* New York; Penguin Books, 1992.

Tanz, Jason. *Other People's Property: A Shadow History of Hip-Hop in White America.* New York: Bloomsbury, 2007.

Taft, Michael. *The Blues Lyric Formula.* New York: Routledge, 2006.

———. *Blues Lyric Poetry: An Anthology.* New York: Garland Publishing, 1983.

Taylor, Arthur. *Notes and Tones: Musician-to-Musician Interviews.* New York: DaCapo Press, 1993.

Thomson, Graeme. *I Shot a Man in Reno: A History of Death by Murder, Suicide, Fire, Flood, Drugs, Disease, and General Misadventures, As Related In Popular Song.* New York: Continuum, 2008.

Tracy, Steven C., editor. *Write Me a Few of Your Lines: A Blues Reader.* Amherst: University of Massachusetts Press, 1999.

Van Rijn, Guido. *Roosevelt's Blues: African-American Blues and Gospel Songs on FDR.* Jackson: University Press of Mississippi, 1997.

———. *The Truman and Eisenhower Blues: African-American Blues and Gospel Songs, 1945–1960.* London: Continuum, 2004.

Wald, Elijah. *Escaping the Delta: Robert Johnson and the Invention of the Blues.* New York: Amistad, 2004.

Watkins, S. Craig. *Hip Hop Matters; Politics, Pop Culture and the Struggle for the Soul of a Movement.* Boston: Beacon Press, 2005.

Werner, Craig. *Higher Ground: Stevie Wonder, Aretha Franklin, Curtis Mayfield, and the Rise and Fall of American Soul.* New York: Three Rivers Press, 2004.

Recordings

Ain't Times Hard: Political and Social Comment in the Blues. JSP Records JSP77109, 2008.

Boyz N the Hood (Music from the Motion Picture). Qwest/Warner Brothers, 1991.

Can't Keep from Crying: Topical Blues on the Death of President Kennedy. Testament Records, 1994 CD reissue of 1964 LP.

Cap'n You're So Mean. Negro Songs of Protest Volume 2. Rounder LP 4004, 1973.

Coltrane, John. *Live at Birdland.* 1994 CD reissue of 1964 LP.

Ellington, Duke. *Live at the Whitney.* GRP B000003N80, 1972.

Gaye, Marvin. *What's Going On.* Motown CD 440 064 022-2, 2002 reissue of 1972 album.

Lenoir, J. B. *The Topical Bluesman: From Korea to Vietnam.* Blues Encore CD 52017, undated.

Leadbelly's Last Sessions. Smithsonian Folkways SF CD 40068171, 1994.

Johnson, Robert. *The Complete Recordings.* Columbia, C2K 46222, 1990.

Mingus, Charles. *Charles Mingus Presents Charles Mingus.* Candid CD 9005, 1989.

Negro Songs of Protest. Rounder LP 4004, 1973.

N.W.A. *Straight Outta Compton.* Ruthless CDL57102, 1988.

Public Enemy. *Fear of a Black Planet.* Def Jam/Columbia CK 45411, 1990.

Raz. *Slave 323.* Eclipse Muzik Group, 2005.

Roach, Max. *We Insist! Max Roach's Freedom Now Suite.* Candid CCD 79002, 1989 CD reissue of 1960 LP.

Sing for Freedom: The Story of the Civil Rights Movement Through Its Songs. Smithsonian Folkways CDSF 40032, 1990.

Voices of the Civil Rights Movement. *Black American Freedom Songs 1960–1966.* Smithsonian Folkways CD SF 40084, 1997.

4: Women's Lives and Songs

Books

Amort, Teresa, and Julie Matthael. *Race, Gender and Work: A Multicultural Economic History of Women in the United States.* Boston: South End Press, 1991.

Barnett, LaShonda Katrice. *I Got Thunder: Black Women Songwriters on Their Craft.* New York: Thunder's Mouth Press, 2007.

Barnwell, Ysaye M., compiler and editor. *Continuum: The First Songbook of Sweet Honey in the Rock.* Southwest Harbor, ME: Contemporary A Cappella Publishing, 1999.

Bennett, Andy, and Richard A. Peterson, eds. *Music Scenes, Local, Translocal and Virtual.* Nashville: Vanderbilt University Press, 2004.

Bernstein, Jane A., editor. *Women's Voices Across Musical Worlds.* Boston: Northeastern University Press, 2004.

Bufwack, Mary, and Robert K. Oermann. *Finding Her Voice: The Saga of Women in Country Music.* New York: Crown Publishers, 1993.

Carpenter, Mary Chapin. *The Mary Chapin Carpenter Collection.* Milwaukee: Hal Leonard, 2005.

Carson, Mina, Tisa Lewis, and Susan M. Shaw. *Girls Rock! Fifty Years of Women Making Music.* Lexington: University of Kentucky Press, 2004.

Cheney, Joyce, Marcia Deihl, and Deborah Silverstein. *All Our Lives: A Woman's Songbook.* Baltimore: Diana Press, 1976.

De Beauvoir, Simone. *The Second Sex.* New York: Alfred Knopf, 1959.

Dickens, Hazel, and Bill Malone. *Working Girl Blues: The Life and Music of Hazel Dickens.* Urbana: University of Illinois Press, 2008.

DiFranco, Ani. *Best of Ani DiFranco for Guitar.* Milwaukee: Hal Leonard, 2001.

Dobkin, Alix. *My Red Blood: A Memoir of Growing Up Communist, Coming Onto the Greenwich Village Folk Scene, and Coming Out in the Feminist Movement.* New York: Alyson Books, 2009.

Emerson, Ken. *Always Magic in the Air: The Bomp and Brilliance of the Brill Building Era.* New York: Penguin Books, 2005.

Enstice, Wayne, and Janis Stockhouse. *Jazzwomen: Conversations with Twenty-One Musicians.* Bloomington: Indiana University Press, 2004.

Gear, Gillian G. *She's a Rebel: The History of Women in Rock 'n' Roll.* Seattle: Seal Press, 1992.

Heresies #10. *Women and Music.* New York: Heresies Collective Inc., 1980.

Hill, Lauryn. *The Miseducation of Lauryn Hill.* Milwaukee: Hal Leonard, 1999.

King, Carole. *Carole King: Deluxe Anthology.* New York: Warner Bros. Publications, 1986.

Leib, Sandra. *Mother of the Blues: A Study of Ma Rainey.* Amherst: University of Massachusetts Press, 1981.

Lindeen, Laurie. *Petal Pusher: A Rock and Roll Cinderella Story.* New York: Washington Square Press, 2007.

Marcic, Dorothy. *Respect: Women and Popular Music.* New York: Texere, 2002.

Merchant, Natalie. *Natalie Merchant: Collected Songs, 1985–2005.* New York: Cherry Lane Music Co., 2007.

Mitchell, Joni. *The Complete Poems and Lyrics.* Toronto: Random House of Canada, 1997.

Monem, Nadine, editor. Riot grrrl: revolution girl style now! Black Dog Publishing.

Morissette, Alanis. *Alanis Morissette, 20 Greatest Hits.* New York: Warner Brothers Publications, 2001.

Near, Holly. *Fire in the Rain . . . Singer in the Storm: An Autobiography.* New York: Quill, William Morrow, 1990.

―――. *Singing for Our Lives: Music from Imagine My Surprise and Fire in the Rain*. Oakland: Redwood Records, 1992.

Near, Holly, and Jeff Langley. *Words and Music*. Ukiah, CA: Hereford Music, 1976.

Nyro, Laura. *Laura Nyro: Lyrics and Reminiscences*. New York: Cherry Lane Music, 2004.

O'Brien, Karen. *Hymn to Her: Women Musicians Talk*. London: Virago Press, 1885.

O'Brien, Lucy. *She Bop II: The Definitive History of Women in Rock, Pop and Soul*. London: Continuum Press, 2002.

Quirino, Raffaele. *Ani DiFranco: Righteous Babe*. Kingston, Ontario: Quarry Press, 2000.

Reynolds, Malvina. *The Malvina Reynolds Songbook*. 3rd edition. Berkeley: Schroeder Music Co., 1974,

Rosenberg, Rosalind. *Divided Lives: American Women in the Twentieth Century*. New York: Hill & Wang, 1993.

Tucker, Sherrie. *Swing Shift: "All-Girl" Bands of the 1940s*. Durham: University of North Carolina Press, 2000.

Twain, Shania. *Shania Twain's Greatest Hits*. Milwaukee: Hal Leonard, 2005.

Vega, Suzanne. *Bullet in Flight: Songs*. London; Omnibus Press, 1990.

Weller, Sheila. *Girls Like Us: Carole King, Joni Mitchell, Carly Simon—and the Joy of a Generation*. New York: Atria Books, 2008.

Wenner, Hilda, and Elizabeth Freilicher. *Here's to the Women: 100 Songs for and About American Women*. Syracuse, NY: Syracuse University Press, 1987.

Williams, Dar. *The Dar Williams Songbook*. Milwaukee: Hal Leonard, 1999.

Williamson, Chris. *The Chris Williamson Songbook*. Oakland: Olivia Records, 1985.

The Women of R&B: 37 Classic Songs from the Giants of R&B. Milwaukee: Hal Leonard.

Recordings

Amos, Tori. *Little Earthquakes*. Atlantic 7 823582, 1991.

Benatar, Pat. *Best Shots*. Chrysalis F 21715, 1989.

Brown, Sawyer. *Café on the Corner*. Curb 80013KVOKK, 1991.

Carpenter, Mary Chapin. *Come On Come On*. Columbia AAD 4882, 1992.

———. *Stones in the Road*. Columbia 64327, 1994.

Tracy Chapman. *Tracy Chapman*. Elektra 960774-2, 1990.

DiFranco, Ani. *Imperfectly*. RB R003-D, 1992.

———. *To the Teeth*. RB R027D, 1999.

Ethridge, Melissa. *Yes I Am*. Island 12 288660, 1993.

Indigo Girls. *Nomads, Saints, Indians*. Epic EK 46820, 1990.

———. *Come On Now Social*. Epic EK 69914, 1999.

King, Carole. *Tapestry*. Ode, Epic/Legacy EK 65850, 1999 CD reissue of 1971 album.

Mitchell, Joni. *Blue*. Reprise MS2038, 1971.

Near, Holly. *Singer in the Storm*. Chameleon D2-74832, 1990.

Oslin, K. T. *8os Ladies*. RCA 5924-R, 1987.

Phair, Liz. *Whip-Smart*. Matador/Atlantic 92429-2, 1994.

Smith, Patti. *Horses*. Arista B000002VCQ, 1996 CD reissue of 1975 LP.

Williamson, Chris. *The Best of Chris Williamson*. Wolf Moon CRR959, 2005.

5: Protest Music: Music as a Tool for Social Change

Books

Alterman, Eric. *It Ain't No Sin to Be Glad You're Alive: The Promise of Bruce Springsteen*. Back Bay Books: New York, 1999.

Andressen, Lee. *Battle Notes: Music of the Vietnam War*. Superior, WI: Savage Press, 2000.

Baez, Joan. *And a Voice to Sing With*. New York: Summit Books, 1987.

Cantwell, Robert. *When We Were Good: The Folk Revival.* Cambridge: Harvard University Press, 1996.

Cohen, Ronald D. *Rainbow Quest: The Folk Music Revival and American Society, 1940–1970.* Amherst: University of Massachusetts Press, 2002.

———. *Work and Sing: A History of Occupational and Labor Union Songs in the United States.* Crockett, CA: Carquinez Press, 2010.

Crosby, David, and David Bender. *Stand Up and Be Counted: Making Music, Making History.* San Francisco: Harper San Francisco, 2000.

Denisoff, R. Serge. *Great Day Coming: Folk Music and the American Left.* Baltimore: Penguin Books, 1973.

Doggett, Peter. *There's a Riot Going On: Revolutionaries, Rock Stars and the Rise and Fall of '60s Counterculture.* Edinburgh: Cannongate Books, 2007.

Dunaway, David. *How Can I Keep from Singing: Pete Seeger.* London: Harrap, 1985. Revised edition, New York: Villard/ Random House, 2008.

Dylan, Bob. *The Definitive Bob Dylan Songbook.* New York: Amsco Publications, 2001.

———. *Chronicles, Volume 1.* New York: Simon & Schuster, 2004.

Fowke, Edith, and Joe Glaser. *Songs of Work and Protest.* New York: Dover Publications, 1973.

Goldsmith, Peter D. *Making People's Music: Moe Asch and Folkways Records.* Washington, D.C.: Smithsonian Institution Press, 1998.

Green, Archie. *Only a Miner: Studies in Recorded Coal-Mining Songs.* Urbana: University of Illinois Press, 1972.

———, editor. *Songs About Work: Essays In Occupational Culture for Richard A. Reuss.* Bloomington: Indiana University Folklore Institute, 1993.

Greenway, John. *American Folk Songs of Protest.* Philadelphia: University of Pennsylvania Press, 1953.

Guthrie, Woody. *Bound for Glory: 101 Woody Guthrie Songs, Including All the Songs from "Bound for Glory."* New York: TRO, 1977.

Hawes, Bess Lomax. *Sing It Pretty: A Memoir.* Urbana: University of Illinois Press, 2008.

Hampton, Wade. *Guerrilla Minstrels: John Lennon, Joe Hill, Woody Guthrie, Bob Dylan.* Knoxville: University of Tennessee Press, 1986.

Harrah-Conforth, Bruce. *Laughing Just to Keep from Crying: Folk Song, the Field Recordings of Lawrence Gellert.* Unpublished master's thesis, Indiana University Bloomington.

Heylin, Clinton. *Behind the Shades Revisited: Bob Dylan.* New York: William Morrow, 2001.

Huber, Patrick. *Linthead Stomp: The Creation of Country Music in the Piedmont South.* Chapel Hill: University of North Carolina Press, 2008.

Isserman, Maurice. *If I Had a Hammer: The Death of the Old Left and the Birth of the New Left.* New York: Basic Books, 1987.

Kahn, Si. *Si Kahn Songbook: Music from the Albums "New Wood," "Home," "Doing My Job."* Milwaukee: Hal Leonard, 1989.

Lieberman, Robbie. *"My Song Is My Weapon": People's Songs, American Communism and the Politics of Culture, 1930–1950.* Urbana: University of Illinois Press, 1989.

Klein, Joe. *Woody Guthrie: A Life.* New York: Ballantine Books, 1980.

Lomax, Alan, Woody Guthrie, and Pete Seeger. *Hard Hitting Songs for Hard Hit People.* New York: Oak Publications, 1967.

Morgan, Ted. *Reds: McCarthyism in Twentieth-Century America.* New York: Random House, 2003.

Okun, Milton, editor. *Tom Paxton: The Honor of Your Company.* New York: Cherry Lane Music, 2008.

Pratt, Ray. *Rhythm and Resistance: The Political Uses of American Popular Music.* Washington, D.C.: Smithsonian Institution Press, 1994.

Reuss, Richard A. and JoAnne C. *American Folk Music and Left-Wing Politics, 1927–1957.* Lanham, NJ: Scarecrow Press, 2000.

Robinson, Earl, with Eric A. Gordon. *Ballad of an American: The Autobiography of Earl Robinson.* Lanham, NJ: Scarecrow Press, 1998.

Romalis, Shelly. *Pistol Packin' Mama: Aunt Molly Jackson and the Politics of Folk Song.* Urbana: University of Illinois Press, 1999.

Roscigno, Vincent J., and William F. Danaher. *The Voice of Southern Labor: Radio, Music and Textile Strikes, 1919–1934.* Minneapolis: University of Minnesota Press, 2004.

Rotolo, Suze. *A Freewheelin' Time: A Memoir of Greenwich Village in the Sixties.* New York: Broadway Books, 2008.

Seeger, Pete, and Bob Reiser. *Carry It On! A History in Song and Picture of the Working Men and Women of America.* New York: Simon & Schuster, 1985.

Seeger, Pete. *Where Have All the Flowers Gone: A Singer's Stories, Songs, Seeds, Robberies.* Bethlehem, PA: Sing Out Corporation, 1993.

Shelton, Bob. *No Direction Home: The Life and Music of Bob Dylan.* New York: William Morrow, 1986.

Smith, Craig. *Sing My Whole Life Long: Jenny Vincent's Life in Folk Music and Activism.* Albuquerque: University of New Mexico Press, 2007.

Tuso, Joseph F. *Singing the Vietnam Blues: Songs of the Air Force in Southeast Asia.* College Station: Texas A&M University Press, 1990.

Weissman, Dick. *Which Side Are You On? An Inside History of the Folk Music Revival in America.* New York: Continuum, 2005.

Willens, Doris. *Lonesome Traveler: The Life of Lee Hays.* New York: W. W. Norton & Company, 1988.

Willman, Chris. *Rednecks and Bluenecks: The Politics of Country Music.* New York: The New Press, 2005.

Wolfe, Charles K., and James E. Akenson. *Country Music Goes to War.* Lexington: University of Kentucky Press, 2005.

Wolfe, Charles K., and Kip Lornell. *The Life and Legend of Leadbelly*. New York: Harper Collins, 1992.

Recordings

The Bear Family. *Songs for Political Action: Folk Music, Topical Songs and the American Left, 1926–1953*. Bear Family BCD 15720 JL, 1996.

The Best of Broadside, 1962—1988. Smithsonian Folkways SFW CD 40130, 2000.

Classic Labor Songs. Smithsonian Folkways SFW CD 40 166, 2006.

Country Joe and the Fish. *Fixin' to Die Rag*. Vanguard B000000EJS, 1990 reissue of 1967 album,

Kickin' Hitler's Butt: Vintage Anti-Fascist Songs, 1940–1944. Buzzola BZCD 013, 2007.

Songs of Dissent, Live. Revolt in Records 46122, 1997.

Soul of Viet Nam. Risky Business AK 53917, 1993.

That's Why We're Marching. Smithsonian Folkways SF CD 40021, 1996.

6: Spanish-Speaking Groups

Books

Alaniz, Yolanda, and Megan Cornish. *Viva La Raza: A History of Chicano Identity and Resistance*. Seattle: Red Letter Press, 2008.

Allen, Ray, and Lois Wilcken, editors. *Island Sounds in the Global City: Caribbean Popular Music and Identity in New York*. New York: New York Folklore Society and Institute for Studies in American Music, Brooklyn College, 1998.

Aparicio, Frances R. *Listening to Salsa: Gender, Latin Popular Music and Puerto Rican Cultures*. Hanover, NH: Wesleyan University Press, 1998.

Barkley, Elizabeth F. *Crossroads: The Multicultural Roots of America's Popular Music*. 2nd edition. Upper Saddle River, NJ: Pearson Prentice Hall, 2007.

Bourgeois, Philip. *In Search of Respect: Selling Crack in El Barrio.* Cambridge, England: Cambridge University Press, 1993.

Clark, Walter Aaron, editor. *From Tejano to Tango.* New York: Routledge, 2002.

Dickey, Dan William. *The Kennedy Corridos: A Study of the Ballads of a Mexican-American Hero.* Austin: Center for Mexican American Studies, University of Texas at Austin, 1978.

Garcia, David F. *Arsenio Rodriguez and the Transnational Flows of Latin Popular Music.* Philadelphia: Temple University Press, 2006.

Glasser, Ruth. *My Music Is My Flag: Puerto Ricans and Their New York Communities, 1917–1940.* Berkeley: University of California Press, 1996.

Guerrero, Armando Hugo Ortiz, compiler. *Vida y Muerte en la Frontera; Cancionero Del Corrido Norestense.* Monterey, Mexico: Hensa Editions, 1992.

Herrera-Sobek, Maria. *Northward Bound: The Mexican Immigrant Experience in Ballad and Song.* Bloomington: Indiana University Press, 1993.

———. *The Mexican Corrido: A Feminist Analysis.* Bloomington: Indiana University Press, 1990.

Kun, Josh. *Audiotopia: Music, Race and America.* Berkeley: University of California Press, 2005.

Lipsitz, George. *Footsteps in the Dark: The Hidden Histories of Popular Music.* Minneapolis: University of Minnesota Press, 2007.

Loza, Steven. *Barrio Rhythms: Mexican American Music in Los Angeles.* Urbana: University of Illinois Press, 1997.

McDowell, John H. *Poetry and Violence: The Ballad Tradition of Mexico's Costa Chica.* Urbana; University of Illinois Press, 2000.

McFarland, Pancho. *Chicano Rap: Gender and Violence in the Postindustrial Barrio.* Austin: University of Texas Press, 2008.

Miguel, Guadalupe San Jr., *Tejano Proud: Tex-Mex Music in the Twentieth Century*. College Station, Texas: Texas A&M University Press, 2002.

Ospino, Hernando Calvo. *Salsa! Havana Heat, Bronx Beat*. London: Latin American Bureau, 1995.

Paredes, Americo. *A Texas-Mexican Cancionero: Folk Songs of the Lower Border*. Urbana: University of Illinois Press, 1977.

Peña, Manuel. *The Mexican American Orquesta: Music, Culture, and the Dialectic of Conflict*. Austin: University of Texas Press, 1999.

———. *Musica Tejana*. College Station: Texas A&M Press, 1999.

Ragland, Cathy. *Música Norteña: Mexican Migrants Creating a Nation Between Nations*. Philadelphia: Temple University Press, 2009

Robb, J. Donald. *Hispanic Folk Music of Old New Mexico and the Southwest: A Self-Portrait of a People*. Norman: University of Oklahoma Press, 1980.

Roberts, John Storm. *The Latin Tinge: The Impact of Latin American Music in the United States*. New York: Oxford University Press, 1979.

Rondon, Cesar Miguel. *The Book of Salsa: A Chronicle of Urban Music from the Caribbean to New York City*. Chapel Hill: University of North Carolina Press, 2008.

Wald, Elijah. *Narcocorrido: A Journey into the Music of Drugs, Guns, and Guerrillas*. New York: Harper Collins. 2001.

Recordings

Chavez Ravine. Nonesuch/Perro Verde 78977-2, 2005.

Corridos y Tragedies de la Frontera. Arhoolie 7019 and 7020.

Hinjosa, Tish. *Homeland*. A&M CD 5263.

Dr. Loco's Rockin' Jalapeño Band *Movimiento Music*. Flying Fish Records FF 70614, 1992.

The Mexican Revolution: Corridos about the Heroes and Events 1918–1920 and Beyond. Arhoolie 7041-7044.

The Roots of the Narcocorrido, CD 7053.

Rolas De Aztlán: Songs of the Chicano Movement. Smithsonian Folkways SW CD40516, 2006.

7: Rock and Roll

Books

Azerad, Michael. *Our Band Could Be Your Life: Scenes from the American Indie Underground, 1981–1991.* Boston: Little, Brown & Co., 2001.

Berger, Harris M. *Metal, Rock, and Jazz: Perception and the Phenomonology of Musical Experience.* Hanover, NH: Wesleyan University Press, 1999.

Blush, Steven. *American Hardcore: A Tribal History.* Los Angeles: Feral House, 2001.

Charlton, Katherine. *Rock Music Styles: A History.* 4th edition. New York: McGraw-Hill, 2003.

Clover, Joshua. *1989: Bob Dylan Didn't Have This to Sing About.* Berkeley: University of California Press, 2008.

Crazy Horse, Kandia. *Rip It Up: The Black Experience in Rock 'n' Roll.* New York: Palgrave Macmillan. 2004.

Friedlander, Paul. *Rock and Roll: A Social History.* Boulder: Westview Press, 1996.

Garofalo, Reebee. *Rockin' Out: Popular Music in the U.S.A.* 4th edition. Upper Saddle River, NJ: Prentice Hall, 2008.

Harris, Kevin Kahn. *Extreme Metal: Music and Culture on the Edge.* Oxford, England: Berg Publishers, 2007.

Joel, Billy. *Billy Joel Complete, Volume 2.* Milwaukee: Hal Leonard, 1988.

Lahickey, Beth, compiler. *All Ages: Reflections on Straight Edge.* Huntington Beach, CA: Revelation Books, 1997.

Larson, Thomas E. *A History of Rock and Roll.* Dubuque, IA: Kendall/Hunt Publishing Company, 2004.

Mahon, Maureen. *Right to Rock: The Black Rock Coalition and the Cultural Politics of Race.* Durham, NC: Duke University Press, 2004.

Martin, Linda, and Kerry Segrave. *Anti-Rock: The Opposition to Rock 'n' Roll.* New York: Da Capo, 1993.

McNeil, Legs, and Gillian McCain. *Please Kill Me: The Uncensored Oral History of Punk.* New York: Grove Press, 1996.

Myers, Ben. *American Heretics: Rebel Voices in Music.* Hove, England: Codex Books, 2002.

Rage Against the Machine. *Rage Against the Machine.* Milwaukee: Hal Leonard, 1994.

Raha, Maria. *Cinderella's Big Score: Women of the Punk and Indie Underground.* Emeryville, CA: Seal Press, 2005.

Rhodes, Lisa L. *Electric Ladyland: Women and Rock Culture.* Philadelphia: University of Pennsylvania Press, 2005.

Sinclair, John. *Guitar Army: Rock and Revolution with MC5 and the White Panther Party.* Los Angeles: Process Media, 2006.

Stuessy, Joe, and Scott Lipscomb. *Rock and Roll: Its History and Stylistic Development.* 5th edition. Upper Saddle River, NJ: Pearson/Prentice Hall, 2006.

Szatmary, David P. *Rockin' in Time: A Social History of Rock-and-Roll.* 6th edition. Upper Saddle River, NJ: Pearson/Prentice Hall, 2006.

Taylor, Steven. *False Prophet: Field Notes from the Punk Underground.* Middletown, CT: Wesleyan University Press, 2003.

8: The Music of Hate

Books

Burkhart, David, editor. *Soundtracks to the White Revolution: White Supremacist Assaults on Youth Music Subcultures.* Chicago: Center for New Community, 1999.

Glassie, Henry. "Take That Night Train to Selma." In *Folk Songs and Their Makers,* edited by Henry Glassie, Edward D. Ives, and

John F. Swed. Bowling Green, OH: Bowling Green University Popular Press, 1971, 1–70.

Malone, Bill C. *Don't Get Above Your Raisin': Country Music and the Southern Working Class.* Urbana: University of Illinois Press, 2002.

Willman, Chris. *Rednecks and Bluenecks: The Politics of Country Music.* New York: New Press, 2005.

Yurchenko, Henriette. "Skinhead Serenade: The Songs of Neo-Nazis." www.henriettayurchenko.com skinhead.

Recordings

For Segregationists Only: By Popular Demand. Rebel LP-1000, undated.
Numerous Resistance Records titles.

9: The Two Gulf Wars, 9/11/2001, and Afghanistan

Books

Fox, Aaron. A. *Real Country: Music and Language in Working-Class Culture.* Durham: University of North Carolina Press, 2004.

Pieslak, Jonathan. *Sound Targets: American Soldiers and Music in the Iraq War.* Bloomington: Indiana University Press, 2009.

Willman, Chris. *Rednecks and Bluenecks: The Politics of Country Music.* New York: New Press, 2005.

Wolfe, Charles and James Akenson. *Country Music Goes to War.* Lexington: University of Kentucky Press, 2005.

Recordings

Daniels, Charlie. *The Essential Super Hits of the Charlie Daniels Band.* Koch B000V9G42K, 2004.

Earle, Steve. *Just an American Boy.* Artemis Records B0000A0V39, 2003.

Erik B. & Rakim. *Casualties of War.* MCA B0000020KS, 1992.

Green Day. *American Idiot.* Reprise B00020ERIO, 2004.

Greenwood, Lee. *Essential Super Hits*. Sony 8000002BID, 1996.

Jackson, Alan. *Greatest Hits*. Arista B0000BJ1HIV, 2004.

Keith, Toby. *35 Biggest Hits*. Show Dog Nashville B00144VBBS, 2008.

Pearl Jam. *Lost Dogs*. Sony B0000DXJM6, 2003.

Queensryche. *American Soldier*. Rhino R2 517967, 2009.

Rock Against Bush, Vol. 1. With DVD. FAT FAT675-2, 2004.

Rock Against Bush, Vol. 2. With DVD. FAT F87677-2, 2004.

Stevens, Ray. *Osama Yo' Mama*. Curb Records B00005YVKP, 2002.

Trudell, John. *A.K.A. Graffiti Man*. Rykodisc B00008FPXZ.

Williams, Hank Jr. *America the Way I See It*. Curb Special Markets B00000DAIB, 1990.

Wyclef Jean. *Masquerade*. Sony Music Canada B000658NW, 2002.

Young, Neil. *Living with War*. Reprise 44335-2, 2006.

Index

AAA. *See* Agricultural Adjustment Administration

AACM. *See* Association for the Advancement of Creative Musicians

abortion issues, feminism and, 154

"About the Railroad Worker (The Dishwasher),"241–42

"Abraham, Martin and John," 124

Adams, John, 9

Afghanistan. *See* Gulf War (2003)

AFL. *See* American Federation of Labor

African American(s), 1. *See also* blues; jazz; rap music

  American Indians recording with, 51

  banjo as instrument of, 94

  blues recaptured by, 94

  coon songs and, 76–77

  disco music and, 103–4

  entertainers, 1880-1915, 77

  gospel music and, 95–97

  hate music and, 295–97

  interracial romance and, 126–28

  minstrel shows and, 75–76

  pop music and, 97–98

  protest music and, 180–81

  ragtime and, 77–78

  R&B and, 97–98

  secular folk music of, 73–75

  sharecropping and, 73

  slavery and, 63–64

  soul music and, 101–4

  spirituals, origins with, 69–70

  white songs about, 123–26

  World War II and, 94–95

African American slaves

  Civil War and, 72–73

  development/evolution of, 68

  early music of, 64–65

  instruments of, 65–66

  minstrel shows with, 67–68

  music's uses/dangers for, 66–67

  origins of, 64

  religion and, 68–69

  revolts of, 67

  spirituals' content of, 71–72

Africans, in slavery, 23

Afrika Bambaata, 110

Agricultural Adjustment Administration (AAA), 188

A.K.A. Graffiti Man, 50

"Alabama Blues," 91–92
Aldon Music, 144
Alexie, Sherman, 39
"All-American Girl," 163
"All Coons Look Alike to Me," 76–77
Allen, Beau, 5
Allen, Rex, Jr., 54
"Allentown," 289
"All Quiet Along the Potomac," 16
"All These Years," 159
the Almanac Singers
    members of, 184–85
    World War II and, 197
Alstyne, Egbert Van, 30–31
American Bandstand, 275
American Communist Party, 178–80
American Federation of Labor (AFL),
    183–84
American History Songbook (Silver-
    man), 17
American Idiot, 311
"The American Indian Girl," 27
American Indians, 1
    African Americans recording with,
        51
    alcohol and, 44–45
    casinos and, 38–39
    civil rights movement and, 35–38
    classical music of, 60
    disease impacting, 25
    environment and, 55
    European settlers battling, 21–22,
        24–25
    European settlers conquest/removal
        rational with, 25–28
    European settlers' relationship
        with, 23–24
    Ghost Dance of, 31–32
    historical music of, 42–43
    history, nineteenth century, of,
        28–33
    history, twentieth century, of, 33–39
    humor/novelty songs on, 53–54
    hybrid music of, 59–60

interracial romance and, 54–55
lifestyle songs of, 43–45
music, twentieth century, of, 40–42
musical fusion of, 51–53
music business and, 61–62
mystic songs of, 45–46
the New Deal and, 33
peyote and, 32
protest music of, 41, 46–49, 56, 58
racism and, 47, 54
record labels for, 61–62
reservations system and allotments
    for, 30–31
schooling of, 32–33
selling out and, 49
slavery and, 22–23
symbols and, 58–59
traditional music of, 39–40
white commentary on, 53–60
World War II and, 33–35
American music
    social theory and, xi
    textbooks on, xi–xii
American Primitive Music (Burton), 39
American Songbag (Sandburg), 17
Ames, Russell, 67
Amos, Tori, 164
"Anacreon in Heaven," 11
Anderson, John, 58–59
"Anthem of the American Indian,"
    45–46
Apache Spirit, 43
Aquash, Anna Mae, 38
Armstrong, Billy Joe, *312*
Armstrong, Louis, 105–6
"Army Reserve," 287
Arnold, Eddie, 29
Arrested Development, 113
Asch, Moses, 190–91
Association for the Advancement of
    Creative Musicians (AACM),
    108
Audiotopia: Music, Race and America
    (Kun), 261

authenticity
    in blues, 92–93
    the Kingston Trio and, 205–6
    rap music and, 121–23
    of White, Josh, 93
Autry, Gene, 140–41

Badlands: Ballads of the Lakota, 59
Baez, Joan, 142, 161, 210
Bagley, E. E., 18
Ballad for Americans, 186
"Ballad of a Thin Man," 212
"The Ballad of Davy Crockett," 12
"Ballad of Gregorio Cortez," 237–38
"The Ballad of Ira Hayes," 34–35, 58
"The Ballad of October 16th," 188
Ballads and Songs Collected by the Missouri Folk-Lore Society (Belden), 29
Ballard, Louis W., 60
"Ball of Confusion," 99
the Band, 52
banda music, 244
banjo
    as African American instrument, 94
    history of, 65–66
"Bank Failure," 186
Barnes, Tommy, 26
"Battle of Little Big Horn," 29
"The Battle of New Orleans," 11
the Beastie Boys, 120
the Beatles, 216
    beginnings of, 143–44
    imitations of, 144
bebop, 106
Bee, Robby, 46–47, 51
Bee, Tom, 43–46, 48, 61–62
the Bee Gees, 280
Belafonte, Harry, 205
Belden, H. M., 29
Bellecourt, Clyde, 36
Bellmore, Rebecca, 60
"The Bennington Riflemen," 8
Berger, Harris M., 285–86

Bernay, Eric, 188
Bernstein, Leonard, 127
Berry, Chuck, 272, 291
Bessie Smith: Empress of the Blues, 84
BIA. *See* Bureau of Indian Affairs
"BIA Blues," 49
Biafra, Jello, 282
Big Daddy Kane, 117
bilingualism, 235–36
Billings, William, 7–8
bin Laden, Osama, 306, 308
Bird, James, 10
Bitter Tears, 29, 46
"Black, Brown, White Blues," 91
Black America, 77
"Black and White," 125
Blackboard Jungle, 269
"Blackened," 285
Black Flag, 282–83
the blacklist, 204
Black Panthers, 291
Blades, Ruben, 252
Blake, Blind, 82
Bland, James, 76
Blood Struggle: The Rise of Modern Indian Nations (Wilkinson, C.), 25
"Blowin' in the Wind," 207
Blue, 150–51
bluegrass festivals, 228–29
"Blue Indians," 51
Blue Ridge Mountain Singers, 140
blues, 41. *See also* jazz
    African Americans recapturing, 94
    authenticity in, 92–93
    birth/evolution of, 78–89
    British invasion reviving, 90
    Chicago and early, 88–89
    country, 79–80
    festivals for, 228–29
    form of, 79
    lyrics of, 79–83
    migration and, 87–88
    ownership of, 91–92
    preachers and, 86–87

as protest music, 85–86
themes central to, 82–83
vaudeville and, 83–85
white audiences/artists and, 89–93
"Blue Wing," 56
"Bombs Over Baghdad," 302–3
"Bomb the World," 311
Bone Days, 51
Boone, Pat, 273–74
"Born in the USA," 128–29
"The Bourgeois Blues," 195
Braddock, Bobby, 126
Bragg, Billy, 193
Braham, David, 6
British invasion, 143–45
    blues revival by, 90
"Broken Arrow," 58
Broonzy, Big Bill, 91
Brown, Dee, 22
Brown, James, 101–2, 114
Browne, Jackson, 224
"Brown-Eyed Woman," 127
Bruce, Lenny, 214
Bryan, Alfred, 18
Buchanan James, 15
The Buena Vista Social Club, 262–63
Buffalo Bill's Wild West Show, 26, *26*
"Buffalo Soldier," 56
Buffalo Springfield, 58
"Bunker's Hill, a New Song," 8
Bureau of Indian Affairs (BIA), 33
Burning Sky, 56
Burns, Ken, 108–9
Burton, Frederic, 39
"Bury My Heart at Wounded Knee,"
    37, 53, 160
*Bury My Heart at Wounded Knee: An
    Indian History of the American
    West* (Brown, D.), 22
Bush, George H. W., 217, 302, 307
Bush, George W., *305*, 307–8
Butler, Jerry, 318
Butler Act (1922), 177
"Buy, Buy the American Car," 219
Byrd, Robert, 317

Caballero, Lorenzo, 254
"Cactus Tree," 150
Calderon, Tego, 249
"California," 150–51
"Camino para Volver," 253
Campbell, Glen, 121–22
Campbell, Luther, 113–14, 168–69
cantometrics, 267–68
Canyon Records, 61
Carawan, Candy, 208
Carawan, Guy, 208
Carey, Mariah, 165–66
Carpenter, Mary Chapin, 158–59
"Carry the Star," 51
Carter, Rubin "Hurricane," 214
Cash, Johnny, 29, 46
    "The Ballad of Ira Hayes" and,
        34–35
"Casino," 59
casinos, of American Indians, 38–39
Castro, Fidel, 249–50
"Casualties of War," 303
"Catman Jimmy," 222
celebrity, politics and, 316–20
Cerullo, John, xii
Chad Mitchell Trio, 206
Chain Gang, 181, 200
"Chain Gang Song," 141
Chandler, Phil, 209
"A Change Is Gonna Come," 321
The Changer and the Changed, 155
Chaplin, Ralph, 173
Chapman, Tracy, 160
    protest music of, 217
Charles, Ray, 97, 274
Chavez, Linda, 235
Chavez Ravine, 263
Cher, 54
"Cherokee Fiddle," 58
"Cherokee Maiden," 54
"Chester," 7–8
"Cheyenne Autumn," 55
"Chicago," 44, 277
Chicago, blues and, 88–89
Chicano rap, 256–58

Chicano Soul Power, 256
chicken scratch, 41
Chief Joseph, 28
the Chi-lites, 102
Chinese Americans, 6
"Choice of Colors," 292, 318
"Chopsticks," 163
Christian music movement, 316
"Christmas in the Trenches," 219
Chuck D., 60, 112–13, 319
CIO. *See* Congress of Industrial
    Organizations
civil rights
    American Indians and, 35–38
    NAACP and, 94–95
    protest music and, 207–9
    white performers and, 208–9
Civil War, 14–16, 25
    African American slaves and, 72–73
Clapton, Eric, 90
Clark, Dick, 275
classical music, of American Indians,
    60
"Class of '73," 51
the Coasters, 104
Cobain, Kurt, 161, *286*, 287
Cockburn, Bruce, 315
Cohan, George M., 18
Cohen, Ronald, 180–81
Cole, Bob, 77
Collins, Judy, 161, 210
Colon, Willie, 252
Coltrane, John, 319
Combs, Sean, 115–17, 320
Come On, Come On, 158
Come On Now, 160
"Commodity Blues," 48
Communist Party
    music of, 178–80
    protest music and, 202
Cone, James H., 86
Congress of Industrial Organizations
    (CIO), 183–84
Congress of Racial Equality (CORE),
    296

conjunto music
    evolution of, 243
    women and, 244–45
Connolly, John, 242
conservative songs, 177
"El Contrabandista," 259
Cooder, Ry, 262–63
Cooke, Sam, 321
    church origins of, 97
the Coolidge Sisters, 53
coon songs, 76–77
Cooper, Alice, 288
Cooper, James Fenimore, 26
CORE. *See* Congress of Racial Equality
corrido(s)
    "Ballad of Gregorio Cortez," 237–38
    definition of, 236
    immigrants and, 241–43
    importance of, 236–37
    on Kennedy, John F., 243
    labor unions and, 242–43
    on Murrieta, 238–39
    narcocorridos and, 258–61
    structure of, 240
    Texas Rangers and, 238
    themes of, 239–40
    women and, 240–41
Cortez, Gregorio, 237–38
country and western, 40
country blues, 79–80
The Country Blues Songbook, 80
country music, women in, 139–40,
    157–59
Country Music Goes to War (Rudder),
    311
"Courtesy of the Red, White, and Blue
    (The Angry American),"309–10
cover records, in rock and roll, 273–74
Cox, Ida, 139
Craig, Vincent, 43
"Crazy Man Crazy," 268
Creedence Clearwater Revival, 36
Crockett, Davey, 12
"Crocket Victory March," 12
Crosby, Stills and Nash, 277

Crow Dog, Mary, 44
Crudos, 256
"The Cruel War," 16
Cruz, Celia, 253
Cuba(ns)
    exodus and, 249–51
    immigrants from, 250
    Miami sound and, 251–52
    salsa and, 252–53
Cuetara, Laura, xi
Cuney, Warren, 85
"Custer," 29
Custer, George, 28–29
"Cuter Died for Your Sins," 30
"Cynthia Parker," 141
Cypress Hill, 257, *258*
Cyr, Richard, 48

Daddy Yankee, 249
Dahl, Steve, 104
D'Ambrosio, Antonio, 34
"Damn the Filipinos," 17
Daniels, Charlie, 304–5
Danish Emigrants Ballads and Songs
    (Wright & Wright), 5
Davidson, Levette J., 31
Davis, Gary, 87
Davis, Mac, 125
Davis, Miles, 108
Dawes Act (1887), 30
Death of John Doe, 195
"Death of Major André," 8
"The Death of Mother Jones," 141
Dehr, Rich, 205
Deloria, Vine, Jr., 36
"Depression Blues," 86
"The Devil and the Farmer's Wife,"
    133–34
the Diamonds, 273
Dickens, Hazel, 219–20
Dickey, Dan William, 243
Diddley, Bo, 267
DiFranco, Ani, 220, 319–20
Dimitrov, Georgi, 179

Dion and the Belmonts, 124
"Dirty Bitch (Feminist)," 299
disco music, 103–4, 279–80
    punk music compared to, 280–81
"Discrimination," 242
"Dixie," 16
the Dixie Chicks, 159
    politics and, 308–10
Dixieland jazz, 65, 105–6
Dixon, Willie, 88
DJ Jazzy Jeff and the Fresh Prince, 118
Dlugacz, Judy, 155
Donegan, Lonnie, 205
"Don't Call Me Nigger, Whitey," 292
"Don't Give Us a Reason," 302
"Don't Go Near the Indians," 54
Dorsey, Thomas A., 95–96
Douglas, Frederick, 66
"The Downeaster 'Alexa'," 290
Dr. Dre, 120–21
Dr. Loco's Rockin' Jalepeno Band, 256
"Drill, Ye Tarriers, Drill," 3–4
Dupri, Jermaine, 114
Dust Bowl Ballads, 190
Dylan, Bob, 122, 193, 207, *211*, 320, 322
    beginnings of, 209–10
    influence of, 215
    "Only a Pawn in Their Game" and,
        210, 321
    politics of, 210, 213–14
    protest music and impact of, 214–15
    Springsteen compared to, 225
    women in lyrics of, 143

Eagle, Bobby, 43
Earle, Steve, 310
Easy Riders, 205
"Easy Street," 219
"Ebony Warrior," 51
"Education," 287
"80s Ladies," 157–58
"Eight Dollars a Day," 13
"The Eighth of January," 11
Einhorn, Steve, 311

Eisler, Hans, 178–79, 182

"El Buen Borincano," 247–48

Ellington, Duke, 106

Ellis, Bill, 221

Ellis Island immigrants, 2

Eminem, 120–22

The Encyclopedia of Native Music (Wright-McLeod), 52

"En Estados Unidos," 253

Enstice, Wayne, 168

environmental issues, protest music and, 222

Epstein, Dena, 65

Eric B. & Rakim, 303

"Estan Tirando Bomboas," 248

Estefan, Emilio, 251–52

Estefan, Gloria, 251–52

Etheridge, Melissa, 162–63

European settlers. *See also* immigrants
    American Indians, conquest/removal rational of, 25–28
    American Indians battling, 21–22, 24–25
    American Indians' relationship with, 23–24

"The Eve of Destruction," 216

Evers, Medgar, 95

"Everybody Crying About Vietnam," 92

Exile in Guyville, 163

"The Fabulous Fables," 107

"Family Affair," 103, 292

"Farewell Song for German Emigrants Going to America," 3

"Farewell to Ireland," 3

"The Farmer is the Man," 172

Farrakhan, Louis, 95

"The Far Side of Town," 245

"Fast Car," 160, 217

"Father, Dear Father, Come Home to Me Now," 137

Feeney, Anne, 219

The Feminine Mystique (Friedan), 145–46

feminism
    abortion issues and, 154
    Friedan and, 145–46
    Mitchell and, 150
    in 1970s, 153–55
    radical, 146
    solo artists and, 162–65
    Vietnam War and, 147
    Williamson and, 155–56

Fender, Freddy, 246–47

"Fight to Be Heard," 256

Fillmore, Millard, 15

Finson, Jon W., 6

"Firelight," 221

Fisk Jubilee Singers, 71, 76

"Fixing Her Hair," 320

Fletcher, Alice, 39

Fletcher, Ed "Duke Bootee," 111

Folk Blues, 88–89

folk music, 41. *See also* protest music
    African Americans and secular, 73–75
    in 1960s, 142–43
    pop music and crossover of, 204–5
    revival of, 226–29
    women in, 139, 159–61

Folk Song Encyclopedia, Volume II (Silverman), 9

Folkways Records, 61

"Follow the Drinking Guard," 66

Foner, Philip, 172

Footsteps In the Dark: The Hidden History of Popular Music (Lipsitz), 103

Ford, Ernie, 12, 205

For Segregationists Only, 296

Foster, Stephen, 15

Franklin, Aretha, 97, 101–2, 268

Franti, Michael, 311

Freedom Now!, 107, 168

"Freedom of Speech," 117–18

The Freewheelin' Bob Dylan, 209

Fremont, James, 15
Friedan, Betty, 145–46
From the Underworld of Redboy, 52
Fugazi, 283–84

G., Kenny, 109
Gaillard, Sam, 98
Galliard, Slim, 110
Gallogly, Sarah, xii
Gamble, Kenneth, 102
gangster rap, 113–14, 120, 299–300
Garafalo, Reebee, 284
Garland, Jim, 176
Gartrell, Delia, 221
Gaye, Marvin, 99–101, *101*
gay music, 315–16
Gaytan, Jean, 259
Gellert, Lawrence, 67
    collections of, 75, 181
"Genocide in Progress," 47
"Geronimo's Cadillac," 58
"Get Out, Yellow Skins, Get Out," 6
"Ghetto Bastard," 118
Ghost Dance, 31–32
"Ghost Dance," 52
Ghost of Tom Joad, 225
Giant Book of Rock, 169–70
Gilbert, Ronnie, 202–3
Gillespie, Dizzy, 106
"Gimme a Pigfoot and a Bottle of
    Beer," 78
Ginn, Greg, 283
Giuliani, Rudolph, *305*
"Give Peace a Change," 304
Gladstone, Jack, 30
Glaser, Joe, 218
Glasser, Ruth, 247–48
Glassie, Henry, 295–96
Glover, Henry, 274
"God Bless the USA," 302
Goffin, Gerry, 156
"Going Home," 53
"Goodbye Earl," 159
Goodman, Benny, 105–6

"Good Night Irene," 195, 203
"Goodnight Saigon," 289–90
Gordon, Kim, 161
Gordy, Berry, 98–101
gospel music, 95–97
Graham, John, 38
Grandmaster Flash, 110–12, *111*
"Grandmother's Land," 55
the Grateful Dead, 277
Great Depression
    government affected by, 183
    women and, 138–41
Green, Victor, 1
Green Day, 311, *312*
Greenwood, Lee, 302, 308
Griffith, Nanci, 158
"Gringo Ku Klux Klanes," 261
Grossman, Al, 209
grunge music, 286–88
Guard, Dave, 206
Guererro, Lalo, 263
Gulf War (1991)
    music supporting, 301–2
    protest music about, 302–4
    summary of, 301
Gulf War (2003)
    music of, 308–13
    reasons behind, 306–7
    support of, 307
    Vietnam War compared to, 313–14
Gunning, Sarah Ogan, 176
Guns N' Roses, 285
Guthrie, Woody, 85, *191*, 197, 203, 209,
    225, 303, 319
    the Almanac Singers and, 184–85
    Asch patronizing, 190–91
    beginnings of, 189
    legacy of, 193
    "The Ludlow Massacre" and, 191–92
    "Private Property" and, 192–93
    "Roll On Columbia" and, 190
    Seeger, Pete, compared to, 198–99
    "This Land Is Your Land" and, 192
Guy, Buddy, 90

Haggard, Merle, 54, 127–28
"Hail Columbia," 9, 67
halam, 65
Haley, Bob, 268
    "Rock Around the Clock" and, 269
"Half Breed," 54
Halker, Clark, 172
Hammond, John, 209
Hampton, Wayne, 174–75
Handcox, John, 180
Handley, Randy, 28, 56
hard core music, 282–83
Harrigan, Edward "Ned," 6
Harrison, William Henry, 13
Hatch, Orrin, 317
hate music
    African Americans and, 295–97
    neo-Nazi music and, 297–300
"Have You Forgotten," 311
Hayes, Alfred, 175
Hayes, Bill, 12
Hayes, Ira, 35
Hays, Lee, 193, 198. *See also* the Weavers
    the Almanac Singers and, 184–85
Heaps, Porter W., 16
Heaps, Willard A., 16
"Heartbeat," 48
Heartbeat: Voices of First Nation's Women, 53
A Heartbeat and a Guitar: Johnny Cash and the Making of Bitter Tears (D'Ambrosio), 34
heavy metal
    1980s and, 284
    themes in, 284–86
Hellerman, Fred, 202–3
Hendrix, Jimi, 291
Herrera-Sobek, Maria, 240
"He Thinks He'll Keep Her," 158
Hidalgo, David, 263
Highway 61 Revisited, 210
Hill, Joe, 174–75
Hill, Lauryn, 119
Hinjosa, Tish, 245, 320

hip-hop. *See* rap music
Hip-Hop and Rap Lyrics (Leonard), 117
The Hip-Hop Wars: What We Talk About When We Talk About Hip-Hop and Why It Matters (Rose), 121
hippies
    communes of, 147
    rock and roll and, 276–77
historical music, of American Indians, 42–43
Hitler-Stalin pact, 186–89
Hogan, Ernest, 76–77
Hold the Rain, 53
Holiday, Billie, 107
Holly, Buddy, 272–73
Homeland, 245
homeless people, 221–22
"Home on the Range," 55
"Honey Child," 97
Hoover, J. Edgar, 263
Hormel Meat Company, 167–68
Horn, Charles Edward, 27
Hornsby, Bruce, 126
Horton, Johnny, 11
"Hotdogs and Hamburgers," 54–55
house concerts, 227–28
Howard, Frank, 76
Howe, Mary, 141
Huff, Leon, 102
"Humanism," 51
humor/novelty songs, on American Indians, 53–54
Hunter, Meredith, 278
"Hurrah for Rough and Ready," 12
Hussein, Saddam, 307
Hutchinson, Frank, 89
Hutchinson, J. J., 13
The Hutchinson Family Singers, 13, *14*
hybrid music, American Indians and, 59–60

"I, Go," 160
"I Ain't Marching Anymore," 212
"I Almost Lost My Mind," 274

I Am an Eagle: The Music from the Legends Project, 49
"I Am a Suffragette," 136
"I Am a Town," 158
Ian, Janis, 126–27
"I Believe the South Is Gonna Rise Again," 126
Ice Cube, 103
Ice T, 117–18
"I Didn't Raise My Boy to Be a Soldier," 18
"If I Had a Hammer," 207
"I'm a Civilized Man," 179
immigrants. *See also* European settlers
    corridos and, 241–43
    from Cuba, 250
    at Ellis Island, 2
    from Mexico, 234–36
    origins of, 1
    politics of Mexico and, 235–36
    songs about, 5–7
    songs of, 2–5
    stereotypes of, 5–6
    themes in music of, 2–3
Immigrant Songbook (Silverman), 3
"I'm Proud to Be an American," 308
"Independence Day," 159
"The Indian and the Eagle," 46
Indian Appropriation Act (1854), 28
Indian Blues: American Indians and the Politics of Music, 1879-1935 (Troutman), 32
"Indian Cars," 43–44
The Indian Frontier of the American West (Utley), 30
Indian Gambling and Regulation Act (1988), 38
"The Indian Ghost Dance and War," 31
"Indian Giver," 49
"Indian Outlaw," 26
Indian Removal Act (1830), 27–28
Indian Reorganization Act (1934), 33
"Indian Reservation," 26
Indians, Cowboys, Horses, Dogs, 58

"Indian Sunset," 55
"Indian Wars," 56
Indigo Girls, 159–60
the Indigo Girls, 60
Industry Workers of the World (IWW), 172–73
interracial romance
    African Americans and, 126–28
    American Indians and, 54–55
In the Blood, 52
"In the Ghetto (Vicious Circle),"125
"In the Sweet Bye and Bye," 175
Iraq. *See* Gulf War (1991); Gulf War (2003)
"Irma Jackson," 127–28
the Isley Brothers, 103
"It Was a Good Day," 103
I've Got to Know, 303
Ives, Burl, 135, 201
"I Want to Go Home," 71
"I Will Overcome," 208–9
"I Wish I Was a Single Girl Again," 134–35
IWW. *See* Industry Workers of the World

"Jack and Diane," 290
Jackson, Alan, 306
Jackson, Andrew, 27–28
Jackson, Aunt Molly, 176, 180, 185, 196
Jackson, George Pullen, 69–70
Jackson, Janet, 165
Jackson, Mahalia, 96
Jackson, Otis, 96
Jagger, Mick, 292
"James Bird," 10
Jamieson, Stuart, 65–66
Jay Z, 115–16
jazz. *See also* blues
    bebop and, 106
    collectives, 107–8
    complexity of, 104–5
    developments in, 108–9
    Dixieland, 65, 105–6

early, 83–85
New Orleans and, 105
politics and, 107
women in, 138–39, 167–68
Jazz, 108–9
Jazzwomen: Conversations with Twenty-one Musicians (Enstice & Stockhouse), 168
Jean, Wyclef, 306
Jefferson, Blind Lemon, 81, 82
Jefferson, Thomas, 9, 11, 23, 27, 68
Jefferson Airplane, 153, 293
"Jefferson and Liberty," 9–10
Jenkins, Gordon, 202
Jennings, Waylon, 255
Jermance, Frank, xii
"Joaquin," 245
"Joe Hill," 175
Joel, Billy, 289–90, 312
John, Elton, 55
"John Doe No. 14," 158–59
Johnny Damas and Me, 50
"Johnny Has Gone for a Soldier," 8–9
Johnson, J. Rosamund, 77
Johnson, James Weldon, 77
Johnson, Lee, 28
Johnson, Lyndon, 95, 207, 242
presidency of, 275–76
Johnson, Robert, 39, 78, 82, 93
devil and, 87
"John Walker," 310
Joplin, Janis, 277
Joplin, Scott, 78
Jordan, Louis, 97
"Juanita," 246
Juravich, Tom, 219
JV, 258

Kaiser, Henry, 59
"Kajun Ku Klux Klan," 296
Kansas, 55
"The Kansas Contractors," 241
Kanye West, *115*
"Keep On Pushing," 318

Keil, Charles, 92–93
Keith, Toby, 309
Kennedy, Bobby, 215
Kennedy, Jacqueline, *276*
Kennedy, John F., *276*
corridos on, 243
presidency of, 275
Key, Francis Scott, 10–11
Keys, Alicia, *166*
"Kick Out the Jams," 291
Kid Frost, 256–57
"Killing Ground," 303–4
King, B. B., 93
King, Carole
men in songs of, 157
piano work of, 144
themes of, 156–57
King, Charlie, 219
King, Martin Luther, Jr., 95
King Records, 274
the Kingston Trio, 215
authenticity and, 205–6
Kirshner, Don, 144
Kissinger, Henry, 279
Klein, Joe, 189
Knight, Suge, 120
Kravitz, Lenny, 292, 304
Kristofferson, Kris, 310
Ku Klux Klan, 296–97, *297*
Kun, Josh, 261

"La Bamba," 254
labor songs, 74–75
communism and, 178–80
miners and, 175–77
textile workers and, 175–77
Wobblies and, 172–73
women and, 140–41
labor unions
corridos and, 242–43
formation of, 183–84
Ladies of the Canyon, 151
La Farge, Peter, 29, 34, 46–47, 58, 318
Lakota Woman (Crow Dog), 44

"Land of the Free," 48
"Land of the Wanna Be Free," 51
Lange, Robert "Mutt," 165
Larkin, Margaret, 176–77, 179
"The Last Fierce Charge," 29
"Latin Lover," 256
Lawrence, Vera Brodsky, 7, 10
Leadbelly, *194*
   "The Bourgeois Blues" and, 195
   legacy of, 196
   persona of, 193–94
   White, Josh, compared to, 200
Ledbetter, Huddie. *See* Leadbelly
Ledbetter, Lilly, 154
Ledford, Lily Mae, 139
Lee, Arthur, 291–92
Lee, Peggy, 138, 246
Lee, Spike, 292
The Legal Fakebook, 169–70
"Leningrad I," 290
Lennon, John, 216, 315, *317*
Lennon, Sean, 304
Lenoir, J. B., 91–92
Leonard, Hal, xii, 117
"Let My People Dance," 43
"Let's Save Our Mother Earth," 46–47
"Letter to My Teenaged Son," 223
Levenson, Robert, 18
Levy, Jacques, 214
lifestyle songs, of American Indians, 43–45
The L'il Green Songbook, 222
Lilith Fair, 166
Lincoln, Abbey, 107, 168
Lincoln, Abraham, 72
Lipsitz, George, 103, 108–9, 116–17, 255, 263
Little Eva, 145
"A Little Good News," 103
"Little Mohee," 27
The Little Red Songbook, 173
Little Richard, *272*, 273, 291
"Livin' for the City," 100–101

Lomax, Alan, 178, 180, 189–90, 197, 267–68
Lomax, John, 74–75, 171–72
Longfellow, Henry Wadsworth, 26
Longoria, Felix, 242
"Long Way to Hollywood," 125
Lopez, Gustavo Firmat, 253
Los Lobos, *254*, 254–55, 263
"Los Rinches de Texas," 242
Los Tigres del Norte, 258–59, 261, 320
Loudermilk, John D., 26
Love, Courtney, 161
Love, Darlene, 127
"Love at the Five and Dime," 158
"Lovin' Ways," 45
"The Ludlow Massacre," 191–92
"Luka," 159, 216
Lundberg, Victor, 223

MacAnally, Mac, 159
MacKaye, 283–84
Madonna, 163–64, 293
"Maid of Monterey," 12
Maines, Natalie, 308–9
Malavarca, Bernadette, xii
"Malcolm, Malcolm, Semper Malcolm," 319
"Mañana," 246
Manson, Marilyn, 288–89
Manuel, Peter, 248–49
"Many Thousand Gone," 71–72
"Marine Corps Hymn," 18–19
Markham, Pigmeat, 110
Marley, Bob, *57*
   "Buffalo Soldier" and, 56
Marsalis, Wynton, 108
Martin, Don, 46
"Mascot," 47
Mathiesen, Peter, 36*n*
Mayall, John, 90
Mayfield, Curtis, 100, 124, 208, 292
   politics and, 318–19
Mayo, Margot, 65–66
McClain, Billy, 77

McCutcheon, John, 219, 305

McEntyre, Reba, 159

McFarland, Pancho, 256–57

McGraw, Tim, 26

McLachlan, Sarah, 166

"Me and a Gun," 164

Medley, Bill, 127

Melle Mel, 110–11

Mellencamp, John, 54–55, 290

men
  King, Carole's, songs on, 157
  societal dominance of, 146–47
  women compared to, 132

"Merchandise," 283

"Me So Horny," 118

"The Message," 110–12

metal. *See* heavy metal

Metal, Rock, and Jazz: Perception and the Phenomenology of Musical Experience (Berger), 285–86

Metallica, 284–85

Mexican Americans. *See also corrido(s)*
  in Anglo music, 246–47
  Chicano consciousness in music of, 253–55
  Chicano rap and, 256–58
  evolution of music by, 243–45
  music of, 236–40
  World War II and, 253

The Mexican War, 11–12, 233–34

Mexico
  drug wars escalating in, 260
  immigrants from, 234–36
  politics of immigrants from, 235–36
  Spanish settlers warring with, 232–33

Miami sound, 251–52

microphone, origins of, 96

Miller, Bill, 46, 287–88

Miller, Bob, 185–86

Miller, Frank, 205

Miller, Jay, 297

Miller, Mitch, 274

Miller, Randy, 246

miner labor songs, 175–77

Mingus, Charles, 107, 151

minstrel shows
  African Americans and, 75–76
  African American slaves and, 67–68

Mirabel, Robert, 52

misogyny, in rap music, 118

"Miss Otis Regrets (She's Unable to Lunch Today),"123–24

Mitchell, Joni, *152*, 217, 278
  Blue and, 150–51
  career path of, 151
  feminism and, 150
  legacy of, 153
  Song to a Seagull and, 149–50

"Mojado," 262

mojados, 261

Montano, Frank, 48

Monterey Pop Festival, 278

Moore, Chauncey O., 10

Moore, Ethel, 10

Morello, Tom, 291

Morissette, Alanis, 164

Mormons, 6–7

Motown Records, 61
  "The Sound of Young America" and, 275
  women in, 145
  writers/producers at, 98

Ms. Sancha, 257

Murphy, Michael, 58

Murray, Anne, 103

Murrieta, Joaquin, 238–39

Musica Tejano (Peña), 242

Music for Patriots, Politicians, and Presidents: Harmonies and Discords of the First Hundred Years (Lawrence), 7

"Mutilation Is the Most Sincere Form of Flattery," 289

"My Country 'Tis of Thy People You're Dying," 48

"My Indian Girl," 49

My People, My Land, 53

mystic songs, of American Indians, 45–46

N. W. A., 113, 118, 319
NAACP. *See* National Association for the Advancement of Colored People
Nakai, R. Carlos, 41–42
Narcocorrido: A Journey into the Music of Drugs, Guns and Guerrillas (Wald), 259–60
narcocorridos, 258–61
Nash, Graham, 277
Nathan, Syd, 274
National Association for the Advancement of Colored People (NAACP), 94–95
National Organization for Women (NOW), 145
National Woman's Suffrage Association (NWSA), 135–36
Native Americans. *See* American Indians
naturalism, rap music and, 112–13
Naturalization Act, 9
Naughty by Nature, 118
"Navajo, Navajo," 30–31
"Navajo Code Talker," 43
Near, Holly, 156
Nelson, Oliver, 107
Nelson, Willlie, *309*, 309–10
neo-Nazi music, 297–300
Nettl, Bruno, 39
Nevins, Al, 144
New Age, 41
the New Deal, 33
New Lost City Ramblers, 227
the New Lost City Ramblers, 17
Newman, Randy, 290
New Orleans, jazz and, 105
Newport Folk Festival, 210
"Nigger-Lovin' Whore," 297
"Niggers Came Over," 299
"Night in the City," 150

9/11, 304–6
Nirvana, 286–87
Nixon, Richard, 279
"Nobody in the World Is Better Than Us," 196
"No Irish Need Apply," 4–5
North American Folk Music and Dance Alliance, 228
"No Segregation in Heaven," 96
"Nothing Could Be Finer Than a 49er," 44
"Not in My Name," 305
Novoselic, Krist, 287
NOW. *See* National Organization for Women
"Now That the Buffalo's Gone," 28
NWSA. *See* National Woman's Suffrage Association
Nyro, Laura, 124, *148*
    lyrics of, 149
    style of, 148–49

Obama, Barack, 154, 308
Ochs, Phil, 209
    career of, 212
O'Connor, John, 219
Odum, Howard, 74, 78
Oh Brother, Where Art Thou?, 229
"Ohio," 277
the Ojays, 102
Old Time Music Gathering, 227
"Oleana," 3
Olivia Records, 155–56
"Once upon a Genocide," 47
"100 Miles and Runnin'," 118
"One in a Million," 299
"Only a Pawn in Their Game," 210, 321
Ono, Yoko, 304
Orchestre de la Luz, 253
orquesta, 243–44
Ortega, A. Paul, 44–45
"Osama Yo' Mama," 305
Oslin, K. T., 157–58
"Our Line's Been Changed Again," 218

"Out of Control," 220
"Over There," 18

pan-Indian music, 42–43
Paradis, Roger, 23
Paredes, Americo, 236–37
"Parents Don't Understand," 118
Parman, Donald L., 34
Parton, Dolly, 153
"Pass Down de Centre," 76
Patriot Act, 306–7
Paxton, Tom, 212–13
Pearl Jam, 287–88, 303, 313
Peltier, Leonard, 37
Peña, Manuel, 242
"People Get Ready," 124, 208, 318
"People Got to Be Free," 124
People's Songs
   collapse of, 202
   Progressive Party and, 201–2
   Seeger and, 198
"In the Persian Gulf," 43
Peter, Paul, and Mary, 8–9, 142
   beginnings of, 206–7
   protest music of, 207
peyote, 32
"Peyote Healing," 52
peyote songs, 40
Phair, Liz, 163
Phillips, John, 273
Phillips, Sam, 269–70
Phillips, Utah, 220, 303–4
Piantadosi, Al, 18
Pierce, William, 298
Pieslak, Jonathan, 313
Planalp, Susan, xii
"Plastico," 252
"Please Mr. Custer," 54
"Pobre Borinquen," 248
de Poe, Peter, 255
"Political World," 214
politics
   "Born in the USA" and, 128–29

celebrity/music's influence on,
   316–20
the Dixie Chicks and, 308–10
of Dylan, 210, 213–14
jazz and, 107
Mayfield and, 318–19
of Mexican immigrants, 235–36
of 1960s, 275–76
of punk music, 281–82
in rap music, 111, 117–18
songs and, 9–10, 19
"Pompeyu Smash," 12
"Poor Cambodia," 3
pop music
   African Americans and, 97–98
   folk music crossing over to, 204–5
   selling out and, 322
   women and, 138
Porter, Cole, 123–24, 128
"The Power and the Glory," 212
powwow songs, 40
Pozo, Chano, 252
"Prairie Fire," 55
Prather, W. H., 31
preachers, blues and, 86–87
Presley, Elvis, 89, *270*
   discovery of, 270
   impact of, 271
   "In the Ghetto (Vicious Circle)"
      of, 125
Preston, Johnny, 53
Primitive Tribes, 49, 51
Prince, 292
"Private Property," 192–93
Progressive Party, 201–2
protest music. *See also* folk music
   African Americans and, 180–81
   the Almanac Singers and, 184–85
   American Indians and, 41, 46–49,
      56, 58
   audiences and, 196
   blues as, 85–86
   of Chapman, 217
   civil rights and, 207–9

Communist Party and, 202
conservative songs in, 177
contemporary, 216–25
Dylan's impact on, 214–15
environmental issues and, 222
future of, 225–26
on Gulf War (1991), 302–4
Hitler-Stalin pact and, 186–89
homeless and, 221–22
1960s and, 209–16
of Peter, Paul, and Mary, 207
popular, 224–25
of Robinson, 186
rock and roll and, 216
Spanish Civil War and, 181–82
of Springsteen, 224–25
Vietnam War and, 220–21, 223
of the Weavers, 203
of White, Josh, 200
Psycho Realm, 257
Public Enemy, 113, 319
Puerto Ricans, music and, 246–48
punk music
    disco compared to, 280–81
    hard core music and, 282–83
    politics of, 281–82

Queen Latifah, 168

race, rock and roll and, 267–68, 291–92
racism, American Indians and, 47, 54.
        See also hate music; slavery
Rage Against the Machine, 290–91
"Raggedy, Raggedy," 180
ragtime, 77–78
Rainey, Ma, 84, 139
"Rain on the Scarecrow," 290
the Ramones, 280, 281
Ranchero music, 243–44
Rankin, Jeannette, 135
Rap: The Lyrics (Stanley), 117
RAPM. See Russian Association of Pro-
    letarian Music
rap music

authenticity and, 121–23
boasting in, 110, 117
Chicano, 256–58
current issues in, 115–17
early, 110–12
gangster, 113–14, 120, 299–300
lyrics by category for, 117–20
misogyny in, 118
naturalism and, 112–13
obscenity in, 113–14
origins of, 109–10
as party music, 118
politics in, 111, 117–18
respect and, 120
sampling in, 114–15
violence in, 118, 122–23
whites in, 120–21
women and, 122, 155
"Rapper's Delight," 110
Ray, Amy, 60, 160
R&B. See rhythm and blues
Reagan, Ronald, 128–29
Rebel, Johnny, 296
Recapturing the Banjo, 66, 94
Red, Tampa, 86
Redbone, 255
Red Bow, Buddy, 42, 44–45, 49
Redding, Otis, 101–2
"Rednecks," 290
Red Thunder, 48
Redwood Records, 156
Reece, Florence, 140, 177
reggae, 41
Reid, Vernon, 292
Reitz, Rosetta, 138
religion
    African American slaves and, 68–69
    gospel music and, 95–97
"Relocation," 48
Relocation Act (1956), 35
Reservation Blues (Alexie), 39
"Reservation Road," 46
Resistance Records, 298
"Respect," 102

"Reuben James," 197
Revolution, 310
Revolutionary War, 24
the Revolutionary War, 7–9
"Revolution Daze," 48
"The Revolution Starts Now," 310
Rhone, Sylvia, 170
rhythm and blues (R&B)
    African Americans and, 97–98
    origin of, 88
    whites covering, 274
"Rhythm Nation," 165–66
Rice, Condoleezza, 310
Rice, Thomas D., 75
"Rich Man's War," 310
right-wing songs, 222–23
riot grrrl movement, 162
Ritchie, Jean, 13
Rivera, Jenni, 259
Rivera, Pedro, 259
Roach, Max, 107, 168, 319
Robertson, Robbie, 52
Robinson, Earl, 175
    protest music of, 186
Robinson, Smokey, 98, 271
Robison, Emily, 310
de la Rocha, Zach, 290–91
rock and roll, 142. *See also* disco music;
    heavy metal; punk music
    cover records in, 273–74
    drugs and, 276
    grunge music and, 286–88
    hippies and, 276–77
    history of, 266–68
    mainstream artists in, 289–90
    1980s and, 284
    protest music and, 216
    race and, 267–68, 291–92
    in Spanish, 261–62
    today, 294
    white supremacy in, 271–73
    women and, 293–94
"Rock Around the Clock," 269

*Rockin' Out: Popular Music in the
    U.S.A.* (Garafalo), 284
"Rockin' the Res," 50
"The Rock Island Line," 205
"Rock n' Roll Nigger," 289
"Rock the Boat Baby," 280
Rodgers, Jimmie, 90
the Rolling Stones, 90, 278
Rollins, Sonny, 107
"Roll On Columbia," 190
Romero, Robby, 48
Roosevelt, Franklin Delano, 33, 94
Roosevelt, Theodore, 17
"The Roosevelt Song," 195
Roque, Julio, 247
Rose, Axl, 285, 299
Rose, Tricia, 121, 155
Rosenfeld, Morris, 5
Rounder Records, 181, 227
Rudder, Randy, 311
"Running Bear," 53–54
"Run to Jesus," 66
Russell, Tom, 56, 58
Russian Association of Proletarian Music (RAPM), 178–79

"Sail Away," 290
Sainte-Marie, Buffy, 28, 37, 46, 48,
    121–22, 160, 318
salsa, 252–53
"The Same Old Merry-Go-Round,"
    201
sampling, in rap music, 114–15
Sanchez, Rosalino "Chalin," 259
Sandberg, Larry, xii
Sandburg, Carl, 17, 139
"Santy Anno," 13–14
Saturday Night Fever, 280
"Save the Country," 124, 149
"Say It Loud, I'm Black and I'm
    Proud," 102
Schlitz, Don, 158
"School's Out," 288
Secola, Keith, 41–44

Sedition Act, 9

Seeger, Charles, 179–80

Seeger, Pete, 29, 85, *187*, 193, 201, 206–7, 210, 319. *See also* the Weavers
  the Almanac Singers and, 184–85
  Guthrie compared to, 198–99
  People's Songs and, 198

selling out
  American Indians and, 49
  pop music and, 322

"Seminole Wind," 58–59

Sequra, Knifewing, 46

Seventh Fire, 60

Sex Pistols, 280

Seymour, Chris, 67

"Shadow over Sisterhood," 50

"Shake, Rattle and Roll," 268

sharecropping, 73

Shaw, Artie, 106

"She'll Be Coming Round the Mountain," 246

Shenandoah, Joanne, 41, 43

"She Thinks His Name Was John," 159

Ship Ahoy, 102

"Ship Those Niggers Back," 297

Shorris, Earl, 232

Siembra, 252

Silber, Irwin, 19, 203

Silent Warrior, 46

Silkwood, Karen, 220

Silverman, Jerry, 3, 9, 17

Silver Wave Records, 61

Simmons, Gene, 26

Simmons, Russell, 115–16, 320

Sinclair, John, 291

singer-songwriters, 148–53

The Singing Sixties: The Spirit of Civil War Days Drawn from the Music of the Times (Heaps, P. & Heaps, W.), 16

Sitting Bull, 28

1650 Broadway songwriters, 144

"Six Clicks," 220–21

Six Songs for Democracy, 182, 188

"Sixteen Tons," 205

"The Skidmore Guard," 6

Skull and Bones, 257

Slash, 299

slavery, 14–16. *See also* African American slaves
  African Americans and, 63–64
  Africans for, 23
  American Indians and, 22–23
  in Southwest, 232

Slave Songs of the United States, 71

Sleater-Kinney, 162

Slick, Grace, 153, 293

Sly and the Family Stone, 102–3, 292

"Small Town," 290

Smith, Bessie, 78, *83*
  subject matter of, 84–85
  "Young Woman's Blues" of, 85

Smith, J. M., 27

Smith, Julia, 141

"Smooth Operator," 117

SOAR, 61–62

social theory, American music and, xi

"Society's Child," 126–27

"The Soldier Boys," 29

"Solidarity Forever," 173, 321–22

"So Long It's Been Good to Know You," 190

"Somebody's Kind," 50

"Something About the Rain," 245

the Song Catchers, 45

song circles, 227

"Song for America," 55

songs
  assembly concept for, 75
  about immigrants, 5–7
  of immigrants, 2–5
  political, 9–10, 19
  of Revolutionary War, 7–9
  by whites about African Americans, 123–26

Songs America Voted By (Silber), 19

Songs for John Doe, 188

Song to a Seagull, 149–50

Sonic Youth, *161*
"So This Is America," 46
soul music, 101–4
Soul of Vietnam, 221
"The Sound of Young America," 275
"The Southern Cotton Mill Rhyme," 140
Southwest
 slavery in, 232
 Spanish settlers in, 231–32
the Spanish-American War, 16–17
Spanish Civil War, 181–82
Spanish rock and roll, 261–62
Spanish settlers
 Mexico warring with, 232–33
 in Southwest, 231–32
Spencer, Jon Michael, 86–87
In the Spirit of Crazy Horse (Mathiesen), 36*n*
spirituals
 African American slaves and content of, 71–72
 African Americans/whites, origins of, 69–70
Spitalny, Phil, 167
Springfield, Buffalo, 277
Springsteen, Bruce, 128–29, 157, 193, *225*
 Dylan compared to, 225
 protest music of, 224–25
Stamp Act (1766), 7
Stanley, Lawrence A., 117
the Staples Singers, 97
Starr, Edwin, 99
"The Star-Spangled Banner," 10–11
Stax Records, 98–99
"Staying Alive," 280
"Steal Away," 67
Stevens, Ray, 305
Stewart, John, 206
Stills, Stephen, 277
Stockhouse, Janis, 168
Stones in the Road, 158
Storyville, 105

Strachwitz, Chris, 242–43
Strandberg, Julius, 5
"The Streets of Laredo," 44–45
"Strike for Your Rights, Avenge Your Wrong," 12
Stuart, Marty, 59
Sugar Hill Gang, 110
Sun Records, 269–71
Superfly, 319
Supposed Former Infatuation Junkie, 164
Swing Shift (Tucker, S.), 167

"Talkin' 'Bout a Revolution," 160, 217
Tapestry, 156–57, 164
the Tarriers, 205
Taylor, Johnny, 97
Taylor, Otis, 66, 94
Taylor, Zachary, 12
"Tchepone," 221
teenagers, discretionary income and, 266
tejano music, 243
the Temptations, 99
Termination Act (1953), 35
Testament, 285
Texas Rangers, 238
textile worker labor songs, 175–77
Tharpe, Rosetta, 96
"That's the News," 310
"That's What the Red, White and Blue Mean," 18
"Things 'Bout Comin' My Way," 86
"This Ain't No Rag, It's a Flag," 304–5
"This Is My Country," 318
"This Land Is Your Land," 192
"Three Generations," 45
"Thunder Warrior," 49
Thurmond, J. Strom, 201
the Tijuana No Band, 261
Till the Bars Break, 59
The Times They Are a-Changin', 209
Tindley, C. Albert, 95
Tin Pan Alley, 138
"Tippecanoe and Tyler Too," 13

The Topical Bluesman from Korea to Vietnam, 91–92
Tosti, Don, 263
"Trail of Tears," 28, 49, 56
"Travelin' Soldier," 310
Travis, Merle, 205
"Travis John (The Return),"311
"Trouble," 160
Troutman, John W., 32
Trudell, John, 302–3
    history of, 49–50
    songs of, 50–51
Truman, Harry, 201
Tucker, Sherrie, 167
Tucker, Tanya, 126
Tuft, Harry, xii
Tupac, 120
Turbulent Indigo, 151
"Turn, Turn, Turn," 207
Turner, Big Joe, 268
Turner, Nat, 67
"Tutti Frutti," 273
Twain, Shania, 165
1200 Curfew, 160
The Twentieth Century West (Parman), 34
"Two Gendarmes," 18
Two Live Crew, 113, 118
Tyson, Ian, 246

UAW. *See* United Automobile Workers
Ulali, 53
UMW. *See* United Mine Workers
"Uncle Sam," 200
"Uncle Theo," 52
"Underneath the Bamboo Tree," 77
unions. *See* labor unions
"Union Sundown," 214
United Automobile Workers (UAW), 184
United Mine Workers (UMW), 184
"Universal Soldier," 121–22
Urban Blues (Keil), 92–93
Utley, Robert, 30

"Valley of the Little Bighorn," 30
Vanilla Ice, 120
vaudeville, 83–85
Vecindad y Los Hijos del Quinto Patio, 262
Vedder, Eddie, 287–88, 303
Vega, Suzanne, 159–60, 216
Verne, Larry, 54
"Vietnam," 43
Vietnam War, 279
    feminism and, 147
    Gulf War (2003) compared to, 313–14
    protest music and, 220–21, 223
    the Village People, 104, 279–80
    violence, in rap music, 118, 122–23
"Visions of History," 42
Voice of the Homeless, 222
Voices from the Front Line, 312
The Voices That Are Gone: Themes in Nineteenth-Century American Popular Song (Finson), 6

"The Wagoner's Lad," 134–35
"Waist Deep in the Big Muddy," 29, 207
Wald, Elijah, 259–60
Walela, 53
Walking Elk, Mitch, 51
"Walk Your Road," 45
Wallace, Henry, 201
"War," 99
"War No More," 306
War of 1812, 10–11, 24
War Story Book I, 257
"Wartime Blues," 81
"Was He a Fool (Columbus),"47
Washington, George, 8–9, 23
Watergate scandal, 279
Waters, Muddy, 88, 90
"The Way It Is," 126
WCTU. *See* Women's Christian Temperance Union
"We Are the Iroquois," 43

the Weavers
  blacklist and, 204
  protest music of, 203
  success of, 202
"We Didn't Start the Fire," 290
"We Shall Overcome," 208, 321
West, Rebecca, 155
Westbrooks, Wesley, 87
Westerman, Floyd "Red Crow," 30, 47–48
Weston, Randy, 107
"We Were All Wounded at Wounded Knee," 255
"What Ever Happened to Peace on Earth?,"309–10
"Whatever Happened to the Eight Hour Day?,"219
What's Goin' On, 100
"When I Was Single," 135
"When the President Talks to God," 310
"Where Have All the Flowers Gone?,"206
Where Have All the Flowers Gone (Seeger, Pete), 184
"Where Were You," 306
"Which Side Are You On?,"140, 322
white(s)
  American Indian commentary of, 53–60
  blues and, 89–93
  civil rights movement and, 208–9
  in rap music, 120–21
  R&B covers by, 274
  rock and roll and supremacy of, 271–73
  songs on African Americans by, 123–26
  spirituals' origins and, 69–70
White, Josh, 85, 181, 202
  authenticity of, 93
  early career of, 199–200
  Leadbelly compared to, 200
  protest music of, 200

White, Tony Joe, 124–25
White and Negro Spirituals, Their Life Span and Kinship (Jackson, G. P.), 69–70
"White Trash," 289
Whitfield, Marvin, 99–100
Wiggins, Ella Mae, 176
"Wild Women Don't Have the Blues," 139
Wilkins, Robert, 87
Wilkinson, Charles, 25, 38
Wilkinson, Frank, 263
Williams, Claude, 180
Williams, Hank, Jr., 302, *302*
Williams, Hank, Sr., 268
Williams, Harry N., 30–31
Williams, Mary Lou, 167
Williamson, Chris, 55
  feminism and, 155–56
"Willie and Laura Mae Jones," 124–25
Willkie, Wendell, 186
"Will the Wolf Survive," 255
Wilson, Dick, 36
Wilson, John, 32
Wilson, Woodrow, 17
"Wind River Song," 56
"Winds of Life," 45
WITCH. *See* Women's International Terrorist Conspiracy from Hell
Without Reservation, 47
Wobblies, 172–73
women. *See also* feminism
  conjunto music and, 244–45
  corridos and, 240–41
  country music and, 139–40, 157–59
  current artists and, 166–67
  Dylan's lyrics and, 143
  in folk music, 139, 159–61
  Great Depression and, 138–41
  instruments and, 132–33
  jazz and, 138–39, 167–68
  labor songs and, 140–41
  men compared to, 132
  in Motown Records, 145

music industry and, 170
music movement of, 155–57
1950s and, 141–42
1960s and, 141–43
in 1990s, 161–66
pop music and, 138
rap music and, 122, 155
riot grrrl movement and, 162
rock and roll and, 293–94
roles of, 131–33, 168–69
romantic love and, 133–34
as singer-songwriters, 148–53
single and married, 134–35
World War I and, 135–37
Women's Christian Temperance Union (WCTU), 136–37
Women's International Terrorist Conspiracy from Hell (WITCH), 146
Wonder, Stevie, 99–102
"Woodstock," 278
Woodstock music festival, 278
Work, Henry C., 137
Work and Sing: A History of Occupational and Labor Songs in the United States (Cohen), 180–81
Workers Music League, 178
work songs. *See* labor songs
"World Falls," 160

World War I, 17–19
women and, 135–37
World War II
African Americans and, 94–95
the Almanac Singers and, 197
American Indians and, 33–35
Mexican Americans and, 253
prosperity after, 265–66
Worley, Darryl, 311
"Wounded Knee," 42
Wright, J. Leitch, Jr., 22
Wright, Robert L., 5
Wright, Rochelle, 5
Wright-McLeod, Brian, 51–52
Wynette, Tammy, 153

Yarrow, Peter, 316
"Yellow Ledbetter," 303
"Yellow Ribbon," 303
"YMCA," 279–80
"You Haven't Done Nothin'," 101
Young, Neil, 58, 157, 246, 277, 311, 322
"The Young Man Who Wouldn't Hoe Corn," 188
the Young Rascals, 124
"Young Woman's Blues," 85
"You Really Got a Hold on Me," 271
Yurchenko, Henrietta, 299

Lyric Permissions and Photo Credits

Lyric Permissions

"We Are the Iroquois," by Joanne Shenandoah, courtesy of Joanne Shenandoah. "Indian Cars," by Keith Secola, courtesy of Keith Secola, used by permission. "Chicago," by A. Paul Ortega, courtesy of A. Paul Ortega. "The Generations," by D. C. Cooper, courtesy of D. C. Cooper. "Alaska 49th State," courtesy of Peter La Farge, c/o EB Marks. "BIA Blues," by Floyd "Red Crow" Westerman, courtesy of Floyd "Red Crow" Westerman. "Heartbeat," by Robby Romero, courtesy of Robby Romero. "Land of the Free," by Richard Cyr, courtesy of Richard Cyr. "Revolution Daze," by Joseph Manuel, courtesy of Joseph Manuel. "Commodity Blues," by Frank Montano, courtesy of Frank Montano. "Somebody's Kind," by John Trudell, courtesy of John Trudell. "Carry the Star," by John Trudell, courtesy of John Trudell. "Hotdogs and Hamburgers" by John Mellencamp, courtesy of EMI Full Keel Music. "Song for America," by Kerry Livgren, courtesy of Kirshner CBS Music Publishing. "Wind River Song," by Randy Handley, courtesy of Randy Handley. "A Little Good News" by Tommy Rocco, Rory Bourke, and Charlie Black, courtesy of Warner Chappell Music, Rhythm Ranch Music, and Universal Music Group. "Language of Violence," by Franti Michael and Mark S. Pistel, courtesy of Universal Songs of Polygram. "Long Way to Hollywood," by Stephen T. Young, courtesy of Warner-Tamerlane Publishing Corp. "Night in the City," by Joni Mitchell, courtesy Crazy Crow Music. "Cactus Tree," by Joni Mitchell, courtesy of Crazy Crow Music. "Hell Is for Children," by Pat Benatar, Roger Capps, and Neil T. Giraldo, courtesy of Chrysalis Music Group, Inc. "Stones in the Road," by Mary Chapin Carpenter, courtesy of EMI April Music, Inc., and Getarealjob Music. "John Doe No. 14," by Mary Chapin Carpenter, courtesy of Why Walk Music. "Trouble," by Emily Ann Saliers and Amy Elizabeth Ray, courtesy of EMI Virgin Songs, Inc., and GODHAP Music. "All American Girl," by Melissa Etheridge, courtesy of M L E Music. "Chopsticks," by Liz Phair, courtesy of Civil War Days. "Me and a Gun," by Tori Amos, courtesy of Sword and Stone Publishing, Inc. "There's Got to Be a Way," by Mariah Carey, courtesy of EMI and Universal Music. "Fixing Her Hair," by Ani DiFranco, courtesy of Righteous Babe Music. "The Ballad of October 16th," by Millard Lampell and Lee Hays, courtesy of StormKing Music, Inc. "Uncle Sam," by Josh White, courtesy of Folkways Music Publishers, Inc. "I

Got a Ballot," by Alan Lomax, courtesy of Folkways Music Publishers, Inc. "The John Birch Society," by Michael Brown, courtesy of Michael Brown. "Christmas in the Trenches," by John McCutcheon, courtesy of Appalsongs. "Can't You See What You Done," by Delia Gartell, courtesy of Delia Gartell. "Ballad of Gregorio Cortez," by Chris Strachwitz, courtesy of Olmos Music. "Joaquin Murrieta," by Leal Felipe Valdez, courtesy of EMI April Music, Inc. "Something About the Rain," by Tish Hinojosa, courtesy of Manazo Music. "Joaquin," by Tish Hinojosa, courtesy of Manazo Music. "El Buen Borincano," by Hernandez Marin Rafael, courtesy of APRS. "Pobre Borinquen," by Hernandez Marin Rafael, courtesy of APRS. "Siembra," by Willie Colon, courtesy of EMI Longitude Music. "La Raza," by Arturo Molina, Jr., courtesy of EMI Virgin Songs, Inc. "Chicago," by Graham Nash, courtesy of SONY/ATV Music Publishing. "Ohio," by Neil Young, courtesy of Wixen Music Publishing, Inc. "Suggestion," by Ian MacKaye, courtesy Fugazi Songs. "Cropduster," by Eddie Vedder and Matthew Cameron, courtesty of Innocent Bystander. "Rednecks," by Randy Newman, courtesy of WB Music Corp. "Casualties of War," by Eric Barrier and William Griffin, courtesy of EMI Blackwood Music, Inc. "American Idiot," by Billie Joe Armstrong, Mike Pritchard, and Frank E. Wright, courtesy of Green Daze Music.

Photo Credits

Group waiting at Ellis Island, pg. 2, and Steelworker in Homestead Pennsylvania, pg. 4: Photography Collection, Miram and Ira D. Wallach Division of Arts, Prints, and Photographs, The New York Public Library, Astor, Lenox, and Tilden Foundations. "The Old Granite State," by the Hutchinson Family, pg. 14: Music Division, The New York Public Library, Astor, Lenox, and Tilden Foundations. Wichita Indians giving war song, pg. 24 and the Tipica Orchestra, pg. 244: Picture Collection, The New York Public Library, Astor, Lenox, and Tilden Foundations. Buffalo Bill's Wild West Show, pg. 26: Billy Rose Theatre Division, The New York Public Library for the Performing Arts, Astor, Lenox, and Tilden Foundations. Astoria Work Experience Center, pg. 133: Photographs and Prints Division, Schomburg Center for Research in Black Culture, The New York Public Library, Astor, Lenox, and Tilden Foundations. Suffrage Parade, pg. 136: National American Woman Suffrage Association Records, Manuscripts, and Archives Division, The New York Public Library, Astor, Lenox, and Tilden Foundations. From the Library of Congress Prints and Photographs Division: Segregation, pg. 92: photo by Jack Delano. Southwestern musicians, pg. 176: photo by Lee Russell. Picket at a textile mill in Greensboro, Georgia, pg. 183: photo by Jack Delano. Pete Seeger, pg. 187: photo by Joseph A. Horne. Latina singing folk songs, pg. 250: photo by John Collier. All other interior photos and all cover photos are from Photofest.